DRIVEN

Notes of a Neurotic Entrepreneur:
His Trials, Failures & Victories

By Max Barnet

STONES POINT PRESS
P.O. Box 384
Belfast, ME 04915

COVER by Mary Reed/Imageset Design
EDITED by Barbara Feller-Roth

FIRST EDITION

Barnet, Max
DRIVEN, Notes of a Neurotic Entrepreneur: His Trials, Failures & Victories
Library of Congress Catalog Card Number: 93-085983
ISBN 1-882521-01-3

$15.00 Softcover
Printed in the United States of America

This book is dedicated
to all the courageous souls in business,
those who succeed and those who fail.

Perpetual devotion to what a man calls his business, is only to be sustained by perpetual neglect of many other things.

Robert L. Stevenson

No man can see all with his own eyes or do all with his own hands. Whoever is engaged in multiplicity of business must transact much by substitution and leave something to hazard, and he who attempts to do all will waste his life in doing little.

Samuel Johnson

TABLE OF CONTENTS

FOREWORD

Presumably Max Barnet asked me to write this Foreword because he knows that I, too, am an entrepreneur. His subtitle: "Notes of a neurotic entrepreneur" makes me wonder what else he knows.

No matter. What I *don't* wonder about is Barnet's knowledge of what's really involved in making a business work. Sure, he knows about spreadsheets, inventory control, and cash flow—the mechanics of business. But happily he knows much that's far more important: that all that mechanistic stuff doesn't actually drive the people in business . . . it sort of tags along.

Barnet has it absolutely right and, as this book compellingly demonstrates, peoples' emotions, needs, aspirations, frailties and strengths represent the untidy and uncontrollable drivers of a business. (Or, for that matter, perhaps *even* a business school.)

As such, here is a novel that's also truly a textbook. Just yesterday our local paper highlighted the iconoclastic orientation of the new dean of our university's business school. He claims that business schools have tended to be much too insular and that they must operate at the intersection of theory and practice. He adds, shockingly, that: "You would think that managers [rather than academics] would train managers." Right on, dean.

We have watched the business schools, often peopled by unsoiled theorists, lead our innnocent MBA candidates quite astray by implying that a business is an exercise in rationality. It's rather like teaching neurosurgery from a manual with nary an exposure to blood or the possibility of an accidental needlestick following the needle's use on an HIV-positive patient.

Now as long as I still have the floor, I'd like to reinforce the above prejudice and so offer the following as further evidence of business school insularity: I recently received a notice of a new academic business-to-business marketing journal with a 28-member editorial board. Every last one of this admittedly august assemblage hails from academe. Regrettably, not a single Max Barnet amongst them. In all fairness, some of these good people may well have had previous stints in the real business world, but is that really good enough?

So, I think that DRIVEN is a most welcome antidote to all that business school myopia. It takes us far beyond the clichés and lets us soak up business realities that include, but transcend, mere number crunching.

For all these reasons, it might well be appropriate to make receipt of the MBA sheepskin contingent upon prior immersion in DRIVEN. It would also not hurt would-be entrepreneurs or, for that matter, all the other saints and sinners already in business. Amen.

GEORGE NAIMARK, Ph.D.

Dr. Naimark, a management consultant, has been a director of seven companies and is president of Naimark & Barba, Inc., Florham Park, NJ. He has written for management, marketing, advertising, scientific and medical journals and has authored two books: COMMUNICATIONS on COMMUNICATIONS *and* A PATENT MANUAL FOR SCIENTISTS AND ENGINEERS.

PREFACE

Why this book? To give the reader insight into what being in business is really like? Quite obviously. To show how being in business impacts the personal life of the CEO and those around him? Definitely. To ask—and answer—whether it's worth it to endure the constant struggle that being in business involves? Perhaps.

To be honest, when I began the book I had barely an inkling of why I was writing it. As I got into it, the above reasons seemed as good as any. Now, five years after the last sentence was cast, I can see that none of those reasons addresses what this book is mostly about, and that is how to deal with the chaotic world.

The chaos peculiar to ordinary life is compressed and intensified in business. Momentous things happen more frequently, and usually more dramatically. One of the reasons for this phenomenon is that so much is at stake, often the very survival of the business. Why would anyone wish to expose him- or herself to such extreme uncertainties?

One answer is found in the following excerpt from Theodore Dreiser's *Jennie Gerhardt*:

> To be a forceful figure in the business world means, as a rule, that you must be an individual of one idea, and that idea is the God-given one that life has destined you for a tremendous future in the particular field you have chosen. It means that one thing, a cake of soap, a new can-opener, a safety razor, or speed-accelerator, must seize on your imagination with tremendous force, burn as a raging

flame, and make itself the be-all and end-all of your existence.

So an idea, one idea, is the inspiration, giving purpose to the entrepreneur's struggle. But the motivation runs deeper. Although always striving for security and minimizing risk, the entrepreneur thrives on conflict and is driven in a quest to outsmart and control the chaos. The entrepreneur does this by creating order, building an organization, inspiring a cadre of employees, developing strategies, and finding an edge—or, as economist Joseph A. Schumpeter put it, by creating "a private kingdom."

The chaos of life is more than just the devil to be defeated, it is also the most fascinating opponent a businessperson can imagine. Every problem is a challenge, every challenge a test of competence; every success is a triumph, every failure a goad to try again. Without this provocation the "raging flame" would soon die.

MAX BARNET

CHAPTER I
Year Zero
1966

I have heard that only about 10 percent of the population possesses the qualities necessary to be a leader. Among other things a leader is a risk taker. And a risk taker is a kind of fanatic. Fanatical, risk-taking leaders are basically insecure, untrusting bastards. We weren't born that way, but something happened in our early lives that made us think we couldn't trust. Maybe we felt we weren't loved. Then the things we often do to get love just aren't very loving. So we keep trying anyway even if it's hopeless. Basing our actions on the premise that love and survival depend on success, those of us born with the gift of competence make it.

I had this dream of owning my own business ever since I was a kid waiting on the counter in my father's neighborhood convenience market. Most men have this dream too, at least most men I know. Even those who are too fearful to take the risk, and know deep down their dream will stay only a dream, hang onto it like life after death. As for me, I knew that owning my own business was in my destiny. Basically I was a loner, an iconoclast, despite my conservative suits and low-key selling line to the contrary. Everyone took me for a don't-make-waves guy, definitely not the uptight, introspective power-mad renegade I really was.

But let's start at the beginning, when I was a salesman. I loved my job out there on the road, free as can be, selling plastic materials to manufacturers of all kinds of plastic items, from rope to frames for sunglasses, toys to radio cabinets. I say free because Cal, our vice president and manager of the New England plant, gave me complete autonomy, as he did all his employees. Never raising his voice, never critical, a compulsive optimist, he was, in short, an ideal boss. Because of him I learned a skill, a specialty, which is what you need in this world to make it.

Those were great days back in the sixties. The plastics industry was booming and MPI (Majestic Plastics Industries) was riding the crest.

On a snappy January morning in 1964, I called Cal at the office from an outdoor phone booth, as was my custom every day when I was on the road.

"What do you think about our getting into the color concentrate business?" Cal asked.

I had spoken to Cal several times about the appearance of color concentrate on the scene, and suggested that it might well be the wave of the future. Couldn't we manufacture and offer such a product, if only to protect ourselves? Cal always seemed receptive but noncommittal. I figured I was only talking against the wind.

"You know what I think," I yelled excitedly. "I'm sure I can sell tons."

"Hell, you won't be selling color concentrate," he responded.

"What do you mean?"

"You'll be making it. It'll be your baby. A separate division."

"Making it? I don't know how."

"Nobody else does either. You'll have to learn."

"I'm a salesman, Cal. You've got the wrong man."

"I don't think so. And Henry [our president at headquarters in Chicago] thinks you're the best man too.

It'll be a challenge, Harry, and I believe you're the sort of guy who likes a challenge."

By putting it that way, he hit me where I'm most vulnerable. I opened the door to the phone booth for some fresh air.

"When would I start?"

"Right now. Drop what you're doing and come on in. Let's talk some more."

On the forty mile trip back to the plant in my Chevy station wagon, I broke every speed limit.

Cal somehow looked smaller than he was, always spoke in a measured, gentle, sincere way. He seemed wise for a man not yet forty. Over lunch at a local restaurant he said, "You'll be responsible for everything: production, sales, hiring, firing—the whole shooting match."

I was euphoric. Even though it wouldn't be my own business, it was the next best thing.

"I appreciate your faith in me, Cal."

"Henry's giving us a year. If the division doesn't make it, he'll shut it down."

"A year. Christ. I don't know."

"I told him you can do it."

"Boy, oh, boy."

Cal grinned. "Yeah."

During that first year as a semi-entrepreneur—that is, risking someone else's money rather than my own—I couldn't have been happier. I was making a new business grow and building an organization from the beginning. After six months I hired Francis, the local salesman of a competitor in New Jersey. A very high-powered man in his early thirties, Francis was tall, sharp featured, a good-looking all-American type with a butch haircut. He talked in a precise, authoritative way that impressed our customers. But underneath he was a controlled Vesuvius.

"My life's on a definite schedule," he announced one day. "I plan to be a millionaire by the time I'm forty."

"I don't believe a man can plan his life," I said. "Or should."

"Watch me, Harry."

I wondered whether he meant "watch out." Anyway, though I thought his schedule for success was ridiculous and possibly dangerous, I was pleased with his performance.

By the year's end my division had made it: a million dollars in profitable sales. But during that first year, the rest of the company had been sinking. The division's profits were not significant enough to offset MPI's total losses. If Cal was a good boss, he was a bad manager; by January 1965 the operation had run out of funds, had exhausted its bank credit, and was no longer able to support its enormous receivables. Our runaway finished goods inventory, consisting mostly of returned defective or obsolete plastic materials, was worthless. We were in serious trouble.

For two days and one night the auditors huddled with Cal behind the closed door of his office, which had a private shower and bar. Then in April, three months later, Imperial Oil took us over after paying a ridiculously high figure. The negotiations had been conducted in secret. The employees didn't know until the sale was a fait accompli. Some of us were sad, others pleased that now we were rich.

Money was everything when we didn't have enough. But after we had more than we needed, we lost something more valuable: our independence and with it our entrepreneurial spirit. Imperial's management people were all sharp-eyed, smiling eagles in dark suits. They told Cal when to visit the john. His free-wheeling days over, he became serious and secretive, even conspiratorial. The rest of us, too, laboring under the corporate yoke, were no longer a happy crew, except for Francis who was strangely turned on.

After eight months, in December 1965, the chief eagle down on Wall Street asked Cal to resign voluntarily—a face-saving sacking. I was very upset; Cal was the only reason I had stuck around. He had shielded me from the bullshit that was issuing from headquarters.

The day he departed, he said to me: "I don't think you'll last much longer around here. Look me up before you do anything. You know where to find me."

I heard that Francis was behind Cal's demise. Ostensibly he told the eagles in New York that Cal had intentionally misrepresented the value of the inventory when they bought the company and that it was Cal's mismanagement that had almost brought MPI to ruin.

Francis was then appointed Cal's replacement, thus becoming my boss rather than, as before, the other way around. This was hard to take, particularly after what he'd allegedly done to Cal. Could I trust him? He seemed ambitious only for himself. I considered my career at Imperial stymied. Cal was right: I had to quit.

Five months later in May 1966, finally working up enough courage to take a leap into uncertainty, I visited Cal at the marina he'd bought after his departure from Imperial. We sat on a bench on the dock staring at the big white power yachts heaving in their slots.

"Were you serious about my seeing you before I did anything?" I said.

"Absolutely."

"Well I'm thinking about getting into the color concentrate business. It's all I know."

"I've been waiting, Harry."

"Waiting?"

"Keep this under your hat. I own a piece of Magic Colorants with Rob Starr."

"What!"

This was stunning news. Magic Colorants Inc. was a small dry-color house founded two years before by Cal's former production manager, Neil. Handsome, only in his twenties, a barfly and womanizer, Neil didn't tend to business, so his company was losing money and the banks were breathing down his neck. He sold the company to Rob Starr, a customer, for the assumption of the debt.

"Yeah, I signed a three-year, no-compete agreement when I left Imperial," Cal said.

"But Magic Colorants only makes dry-color. Magic isn't competing."

(Dry-color is a recipe of pulverized powdered pigments formulated to match a color target. It is a simple and cheap way to color plastics, but it is not always the most effective way.)

"But we will be," Cal explained, "when we begin making color concentrate. I have to stay silent for another eighteen months." He smiled in oily satisfaction. "I own 25 percent, Rob Starr owns the rest. Randy has a stock option on 25 percent. You could have a 25 percent option too. How's that sound?"

It was more than I thought I would ever have.

"What's the money situation at Magic?" I asked.

"Terrific," Cal said convincingly. "Rob's loaded and his father-in-law is on the board at the bank. We've got all the money we need. The company's losing a little, but once you're aboard that'll change."

I knew I couldn't miss this opportunity to be my own master. No longer would I have to put up with other people's incompetence—just my own. Seeing the mistakes made all around me at MPI, I knew what not to do. I thought I could perform better than others, and I was willing to pay if I couldn't. Of course, I was naive about how high the price would be.

Trusting soul that I was, I never asked Cal to see Magic's financial statements. I wanted a piece of Magic Colorants so badly that I would have dismissed bad news anyway.

My wife, Janet, cautiously supported me in the venture. While not a risk taker, she was a blind believer in me, though I couldn't imagine why. For the first five years of our marriage I rarely held a job for longer than a year. And we had three small children to think of.

"With our savings and a small salary, we'll have enough to last a year," I said. "But we'll have to tighten our belts, eat hamburg instead of steak, give up going out to dinner and movies. It's now or never."

I was forty-two and thinking that I was starting late. Janet was willing to sacrifice. Material things weren't important to her then. Only the kids were, and me.

"If that's what you must do, then do it," she said.

"For a year," I promised.

Janet gave me all that I asked for. After ten years of marriage, we were still devoted to each other, holding the conviction that our being together made us stronger. I needed her love in the early years while I was unemployed and felt worthless. When people would ask, "And what are you doing now?" I was humiliated. Accepting anything available, I was often reduced to waiting on counter, mopping floors, and cleaning restrooms in a restaurant. It wasn't what I'd had in mind doing when I was a serious college student. I felt demeaned and cheated. Believing a man's purpose is to support his dependents, and ashamed of my failure, I had asked Janet to leave, to go to live with her rich sister where she would be more comfortable.

Instead, she hired a baby-sitter and returned to being a nurse to keep us going. Janet was good when I was down. I believed in her as much as she believed in me.

In June, Janet and I and the kids went on a two week vacation at the seashore, where I walked the beach formulating plans to make Magic Colorants grow and prosper. When I returned to Majestic Plastics, Francis angrily confronted me.

"I hear you're giving notice." He was sitting stiffly on the edge of his chair behind Cal's former desk. His secretary, ten years older than himself, with whom he had a suspicious rapport, was at her desk, which was butted up to his.

"Where'd you hear that?" I asked, puzzled and annoyed that the word was out.

I hadn't planned to leave until the end of summer, until all future plans for Magic were mapped out and agreed upon and the necessary legal papers for my participation were drawn up. Furthermore I wanted to accumulate several more weeks of salary.

"Is it true?" he asked.

"Kind of."

"Kind of, hell. You're a partner in Magic Colorants."

The accuracy of his information was uncanny.

"Well, I don't want to leave you in the lurch," I responded. "I intend to stick around as long as you need me — within reason." Although I didn't admire Francis, I found him likable. My offer was mostly sincere.

"Then I've got it right — it's Magic Colorants."

"Where'd you hear that?"

"Randy told his cousin, who works here in production."

Randy was a color technician who used to work in the lab at MPI. When Neil was fired from MPI and formed

Magic Colorants, he persuaded Randy to join him.

So Randy talked despite our agreement that my participation must be kept secret. Randy had been running Magic. Rob and Cal depended on him alone. Perhaps he resented my coming in and diluting his indispensability. Why else would he talk? Trouble already before I had begun.

"I'm not giving notice, yet, Francis."

"Oh, yes you are. I don't want you around anymore."

I was astonished at his reaction. We weren't close, but he knew me to be honorable and considerate.

"Do you really think I'd do anything to harm Majestic? You know you can trust me." My eyes were watering.

"You sonofabitch. Why didn't you tell me you were looking to be on your own? You could have approached me. We could have worked a deal together. I'd stay here while you got things started. We'd have formulations, prices, all kinds of valuable information at our disposal."

I thought Francis was a corporate thoroughbred and Majestic was his future. I never imagined he'd be disloyal to his company, nor that he'd take my departure as a personal betrayal.

"You're my boss," I said. "How could I tell you?"

He stared at me with contempt. After I cleaned out my desk I walked through the plant and the lab and the office and said good-bye to everyone, realizing sadly that from then on that team would be the other side and wishing it could be otherwise. Life is so full of opposites. So long everybody, so long. I was kissing off six mostly happy years. It was 1966. The country was consuming itself in Vietnam and business was rocketing to new levels everywhere. It was a great time to be an entrepreneur and I didn't think about much else.

CHAPTER II
Year One
1967

Sales: $103,000
Profit: ($21,000)
Debt: $64,000
Net Worth: ($13,000)

This first day in my own business I feel like a man just freed from prison. Until today I didn't know how frustrating my life as an employee has been. On this day my feet are marvelously light, I seem taller than before, I breathe pure oxygen. No man again will tell me what I must do. The future is as open as the sky, and I am a soaring rocket. I drove to the Magic plant this morning wondering whether I'm mistaken, whether it's only a dream, and for a moment at an intersection I almost took the road to MPI.

It was a feeling I had only twice more: the day I no longer had partners and the day I no longer owned my own business.

Magic Colorants is in a wood-framed one-story building of about three thousand square feet, tucked onto a narrow, short street of crumbling three deckers in an old section of Little Falls, a defunct textile town in central Massachusetts. A section of the structure's floor is dirt, and the roof leaks. When it rains or snows we have to dodge a dozen buckets scattered around the floor and on the desks and workbenches. In cold weather a coal stove hardly warms more than a ten-foot area around it. Next door is a soft drink storage garage. When our neighbor stacks a shipment of soda cases against our common wall, the entire building rattles and shakes and lets loose puffs of hundred-year-old dust. Best about the place is the cheap rent.

Walking in this first day, I am repelled by the mess: Dust is everywhere, business papers are strewn about, stacks of opened and torn cartons lean into the air like drunks ready to topple. The toilet, so filthy I'll only urinate in it, is my first cleaning project.

Randy, freckled faced, looking younger than his forties, greets me with a big smile and pumps my hand hard. "Welcome aboard," he says, laughing. "It'll be like old times, right?"

Back at MPI he and I used to have chats about the company and the customers. I find him a bit too effusive, too smooth. I suspect such people of laying it on. Still I'll wait and see. We talk about our responsibilities, our duties.

"You be the boss, Harry. We can't have two bosses, right?" he says, grinning still.

"Why do we need a boss if each of us does our job?" I say. "You run production and the lab; I'll run sales and the office. You'll be your boss and I'll be mine. Isn't that why we're in business, to be our own bosses?" We laugh together since we have no other employees to be boss of.

"That's perfecto," he says.

We are beginning at the beginning with the most elementary organization possible. I relish the simplicity and directness of it. I'll be happy if it stays this way. I just want to make a living, a good living of course, that's all. I have no great ambition to be the biggest or even the best, just to be free and my own man.

DRIVEN

After spending two days cleaning up and organizing the place, including hanging a faded Utrillo print in the small foyer, which is barely big enough for my mother's old gate-leg table and a folding chair, I hit the road, calling on my old customers, the very ones I used to sell to at MPI. Since Magic can't afford a car, I use my own, inconveniencing Janet, but she doesn't complain. Without exception, the customers are friendly and welcoming, most promising me business.

On a typical day I leave the house at eight in the morning and call on as many customers as I can, perhaps ten or twelve, until two in the afternoon, then drive two to three hours to the plant. There I take care of the necessary paperwork, return phone calls that Randy has taken, and make appointments for my itinerary the next day. After changing from my business suit to old work clothes, I help Randy in the room with the dirt floor, operating our special machines, a high-intensity mixer and a micropulverizer. In short order I look like a painted clown covered from head to foot with brilliantly colored pigment dust. Often I work until eight or nine at night to meet a customer's delivery demand. Magic is already a going, if not successful, concern with a half dozen customers.

After furnishing last month's raw figures to the accountant, a nervous, highly excitable man with a black mustache, a friend of Rob Starr's, I meet with him in our office Saturday morning. We're in the red still, having lost $5,000, 50 percent of sales. The accountant sees the red as being black as doom and screams that I had better get our act together. This guy has got to go. I need a calm, level voice around me, one that encourages and doesn't blame.

I nearly go into shock when he shows me the current balance sheet. Our net worth is negative. He says Magic lost thirty thousand dollars last year, 30 percent of annual sales. That isn't what Cal told me. I can't believe he would deliberately misrepresent the figures. He may be a loose, casual guy but certainly not in such matters. Immediately I phone him at the marina.

"Why didn't you level with me? Christ, you said—"

"Nothing to worry about, Harry," he says as if I was being ridiculous.

"Not worry! Hell, we're below zero. If I had known the story—"

"You're forgetting, I told you we can get all the cash we need from Rob. As I said, his father-in-law is on the bank board. I've got a few bucks to put in too. And in a little while you'll be bringing in more sales. Relax, Harry. No need to panic."

"I'm carrying a pretty heavy load, y'know," I say. "It's slow going—only me on the road."

"Sure, Harry, I know you're working your balls off."

"I'm anxious for you to come aboard in November," I say, reminding him of our prior agreement that he become active as soon as his no-compete agreement with Majestic expires.

"I'm anxious too," he says. " 'Course, first I've got to find someone to take over the marina."

Cal can sell condoms to eunuchs. He exudes an amazing self-confidence. When he speaks, you feel reassured. His entire manner reflects a superior wisdom. You simply know you can trust him. That's partly why I didn't dig deeper into the hard facts before coming aboard. And I must keep that trust going. I don't think I'm a good salesman, certainly not in Cal's league. The plan is that ultimately I will manage inside, handle the administration of the business, my forte, and Cal will run sales. With such a combination, I feel we can't lose.

I call Rob Starr.

"No problem," he says. "When the checking account runs low, let me know how much you need."

What a relief. Why did I doubt Cal? I feel stinko for it.

Being a successful man, Rob certainly is not to be doubted. Doesn't he own three businesses, a shiny new factory building in the industrial park near the turnpike? Isn't he married to a woman whose father is not only on the bank board, but also chairman of the largest shoe manufacturer in the state? Doesn't her father know the governor personally, frequently have dinner with the chief justice of the state supreme court, and have a signed photograph of the president of the United States hanging in his office? Indubitably Rob has access to a rarefied circle of powerful people.

In September we rack up another hefty loss. The accountant has a conniption fit. Rob and Cal are staying cool. I'm living on faith that if I work hard enough, I'll make it. It may be a naive way of looking at things, a blind belief in justice and the American system, but it works for me. That is until I go beyond the point of salvation and where that is, is not clear. After all, I am a realist. I don't kid myself.

I notice Randy is easing off. Twice when I arrived at the plant in the late afternoon, it's locked up—no sign of Randy.

Tuesday morning, instead of hitting the road, I go directly to the plant, arriving at about 8:30. Randy traipses in about an hour later.

"Y'know Randy, we're not running a bank here," I comment.

"Right. Well, I'm caught up on all the orders, and the lab work's done, so I figured I'd sleep late."

"Didn't you take off at three in the afternoon the other day?"

"It was quiet around here. I played some golf."

"Golf! Our hours are eight to five. Customers expect us to be here to take their calls." My voice is taut.

"Hey, Harry, they'll call back if nobody answers. Right?"

"Hell they will. They'll think we're running a rinky-dink outfit, go someplace else." I'm starting to boil. "Look, we're in the red. Understand?"

I fear most my anger running amok. Since I've been in business, I find myself on the brink of bursting. I don't have patience. Suddenly everything I do has to count for so much more than it used to. I feel the world is snapping and snarling at me, trying to rip at my flesh. At each turn someone's there with their hand out. Nothing's coming in, everything's costing. Our plight is dire. Am I overreacting?

"Sure, I understand," Randy says. "What do you want of me? If you'd bring in more sales, I'd be busy. Instead you're out there having a good time wining and dining the customers while I'm back here plugging away like some fucking peasant."

He isn't smiling now. His face is as red as a sunset. And mine no doubt matches his.

"Do you think I'm having a lark? Is that what you think? Most days I'm putting in more than twelve hours. I'm drawing peanuts for pay and living off savings when I could still be back at Majestic making a buck. But I believe this business is a once in a lifetime chance, and I'm not going to let you or anyone else kill it."

I slam my fist against the wall, rattling the soda cases on the other side. My hand is bleeding and in considerable pain. Randy's eyes widen with fear.

"Now goddamn it, either you work the hours we agreed on, eight to five, or I'll go to Rob and Cal and tell them it's either you or me."

DRIVEN

Breathing hard and trembling, I'm shocked at the enormity of my anger, probably enhanced when I hurt myself instead of Randy, whom I intended to hurt.

He has to know I am behind the wheel. Everyone realizes the success of the company at this stage hinges on me. I don't mean to underrate Cal's future contribution. But no one in the company will work as hard as I do. My dedication borders on fanaticism. I am the type who, once committed to a cause, ignores all else and makes a revolution. They call us overachievers. Not Cal, who'd rather play captain on a power yacht or beat par on the golf links. Cal works in spurts, is easily distracted. He doesn't stay with a project to its conclusion. Randy knows this too. The truth is I'm Magic's only hope for survival.

My sixth month almost over, having secured very little new business, with losses still mounting, I'm frustrated and puzzled. Why don't the old customers, who used to give me 100 percent of their business when I was with MPI, come my way? Not that I expect a complete switch, only a share of their business. Sure, they're always polite and make promises, but promises aren't real orders. What am I doing wrong? "You lack credibility," one customer says. How can he be sure I'll still be around in six months or a year? He isn't about to switch, go through costly and time-consuming evaluations of my products. But how am I to make it if no one will gamble on me? There's the catch. I have to prove myself before they'll buy, but if they don't buy I have no way to prove myself.

Perfection Toys, whom I've been calling on for five years while at MPI without making a single sale, has just given me our first order of any consequence. Although Howard Carl — sixtyish, thin, rock faced, low keyed—Perfection's president, has never given me much encouragement, he never turned me away either. I've kept calling. Sitting in his office he ruminates about the economy, the state of the industry, his business and its problems and his plans for its future. I simply listen. His manner is always friendly but distant and noncommittal. Then yesterday at eleven in the morning I walked in at exactly the right moment. He was in trouble. My New Jersey competitor had sent him some defective color and refused to act fast enough to rescue him, this after he had patronized the outfit with all his business for the last ten years.

"The bastards let me down," he raged. "You can count on every penny of my business if you'll get me out of trouble. I need color now. I mean NOW."

"How about this afternoon?" I said.

"Okay, Harry, if that's the best you can do," he answered in mock seriousness.

I hightailed it back to the plant, an hour away, then Randy quickly formulated the color and together we produced the order through lunch hour. Two hours later, still taking no time for lunch, I delivered it to Perfection. How ironic that I made my first major sale at Magic from my least expected source, from a prospect I had almost given up on. In business who are your friends? Who is willing to believe in you, take a risk for your sake? So the world's tough, nothing new. It's not the kind of world I like, but there it is. I'm learning how it works, lowering my expectations. I've got to get tougher.

Even all of Perfection's business isn't enough to put us in the black. February was another loss month. I had counted on Cal coming aboard by now, so he could use his magic and save us from these habitual losses. What will it take to break the pattern? How do companies make money? What's their formula?

But Cal is still fooling around at the marina. I remind him of our deal: "By now you should be on the road, plugging away for Magic."

He keeps hemming and hawing, claiming that he has to wind up a few more things at the marina. He's been saying the same thing for months. Finally he levels with me: "The marina is losing money and I can't afford to hire anyone. I'm looking for an investor to put up some cash. After I find one, I'll be free."

I pray that an angel will turn up.

Two weeks ago Cal found an angel, a loaded but questionable character who owns a granite quarry and who, it seems, has Mafia connections. The guy is paying off some officials to secure a lease on state-owned land adjoining the marina so Cal can expand. Then Cal tells me, "The expansion will need all my attention, Harry. Don't count on me. I'm sorry."

"Damnit," I reply, "you know what Magic can become. It has national potential. You're the best salesman in the business; you've got the best connections. I know I'm a damn good administrator; we can avoid all the mistakes MPI made. Our combination can't lose. How can you just toss it all away?"

"Yeah, I really love the plastics business," he says as if he were referring to a friend who has just died. "It's a tough decision. I've talked it over with the wife, agonized over it, but the marina comes first."

The fact is I can't hack it by myself much longer. I'm getting tired from the long hours and the stress of constantly losing money. Our creditors are making noises too. If only there was some sign of progress, something positive to cling to.

I tell Rob of my discouragement.

"Sounds to me like all you need is more money," he says with a cackle.

"And more time," I agree, leaning back in the soft upholstered chair across from his mirror-topped desk. The richly overdone decor of his office shows what money can do. He lights a cigarette with a silver lighter shaped like a miniature blowtorch.

"So let's apply for an SBA [Small Business Administration] loan," he says. "It'll be a breeze. I know a lawyer who has friends there. We'll go for 25 G's. Okay?"

They say time is money, but right now money is time. If we keep losing say two thousand dollars a month on the average, twenty-five thousand would give me another twelve months to make or break it, unless it breaks me first.

"Terrific," I say, exhilarated.

Maybe Rob's not investing his own money, but his connections and status are crucial. Without Rob we'd go no place. He's my angel.

Rob's lawyer friend, a dart of a man resembling Edward G. Robinson, guarantees us the SBA loan for a percentage fee. "You'd never qualify with your balance sheet," he says. We are in his office. He looks like a midget sitting in a high-back chair behind his vast desk. "Leave it to me. The money's yours."

I don't like his shadiness, his overblown sense of self-importance based on influence. He's one of those arrogant little people who try to compensate for their size. He peppers me relentlessly with questions as if I were on a witness stand.

DRIVEN

A year later he was found dead floating off Block Island in his power yacht, shot through both eyes, his tongue cut out: a Mafia-style murder for sure.

Rob and Cal expect me to cosign the SBA note with them.

"But I thought you guys were supposed to be the money men," I protest.

After all, Rob's comfortable with other businesses and a rich wife, and Cal has a marina, two Mercedes, and a big house decorated by a professional. How can they expect me, with only a few dollars in savings and a mortgage, to go out on a limb?

"Don't you believe we'll make it, Harry?" Cal asks.

"Sure I do. Or I wouldn't stick around."

"Signing shows you mean it. If you have any doubts, you can—"

Rob interrupts. "In other words, Harry, you've got to believe in yourself or forget it."

That's a telling point. But the SBA requires my car, my house—everything I have except my wife and kids—as collateral.

"If we go belly-up, I lose everything. You guys will still have plenty."

"Maybe you'd want to forfeit your stock option—" Rob offers.

"In that case I wouldn't stay on just as an employee." I retaliate.

Nor will I give up my dream of ownership. It's too soon to do that. Nothing risked, nothing lost or won, only the boring status quo. The possibilities of the future are so seductive. I'm driven like the voyager in pursuit of the next horizon. I've got to find out what's beyond it.

"Then be an owner," says Cal, "and do what every owner does."

I sign, realizing there's no free ride.

That was my first lesson in entrepreneurship among many that would follow on a far grander scale. And it was the least risky. Back then I thought I was putting so much on the line. But what did I have to lose? A mortgaged house? A five-year-old car? That's all. No matter, that's how I felt, so I can give myself credit for showing courage.

But Randy refused to sign after his wife threatened to leave him if he did. Rob retained Randy's shares, becoming a 75 percent shareholder, and against my advice granted him a five-year employment contract with a guaranteed salary. Randy was incapable of seeing beyond himself, of dedicating himself to a purpose. His narrow personal interest and convenience always came first. I never doubted that the company came before me. Like being in love, I was willing to sacrifice my own needs to the object of my love. It got the very best I had to give right to the end. Our survival became identical. Few employees feel this way about their company. Why should they? Often I had to remind myself that they didn't. I had to learn to expect less from people, lower my demands.

Although the past two months show a slight improvement in sales, it's not enough to put us in the black. I really wonder, have I lost my touch as a salesman? I keep asking myself, what am I doing wrong? I've been calling on the trade for ten months now, proof enough, I think, of our staying power. Does Magic have some kind of stigma; are we a dirty word?

My savings account is running low. Of course I knew from the beginning my hundred dollar a week draw wouldn't be enough. Should I begin to think of quitting, look around for other possibilities?

"Didn't you say you'd give it a year?" Janet reminds me.

I need her to keep believing in me, to give me encouragement. Except for a complaint now and then that I'm not spending enough time at home, she's coming through. Without her I think I'd probably give up.

CHAPTER III
Year Two
1968

Sales: $188,000 (+83%)
Profit: $16,000 (+176%)
Debt: $58,000 (-9%)
Net Worth: $3,600 (+127%)

I'm not alone in being discouraged. Cal and Rob are also losing confidence in my ability to turn things around. And Randy lost confidence in me months ago. Cal suggests selling the company, pointing out that I can retain my share even though he and Rob would sell theirs. In other words I would be swapping them for a new partner or partners. I realize it would enable them to salvage their investment as well.

I have no objection. Rather, the more I think about it, the more I like the idea. Cal has turned out to be useless; Rob has made no recent contribution, not even cash, and a new partner might be willing to pour in sufficient working capital to pay me a decent salary and give me more time to build sales.

Burt, Cal, and I meet at the local restaurant for lunch. Burt is the first prospect, a shrewd fellow with a steel plate in his head, having recently sold his plastics materials business to an oil company. (The oil companies were moving into the plastics business, driving out the chemical companies who pioneered and dominated the industry. The chemical companies didn't stand a chance because the oil companies were their raw materials suppliers—petrochemicals are a derivative of oil—and could cut them off or charge outrageous prices, which they often did.) Burt has a round baby face with wobbly jowls; he acts innocent of any evil. He interrogates to disguise his underlying slyness.

"Are you saying, Cal, you'd sell the company for the debt on the books? And you'd stay with it as a salesman?" Burt asks although Cal has said no such thing.

After Cal gives him the correct picture, Burt wrinkles his face thoughtfully: "And Harry, you say you'd be willing to keep working for your present salary?"

"No," I say, having already explained that I expected double my existing draw. Doesn't he understand me?

Cal extols the potential in color concentrates and praises my managerial ability and Randy's technical expertise — "a genius in color formulating." He explains that the asking price of fifteen thousand dollars is a bargain. Of course the company has a negative net worth of more than thirteen thousand dollars. Well, surprisingly Burt went for it. Cal, smacking his lips, tells Burt he'll have to talk to Rob first but he's sure they have a deal.

Right after the meeting as we walk to the car I tell Cal that as far as I'm concerned, there will be no deal.

Cal is amazed. "With Burt's contacts you'd have more business right off the bat than you could handle. And you know he's got money. What more do you want, Harry? I think he's an answer to your prayer."

"Maybe to your prayer, not mine," I say. "I don't trust him. I think it'll be all his show. He's an operator."

Cal keeps working on me but I stick by my guns. Since my concurrence is essential, there is no deal.

The second case is a humdinger, a story all by itself. The main character is a tall, sleek-looking guy about twenty-eight who has inherited a string of textile mills here in the Northeast and in the deep South. His father had spent his lifetime building a business empire before he suddenly died a couple of years ago.

Some inheritors of successful businesses have more arrogance than good sense. Maybe they feel inadequate knowing that their fortune and power are unearned. Maybe they see their inheritance as an opportunity to test and prove their abilities.

The prospective buyer, Brian, wants to break into plastics in the worst way. Today, plastics are increasingly replacing natural materials in the manufacture of textile fibers. In addition the textile industry is highly competitive, mostly due to the importation of low-cost foreign goods. On the other hand, the plastics industry, still young and booming in a market that keeps finding new applications, has plenty of room for everybody.

After our first meeting, Rob and Cal expect that Brian wants Magic Colorants so badly, he would be willing to pay an exorbitant price. They set the figure at fifty thousand dollars, more than three times what they were ready to accept from Burt. I gasp.

"He'll never go for it," I say. "He must see we've got a negative net worth. If we aren't reasonable, we'll kill the possibility of a deal right at the start."

"Not on your life," says Cal. "Trust me. He can taste it. He's looking at the profits Magic can generate down the line. What we're selling here, Harry, is the future."

Who am I to argue with an expert? Cal knows more about making deals than I. As I say, Cal can sell anybody anything. Why not to Brian too?

Again the four of us meet at his Fall River plant in his old-fashioned, high-ceilinged office. Rob, Cal, and I sit in overstuffed dried-up brown leather chairs; Brian sits in a creaky office chair behind his father's old oak desk. After a half hour of light nonsense and beating around the bush,

Cal presents our absurd price. Then Brian springs his surprise.

"You've got a deal," he says. Cal and Rob beam at each other. Of course I am pleased, though somewhat uneasy because it's so easy. "I have one request," Brian says after a few moments of observing our smiling faces. Oh, oh, I think, here it comes: the deal killer. "I insist that you, Cal and Rob, retain your names on the SBA note." He speaks casually, maybe cheerfully.

"I don't see the need for that," Cal says. Rob's jaw moves up and down quietly mouthing agreement.

"The need is, Cal, it protects me against any possible misrepresentation. After all, the financial statements aren't audited; if anything's wrong I've got quick recourse. If everything is as you say it is, there's nothing to worry about. And bear in mind, I'm not quibbling. I'm meeting your asking price."

"In other words our signatures remain on the note, but Magic will meet the obligation and maintain regular payments?" Rob asks.

"That's right. It won't cost you a cent. Magic will make the payments until the note matures. However, I must emphasize, if you can't agree to this condition, there's no deal."

Cal, Rob and I excuse ourselves and huddle in the hot sun outside the front door of the old four-story brick building.

"I don't see a problem," Rob says.

"Neither do I," Cal agrees. "With the price we're getting it's worth the risk."

"Well, what IS the risk?" I ask.

"Practically none," Cal says with Rob nodding in agreement.

"But if Magic doesn't make good on the note some time in the future—it still has five years left to run—won't you still be responsible for it?"

"Always worrying, Harry, aren't you?" Cal says. "I appreciate your concern for our sakes. But this guy is going to invest a fortune in Magic. He wants it to grow. Why would he pull the rug from under it? And even if he defaults three, four years from now, there'll be enough assets to take care of the unpaid balance. Remember, after the IRS, the SBA is number one on the creditor list."

Typically, Cal makes sense. Furthermore I'm impressed with Brian, his calmness and his no-nonsense way of handling his end of the negotiation. The man is a doer, which I admire, and promises well for the future. His father surely taught him the ropes, I figure.

We return to Brian's office pleased with our cleverness at setting the price so high and consent to the deal, sealing it with handshakes all around. As we are leaving, Brian asks, "Could Harry stay behind for a minute. Since he's going to be running the show, we've got a lot of talking to do."

My supposedly future former partners depart, leaving me with my supposedly future boss.

After inviting me to relax in one of the stiff overstuffed leather chairs, Brian describes the ambitious plans he has for Magic. He lights a cigarette and rests his feet on the desktop. Casually he asks how much money I would need to get us into the color concentrate business—a hundred thousand, a quarter million, more?

"Depends on how much capacity you want to start with," I say with some disbelief.

"Enough," he says. "Enough to be a major factor in the industry. My plan is to go national. Are you up to it?"

He's young. How typical and exhilarating to think that everything's possible. "Damn right, I am," I say getting all fired up.

"I'd like you to participate, Harry. I don't mean a mere twenty-five percent. I'm talking forty-nine percent. Take forty-nine percent of, let's say, a quarter million for a starter and you're worth roughly one hundred twenty-two thousand without lifting a finger. What do you think of that?"

"Why?" I say.

"Why? Because I need you. You're the key. I'll need your loyalty and dedication one hundred percent. Do you comprehend me?"

"Brian, I honestly don't know what to say."

This is such an incredible conversation, I rub my eyes to make sure I'm there. Nothing ever came to me so easily. I've always had to work and struggle to achieve anything I wanted—until now, it seems.

"My plan is to make Magic a sales organization, strip its assets, y'know, the machinery and such, and transfer everything to a new manufacturing corporation. You and I will hold stock in the new outfit. See?"

His face is so fresh and clean-cut and his manner so innocent, in such contrast to what I think I am hearing. "Are you saying Magic will become only a shell? Is that what you're saying?"

"You can forget Magic from now on, Harry."

"But my partners—"

"Your ex-partners, Harry."

"Not yet, Brian. Under your plan my partners will continue to hold an obligation for which there will be no collateral. The SBA won't like that."

"Don't concern yourself. It's not your worry. Okay? You don't have to know a thing."

I can feel my heart rate increase from a mounting anger.

"You mean you're going to default on the note."

"That's right."

"And they'll be left holding the bag. With the collateral gone they'll have to make good on the note."

"Fuck them."

My stomach begins to roil and I feel sick.

"This is dirty," I say.

"So's the price I'm paying, and they and you know it. Look, Harry, I'm going to make you a millionaire. Think of that. Do you honestly believe they care about you?"

"Maybe they don't. I don't know. But I care about them."

"You're unbelievable, Harry. I took you for a man who knows his way around. Have you always been this naive?"

He shows only smoothness and composure. I always thought the devil spoke with a forked tongue and had horns. I mistook the package for the contents.

"Tell you what, Brian, I'll inform them of what you plan to do with Magic and if they're still willing to go along, so will I."

"You know what their answer will be," he says with contempt. "You're a fool, Harry, a real fool. Frankly, I'd given you more credit; it seems I misjudged you."

"That you did, Brian, my boy, that you did."

First thing in the morning I call Cal, then Rob, and give them the news that the deal they had been so proud of was in fact a royal rip-off. They are incredulous, but they don't say thank-you which hurts. I tell Janet about what happened and I think she's impressed. Maybe not. But it doesn't matter. Anyway, we keep looking.

The third guy who comes along, Melvyn, has a paint business in New Jersey. He drives up to Massachusetts in his new Lincoln with an entourage of three executives to look us over. Mel is a large, aggressive, blustering man who wears a shiny custom-made suit. His men seem to be always scurrying around him like puppies. After examining the books for hardly five minutes, he makes an offer of fifteen thousand dollars for Rob and Cal's shares which is ten thousand less than their revised asking price. On striking a compromise at twenty thousand, there seems to be a deal. I say "seems" because, as the minority partner who would remain with the company, I have some reservations.

"What are your plans for Magic?" I ask Mel. "Short and long range." He evades my eyes, appearing to resent the question.

"Short range, my friend: expand to making concentrates right away. This dry color product you're making has too little potential. Long range: make Magic Colorants the biggest in the industry. Go international."

Funny, why does everybody want to be the biggest? So far, so good, I think, until he says, "Of course, my friend, Massachusetts isn't the place to do it. We'll move the operation to civilization—New Jersey."

"There's good quality labor here in Massachusetts," I say. "Solid, hardworking family men."

"We've got the management, the professionals, in New Jersey, my friend. Management's the name of the game. I'd like you to come on down and visit our plant and see how we run our business. We're a top professional team."

Northern New Jersey—with its swarms of traffic, stinking air, and fast pace—isn't exactly my favorite place. We live in Massachusetts in a nice new home built to our liking in a small community surrounded by unspoiled woods. Maybe it could be duplicated in New Jersey, but here we're happy. Here we want to stay.

Though I have already made up my mind not to go for the deal if it meant moving, I take Mel up on his invitation to visit him. Maybe I can talk him into keeping things put. But it turns out that the moving issue isn't what persuades me to run the other way.

One of his managers meets me at Newark Airport. On the drive to Mel's plant the manager brags about how "brilliant" his boss is. As he recites examples, for "brilliant" I read uncouth. Mel doesn't believe in paying bills on time; his motto is "use the creditors' money, but be tough as nails with customers to see that they pay on time." Buy off-grade, low-quality raw materials where possible. Hire blacks because you don't have to pay them as much as whites. Encourage employee turnover: No one should stay long enough to accumulate company-paid benefits.

As if his plant were a showpiece, Mel proudly gives me a tour. The facility certainly is large, but unimpressive technologywise. Although I am already pretty soured on him, his behavior during lunch hour really knifes any chance of a deal. We are standing in a short line at a classy restaurant in which the receptionist, a spiffy woman in a gown, notifies us that there is a ten-minute wait. Quite innocently, I'm certain, a man engrossed in conversation with a female companion steps into line ahead of us. Mel confronts the man, to my embarrassment.

"We're ahead of you, Buster," he says.

"Excuse me?" the man responds.

"You heard me," Mel presses.

"I'm sorry. I didn't realize," the man apologizes as he steps from the line with his friend.

"Like hell, you didn't," pursues Mel.

During this exchange, I make up my mind: I want nothing more to do with Mel. Though the food is okay, the meal is miserable. I tell Cal and Rob that Mel is out.

DRIVEN

Although Mel's fate is irrelevant, I suppose what happened to him validates the wisdom of my decision. Five years later, Mel was sent to prison. One of his black workers caught him in the act of setting fire to his own plant and reported him.

As Magic keeps losing money, my partners want more than ever to unload because the more we lose, the less the business is worth. I am about to give up finding a so-called "viable partner" when Al Franconi, an old contact from my early MPI days, comes on the scene. Al is president and owns a piece of a very successful company near Boston that makes special plastic compounds.

His company combines two or more materials to change the properties of the plastic host material for a specific use; for instance, by adding certain chemicals a plastic can be made flame retardant or biodegradable and so on. It sounds technical but the process is actually fairly easy, and the product is very, very profitable. He could use his same equipment to manufacture our product. Al is hot for Magic, which he believes would broaden his line and expand his market. Simple. He woos me and Janet like you can't imagine.

He takes us to Durgin Park and Louis', both acclaimed Boston restaurants, and to his ornate home, where his wife prepares marvelous Italian dinners, and to the theater, and to a Benny Goodman concert at Symphony Hall. One afternoon we drive in his Jaguar through the North End, while he reminisces about his carefree childhood on the narrow crowded streets and his family's poverty. He regrets that his immigrant father never lived to see his success. Tears come to his eyes. "Maybe he can see how I turned out from up there. Maybe he knows," he says. I feel warm toward Al even if he is rather pompous, a braggart, and shows off his elaborate trappings. Beneath it all, his humanity and sincerity come through.

"I want you, Harry," he says. "I don't need your company. Actually, it's not much of a business. But I'm willing to pay your partners what they're asking just to get you."

We are departing his childhood haunts. He speaks quietly, almost whispering. "Here's the deal: you'll have shares in my company, a starting salary of twenty-five thousand dollars a year [phenomenal then], a free hand to run your division as you see fit, the best benefits in the industry, and an association with a staff of bright, future-oriented people. Frankly, I don't see how anyone in his right mind could turn it down."

I think hard, especially about Janet and our three children. Since I consider their welfare paramount, I've had pangs of conscience that my ambition has somehow made them pay. Again I ask, would I be selfish by sticking it out at Magic? My sense of responsibility is deeply ingrained; it's necessary for my self-respect. I can't imagine how some men break their marriage vows and abandon their families. My father held a similar view, having worked two jobs during the Depression "to keep our heads above water," as he used to say.

In years since I have known men driven by their need to be "somebody" until it literally killed them. But I didn't see this as a likelihood with me, though I know now I may have been well on my way.

Janet and I hire a weekend baby-sitter and take off for a contemplative weekend on Cape Cod, where we go when I need to think. We bundle up against the early December sea wind and walk the beaches, comparing my options.

"No doubt about it," I say, throwing some pebbles into the foamy green surf, "if I take up Al's offer, we'll have security and live comfortably."

"But will you be happy working for somebody else?" Janet asks, hitting on the most important question.

I am first of all an entrepreneur. I must be my own master, I must be free to react to events, I need to control my destiny no matter how illusory that may be. These needs are so crucial that to live otherwise is to be simply a prisoner of life.

As if finding the answer in the ocean in the next breaking wave, I say, "If I quit Magic now I'll be disappointed, admitting failure before I've run the course. Though I know right now Magic is heading for disaster, I keep thinking there has to be a way to turn it around. And if I don't try I'll lose my . . . my self-respect."

"Then for God's sake call Uncle Rudy," Janet says impatiently. "He's willing to buy out your partners. You wouldn't even consider it the first time he offered. I don't understand why you turned him down. Is it your pride?"

Janet's uncle Rudy is a retired millionaire living in Santa Barbara whom I have come to care about and admire. The fifteen thousand it would take to acquire Cal and Rob's portion is no more than petty cash to Rudy. When Janet told him of Magic's predicament, he immediately offered to buy out the partners for my sake. Though I acknowledged his generosity, I thought he was foolhardy. "It's too risky," I said. "I value our friendship too much."

"I couldn't live with his loss if I don't make it," I explain to Janet now. "No one other than myself must get hurt." I draw her to me. "It's hard enough knowing that if I fail, you'll suffer."

"I'm suffering seeing what you're going through now," she says, touched. "Harry, do whatever your heart says. Whatever you want, whatever you think is best for you is best for me." She holds onto my arm tightly.

I hug her, my eyes misty. She's beautiful through and through. We have never been closer. I love her for loving me. I know I'll make it now.

By the time we head for home on Sunday night, convinced of my destiny, I have hatched a plan that will save Magic. On Monday morning I call Al.

"You'll probably think I'm crazy, Al," I say, "but I have to say no to your terrific offer."

"To tell the truth, I'm not surprised, Harry," he interrupts.

"I guess I've got Magic in my blood. It's just that I've got to see it through to the end. So I'll call you if I don't make it."

"You'll make it, kid," he says. "You know, you're like me. That's why I want you. You're a winner. So, good luck, and look, keep in touch. If I can help—"

"Thanks for everything," I say. "First month I make a profit, I want you to be my guest at Durgin Park."

"You're on, Harry, you're on."

As a postscript to Al's story, ten years later his company's major stockholder, strictly a silent moneyman from New York, sold the company without Al's consent to a multinational corporation. Al got a few bucks from the deal but not enough to retire in his customary style; he stayed on as president. I had lost touch with him over those ten years, until one day for old times' sake I phoned him. He was dispirited and broken-hearted.

"In the old days I made things happen, but now I'm too busy just covering my ass," he said. "Best thing you ever did was turn me down."

"Maybe so, maybe not," I said. "Life at Magic has been no parlor game."

"Of course not, Harry. But no one can ever take away what you've accomplished. You're still yourself. Look at me: I'm someone I don't even want to know."

I need someone to bounce ideas off of, someone intimately familiar with the affairs of Magicolor (our new company name) yet dispassionate, and above all, honest. Such a person need not be a genius, but perhaps more like a mentor, both benefiting by and curious about the progress of my business. Neither Rob Starr nor Cal qualify, since they're too involved; like myself, having no distance, they can't always see things in true perspective. Furthermore they have a conflict between their personal needs and the needs of the business. Our accountant, the panic rouser, is of no use. But the right kind of accountant would be a perfect mentor.

On asking around, I am given the name of one Julius Hillman, a calm, quiet Jewish guy who runs a small CPA firm in Providence. Don't they say you can't go wrong if you have a Jewish accountant and an Irish attorney?

I phone Mr. Hillman.

"I'm very sorry," he says, "but we have about all we can handle. It's our policy not to dilute our attention to existing clients. However, I can suggest someone who—"

I wasn't surprised. Rather I was pleased. Good, competent men are always busy.

"Mr. Hillman, I appreciate what you're saying, which is exactly why I called you. I'm running a small business that's fighting to survive, but I believe it'll make it because I'm prepared to give it everything I can. And it's got great potential. I don't know a lot about balance sheets and P & Ls—not yet anyway. I want someone who'll tell it to me straight, someone who'll point out my mistakes, keep cool and offer solutions. I'll listen."

"What kind of business do you have?" he asks, his curiosity obviously aroused.

"Plastics. You know, from *The Graduate.*"

There is a smile in his voice. "Ah, yes. I suppose if you fail in the plastics business, it will be no one's fault but your own."

"Mr. Hillman, will you do me the favor of at least looking at what I have?"

"Well, I'll tell you, I'll look at your statements, but no promises." His words are spoken slowly, precisely, a good sign. "Come to my home at eight tonight. Bring along your entire financial history and sales and profit projections for the next five years. Or do you need more time?"

"Mr. Hillman, it seems I never have enough time, but I'll be there."

After working the entire day developing projections, I arrive at his home on the fancy East Side of Providence promptly at eight. The living room contains formal tufted furniture and ankle-deep wall-to-wall carpeting, not plain and simple like him, probably his wife's doings. I suspect he blithely tolerates his surroundings. As we sit side by side on the sofa, I lay out the figures on the polished walnut coffee table in front of us. He studies them with the concentration of a biblical scholar poring over an ancient scroll.

"You don't have a cash problem yet, but if you keep losing . . ." he says without lifting his eyes from the figures. "Inventory, receivables, nothing out of line. Are you taking advantage of terms on payables?"

His speech, every motion he makes, is deliberate, measured, gentle. Although not a heavy man, and only five years older than I am, his jowls, chunky body, and slow movements lend him a grandfatherly air.

He is getting right down to the details—my kind of man.

"Sixty, ninety days where possible," I say. "As I see it, all we need is more sales."

"Yes, I can see. You've got things down to the bone, a clean operation."

"Thank-you, Mr. Hillman."

"Julie's okay." He smiles wanly. "How many hours a day are you working?"

"Twelve, fifteen," I brag.

"I'd suggest you cut it down to not more than ten. You're exhausting yourself. You need rest to think straight. I can't discuss your figures if you're muddled."

"Then you'll take us on?"

"You can't afford me," he says, but without finality.

"Maybe not. Right now, as you can see, I can't afford anything. But I can't afford to run things by the seat of my pants either. I don't know what to do about my partners, especially the one who's not pulling his weight, and I have an unreliable key employee. I need someone to talk to, a neutral person I can trust. Know what I mean? Someone I can call up, who'll listen and feed me an honest opinion. I think you fit the bill perfectly. Even if I have to dig into my own pocket, I can't not afford you."

He blinks in astonishment, gazes at me sympathetically and holds up his index finger. "Let me suggest this, Harry. Since you can't afford me, I won't bill you until I see that you can pay."

"You mean you're willing to gamble with me?"

"A calculated risk, certainly—with the odds in my favor, I'd say." He beams, enjoying my surprise. "But don't worry, I'm determined to make up the lost fees. I'm as good a businessman as I think you are."

"You realize it may take years. I could go bust in three, six months," I say. It is remarkable. He just met me.

"That will be a serious problem, but my loss won't compare with yours, will it?"

I extend my hand, which he envelops in both of his, and we say good night.

They say that business is "dog eat dog". I too believed that until I met Julius. What is business really all about? Security. Behind the money, the drive for recognition, the willingness to take risks, to grow bigger, the purpose of business is to provide security. So business brings out the best as well as the worst in people, because such a basic need — security — is at stake. Despite the ego battles and the financial woes and the dirty tricks, as long as I kept that in mind, I understood the struggle.

Comes a miracle — last December is a winner and I end the year in the black. How did Julius know? I didn't.

CHAPTER IV

Year Three

1969

Sales: $275,000 (+46%)
Profit: $13,000 (+6%)
Debt: $131,000 (+126%)
Net Worth: $17,000 (+261%)

The first quarter of the year has been erratic, ending in a small gain. I present Rob Starr with a radical proposal. (He is now the major stockholder, owning 75 percent of Magic after he bought Randy's shares.) I find him at his office at 10 A.M. and I interrupt his perusal of *The Wall Street Journal*, his major daily activity until he leaves for home around three in the afternoon.

"Magic's future looks pretty bleak, don't you agree Rob?" I begin, seated across his clean gleaming desk.

"But don't you think we've turned the corner?" he asks, hiding behind the *Journal.*

"We're barely in the black. I can't ask Janet to sacrifice much longer. I'm reaching the end, Rob."

"I see," he says, lowering the newspaper, revealing bloodshot eyes, "but I think you ought to at least give it another quarter, say through the spring, our second best season."

By then I would be with Magic two years—six months longer than I had given myself to succeed. I may be exaggerating the seriousness of my financial condition. Janet isn't actually complaining. But to make the continued risk worth my while, I want more than is being offered. At the same time, though I believe that given enough time — and money — I'll make it, I'm finding, beyond succeeding itself, that it's the going for it and the getting there that turns me on.

"Well, I've got to tell you Al Franconi's offered me a job that looks too good to turn down," I say, feigning a look of dejection, having, of course, already rejected Al's offer. Neither do I reveal that Al is willing to buy Magic at the asking price just to have me.

"You mean you're quitting?" Rob states, finally closing the newspaper and putting it aside.

"I have no choice. The money situation — "

"If you leave, Harry, I'll shut the place down and pay off the debt. I won't let it go bankrupt; I couldn't take the stigma. So I'll have to take a beating for fifty thousand dollars." His eyes become red rimmed and his heavy face flushed. "Don't make me do that. Just give it one more quarter, that's all I ask. You're the key, Harry."

Rob can't afford to stain the reputation of his wife's rich and influential family with a bankruptcy. His failure would be humiliating enough. I've observed that he is uncomfortable in the presence of his wife's father and her brothers and tries to gain their acceptance by talking up his other businesses and representing Magic as a major enterprise. A sense of unworthiness drives him. That is the premise on which I base my tactics.

"Well, it would be different if I had an incentive, if I owned, say, fifty percent. The way things are, it's not worth it. Cal is only a drag on Magic. He's driving around in a company car and contributing nothing. Why in hell should I make sacrifices?"

Rob is thoughtful for a moment.

"Then why not buy Cal out?"

"With what?"

"Have you got a dollar?"

"A dollar?"

"Offer him a dollar."

"Do you think he'll go for it?"

"What choice does he have?"

"I'll need a third of your stock to make us fifty-fifty."

He pondered again. "You've got it."

"As a gift, I mean."

"Sure, but you've got to see it through."

"To the end," I say, elated.

Though at the time I felt triumphant, later events disclosed that I had made a grave mistake. I was in a strong enough position to demand control, fifty-one percent. If Cal had no choice, neither did Rob. But I lacked the self-confidence and the chutzpah that such a demand required. Instead I rationalized that it would be unreasonable, perhaps unfair, to expect Rob to give up total control. Since then I've learned in business to go for all you can get and then some. But if I was hesitant with Rob, with Cal I was unequivocal. He betrayed his commitment to me and I was merciless.

When I visit Cal at his marina office, he screams foul. It is a busy time for him and he is under pressure. We stand gazing out the picture window of his office at the array of yachts waiting to be made ready for their spring launching.

"Hell, Harry, I brought you into Magic."

"Magic's a disaster area," I scream back, releasing anger that I had been harboring for more than a year. "I had to find out the score for myself, not from you. I came in on the condition that you'd join me."

"We've gone over all that." He turns to me with a helpless look. "Frankly I'd like to get rid of the marina. Seems I'm in bed with the Mafia. I didn't know what I was getting into, and I'm frightened." His lips quiver as he stares at a big motor yacht tied up to the dock, bigger than any of the others.

"You made your choice," I say, startled at my callousness. "Either contribute or get out. I see no other way."

"Not so fast," he says nervously.

"I've gone beyond patience, Cal."

"I have no doubt Magic will be big someday, and I intend to be a part of it," he says firmly.

Removing the key to Magic's door from my key case, I toss it on his desk, where it clinks and bounces. "If you stay, I go," I say quietly. Very deliberately I walk to the door.

"Hold on, Harry. You and I know Magic won't survive without you. Be reasonable. Look, I'll keep just ten percent of the stock. How's that?"

"With ten percent you could control. Your vote would be pivotal. It's out of the question."

"You've got me over a barrel. I didn't think you were like this."

"Neither did I." As I depart I add, "I'll get the papers drawn up."

April:

Last week Cal signed over his shares to me for three thousand dollars, the last of my savings. I also agreed to indemnify him against a possible default on the SBA note, which he had signed. Rob Starr and I are now equal partners.

DRIVEN

That April, the month of the signing, proved to be the turning point in Magic's fortunes. Unrecognized by my partners and me, my plugging away in the territory had been gradually paying off. Enough time had passed for the customers to realize that Magic was on the scene to stay.

From April on, Magic made slow but steady month by month progress. And after that first disastrous year Magic never lost money again. It seemed miraculous at the time. Ridding myself of Cal, being an owner, and having an equal say not only freed me from all constraints, but it also inspired me to a new level of dedication.

Good employees are hard to find. One month after hiring a girl for the office, I fire her for causing a dozen checks to bounce. I replace her with another, Lou (for Louise), who so far seems competent, conscientious, and loyal. Randy now has a female technician to assist him in formulating colors in the lab. We have also just "stolen" a good worker, Jim, from MPI to run production. Meanwhile I still maintain an intense daily pace, calling on the trade from eight to three, then on to other chores at the plant until seven or eight in the evening. We also work Saturday mornings in a more relaxed fashion, often putting work aside for a bull session concerning the company's problems.

Lou is a dedicated employee. She anticipates my wishes, completes assigned projects swiftly, and provides a cheerful atmosphere. Her loyalty is religious. In her late twenties, she is full figured and dark, a Mediterranean beauty. She is the mistress of a philandering married owner of a small convenience market in town. I am powerfully attracted to her but I work to keep our dealings strictly business. Until now I've had no interest in any woman other than Janet. I'm baffled by my erotic stirrings. After all, I'm supposed to be a happily married man.

But am I? Now that I'm a full-fledged owner of Magic, I sense a change in Janet. She is often hostile and complains constantly that I take her for granted and am not attentive enough. And I too have changed: I have more self-confidence than during the early years of our marriage and I'm geared up to meet the challenges of the world. These days Janet and I reach out to each other less and less, and rarely let the other in. We tend to ourselves and not each other. Lou's attention and support are irresistible. If only Janet were more like her, more like she used to be.

Randy is less successful than I in containing his libido. He and his forty-year-old married assistant giggle and parry with each other throughout the day. He is far too tolerant of her frequent mistakes. When I arrived unscheduled from the road during lunch hour yesterday, the two had disappeared into a back storage room for an hour. Lou informs me that this sort of thing goes on often during working hours while I'm on the road.

I confront Randy. "If you want to screw her, do it on your own time and not here."

"You know how it is," he chuckles. "But you're right. I shouldn't mix business with pleasure, huh?"

Nevertheless, two weeks later Lou reports that it's still going on. The man exasperates me.

"Either she goes or you go," I say to Randy.

"What about all the months I've spent training her? She has the best eye for color I've ever seen. And she's got a family, you know. You can't do this to her."

"Okay, I'll keep her. You leave."

"C'mon Harry, be serious." He grins awkwardly.

"I'm dead serious."

"Well, you can't fire me," he sneers. "I've got a contract."

"I know. With a behavior clause. Look again."

Randy has complained to Rob Starr about me, which, for my part, makes the rift between us irreversible. Rob suggested he try to make peace with me. Rob now calls me and asks that I overlook Randy's transgressions. But haven't I already given Randy a second chance?

"Randy doesn't have Magic's interest at heart," I say. "He's selfish, self-centered, disloyal, and sneaky. I don't want him around. Let's pay him off, get rid of them both."

"That would be foolish," Rob says. "How can you get by without a color technician?"

"Randy's not the only colorist alive," I say.

"But they're hard to find. We need him. There's no one as good." His voice sounds worried.

"My God, he's got you believing he's indispensable."

"Well, I think he is."

"Am I running the company or not?" I say.

"Of course, you are."

"Then trust in me and let me do my job. Okay?"

"Okay, okay."

November:

In a week, before letting Randy go, I find another technician, Jamey. He is young and enthusiastic and takes enormous pride in his ability to devise simple, compact formulas. By comparison Randy is a hack. Jamey is a genius.

For years I had to deal with the cult of indispensability. I found it hard to accept that someone with ability can no longer be tolerable. Much of my resistance to accept that fact stemmed from my lack of courage, from fear that somehow an unsatisfactory yet talented person may indeed be indispensable and I would be worse off without him. I had also to face the judgment of my employees, to whom it seemed inhumane to blithely assume that someone is replaceable. It placed them at risk. So, putting blinders on, I adopted four principles: (1) No relationship is forever—people rarely change but things do; (2) no one is indispensable; (3) the replacement may be better but in a different way; (4) the replacement may be worse in which event he or she too can be replaced.

In bitterness, Randy has gotten even. Joining one of our biggest customers, he has set up and runs a color facility sufficient to supply their needs, costing us a 25 percent chunk of our total sales. His contract with us does not contain a no-compete clause, an oversight. It is a hard lesson.

I have just hired George, my next-door neighbor, a divorced forty-eight-year-old insurance man who has been unemployed for six months and unable to find a job because of his age. Although business seeks only the starry-eyed, success-driven young, not the seasoned, appreciative, compromising, mature individual, I approached George. He is the first salesman I've hired, and he has agreed to work for straight commission plus expenses, which is all Magic can afford at this time. So far he has taken to the road with remarkable gusto.

Covering western Massachusetts, all of Connecticut, and part of Long Island for the past month with fiendish dedication, George has had negligible results and appears discouraged. What does he expect? Before hiring him, I explained that generating sales in the color business is a slow, arduous process that will take at least a year, maybe two. Patience and perseverance will be needed. Again and again I remind him of this fact as he calls in from the road with disappointment in his voice.

Unable to avoid his comings and goings next door, Janet says that lately George doesn't depart for work until ten, sometimes eleven, in the morning. In the game of selling, a late start is deadly. It cuts short the time necessary for the salesman to develop a pace. Generally customers aren't interested in seeing salesmen after three in the afternoon. But I'm holding my tongue in the hope that his late starts are temporary. It's a difficult situation. He is, after all, a neighbor.

Janet says that George stays home all day. I have him to the house for a drink. We sit on the sofa in the living room where the kids won't bother us.

"What's wrong, George?" I ask.

"What do you mean?"

"You're not working, are you?"

He sighs, relieved that he's been found out.

"Harry, I can't seem to get myself going each day. I don't know, it's taking too long. Nothing's happening."

"But something is happening, George, only it's not obvious. For almost two years I called on the trade, thinking I was getting nowhere. It was mighty discouraging. Then lo and behold the orders began trickling in. Give it a chance."

George is the only son of rich parents, his father a utility executive and his mother a Boston Brahmin. His former employer, an insurance company, canned him for neglecting his job. His childhood didn't prepare him for dealing with adversity. He ducks life when it isn't easy; he's a big kid expecting instant results.

"I hate to say it, Harry, but I've had enough. Don't get me wrong. I appreciate what you've done for me. I don't want you to think I'm ungrateful."

He gulps down his drink and I make another for him. Drinking is another one of his problems. I don't know whether to pity or disdain him.

"Not at all, George. At least you tried."

"You know, Jim Patrone is starting a car rental business."

"Is that so? Well, I'm not surprised. He's always into something new."

"He's offered to let me buy in."

"I thought you were broke, George."

"Well, I am; I'm refinancing the house."

"It's quite a gamble, going into debt, I mean."

"Oh, I don't think so, not with Patrone."

"I wish you luck," I say skeptically.

Perhaps it's just as well. Now I won't have to fire George. But he's making a grave mistake. Patrone's a high flyer engaged in all sorts of businesses, from auto body repairing to car bars to auto security alarms. He's the richest man in the neighborhood, has the biggest swimming pool, drives a big Lincoln, and is always adding on to his house—a gym, a sauna, a billiard room. It's a lot of show and little substance.

As I feared, in six months Patrone's car rental business is a corpse. He complains that he couldn't compete with the nationals. Though he got out breaking even, poor George, again without a job, is deeply in hock. But he comes up with a brilliant solution, one entirely consistent with his style. Ditching his adoring girlfriend of ten years, he finds and marries a rich woman twenty years older than himself. So he found the easy way, after all. Or did he? What about love? Self-respect? He lost mine.

Sales are building slowly. Our color technician, Jamey, small, thin, and balding despite his youth, is whipping out compact, economical formulations that are both accurate and competitive. His generally sloppy ways and body odor are repugnant but perhaps they are a small price to pay.

Lou, always compulsively neat and organized, finds Jamey intolerable and runs away when he approaches her. Her extreme efficiency sometimes gets on my nerves, but her work is flawless. She becomes very upset when things aren't done according to procedure. She is ever conscious of my welfare, doing little things, such as serving me coffee in the morning without my asking, dressing up my office with flowers, and turning the page of my desk calendar each day. Thinking they are acts of affection, I try to embrace her one Saturday morning when we are alone. She pushes me away.

"Mr. Simon," she says, insisting on using the formal address, though everyone calls me Harry, "I already have a boyfriend. Let's keep it strictly business. Okay, Mr. Simon?"

"Sure, sure," I say, ashamed. "I'm sorry."

"It's okay, Mr Simon. If I didn't have a boyfriend—"

"I don't know what came over me. I've never done this before."

I'm confused. She attracts me. Her loyalty and small kindnesses and her obvious wish to please me stir my passion. I feel like an adolescent in love. But I'm a responsible married man. I don't care.

My life is divided into marriage and business, and the time and attention I give to each are unequal. Though for the past two years, understandably, the business has received the larger share, the two are rarely in sync. It's noteworthy that when I have business problems, the marriage goes smoothly; when the business is going well, Janet and I are at odds. Is this a coincidence? Is it possible that when it's bad with one I seek comfort and support from the other?

For some time now I have felt disenchanted with Janet. During my first year in business, when I was often discouraged, I felt she stood solidly behind me. But now when things are much better and I've regained my self-confidence, she's irritable and critical of me. Perhaps it's no coincidence that I am infatuated with Lou. I must think about this situation some more.

Last night, after a trying day at work, I walk into the kitchen around seven. Janet kisses me but I am remote. I already had supper on the road. I reach for the newspaper and withdraw to the quiet of my study. Janet follows me, babbling about her day with the kids. I half listen, and am unresponsive, trying to read the paper.

"You don't want to listen, do you?" she complains. "The minute you're here you head for the study and bury yourself in a newspaper. The kids don't exist for you, do they? I don't exist."

"I'm tired, Janet. I've had a hard day. It's no cinch out there, y'know."

"Do you think it's easy for me?" I retreat into the paper again. "Listen to me," she demands.

"What do you want of me?" I shout. "I'm breaking my hump—for you. You've got a fine house, plenty to eat, three healthy children."

"For me!" she shouts. "For me! Don't give me that. You're doing it for yourself."

We're at an impasse. What's happening? Thank God for the business. It keeps me sane. And Lou's on my side.

Lou's boyfriend, the so-called family man, is big news around town. His hobby is horses (and Lou's too) and he gives riding instruction in his spare time. He's recently been accused of raping a minor on the horse trail.

"I'd say he was teaching the kid more than horseback riding," I wisecrack, which angers Lou.

"Look, Mr. Simon, he's innocent and I don't think you should say such a thing without knowing the details."

"Well, I was only kidding, really. I don't know whether he's innocent or guilty, but they say where there's smoke—"

Her eyes narrow with indignation.

"For your information, I'm standing behind him one hundred percent because I know him. He'd never do such a thing. Anyway, I keep him happy. We're great together. So I know. Okay, Mr. Simon?"

"Yeah, I guess you do know," I say, realizing that she truly loves her man even though, from what I've heard, he's a skunk.

I admire her for her loyalty and envy her boyfriend. If only I could have the same unquestioning loyalty to my cause from Janet. But after knowing Lou's feelings, I am certainly cured of my infatuation. From now on I see no problem in keeping things between Lou and me strictly business.

Just when we're getting over the blow of Randy's vendetta and I think we're over the worst of our problems, Howard Carl calls. Quiet spoken, a man of few words, Howard is the owner of Perfection Toys, the customer I rescued the year before.

"I think we've got a serious problem," Howard says ominously.

"A problem, Howard?" I say, my heart slamming against my ribs. "What's the trouble?"

I imagine the worst. (The plastics color industry is rife with horror stories. One such case concerns a competitor's color, which after being molded into a million plastic food containers, bled from the host material into the food. The court's award to the plaintiff was frightening.)

"We can't print a decorative pattern on a plastic game made with your color. You'd better get down here right away."

Before leaving for Perfection's plant, I check our formulation and discover that a chemical routinely used in formulations to enhance performance was probably responsible.

The moment I walk into Howard's office, he calmly, almost solicitously, demands an answer. I offer my diagnosis.

"But we didn't know you were going to decorate the item," I say. "Or we wouldn't have used the additive."

"You didn't ask," Howard says evenly. "I'm afraid we'll have to scrap our whole production lot."

That tired truism, "the customer is always right," is the first rule of good customer relations. It's operative unless you think you don't need the customer and you're willing to risk having a reputation of not caring, and possibly a lawsuit. Since Perfection is our biggest customer and growing, Perfection had to be "right."

"How much of a loss are we talking about, Howard?" I ask, dreading the answer.

"I don't know—I guess about twenty-five thousand."

"You mean dollars?" My mouth seems full of cotton.

"That's right."

DRIVEN

I slump into the chair opposite Howard's desk, defeated. It's more money than Magic is worth. A settlement of this size would unquestionably destroy us. I imagine my days as an entrepreneur are finished. If I had any ability as a salesman, this was the time to use it. I raise my eyes.

"Howard, have you been happy with us as a supplier?" I ask.

"Sure have. Your company has been quite satisfactory—until now."

"There's no question we're at fault. I accept responsibility. But we're only a small outfit. A claim of this size would do us in. We couldn't survive it. And you'd be minus a good color supplier."

"Well, I wouldn't want to do that to you."

"Maybe we could work something out. We could make it up in reduced prices over time, something like that."

Tenting his hands, Howard sits back in his desk chair and cogitates silently. I wait. Then, latching his eyes to mine, he says, "It won't be necessary. I'll rework the plastic material and use it in another item. You can forget the whole thing, Harry. Relax."

He stood as I reached across his desk to shake his hand. "I won't forget this, Howard." Smiling, he seems embarrassed.

It is a close call. This is the second instance of kindness and consideration I've experienced in business. (The first involved Julius Hillman, my accountant.) What Howard has done is rare and therefore unforgettable.

Because of the ruthlessness inherent in business, it's easy to be cynical about it. It's the common view. But I find business is like a long drama in which the opposing forces are more clearly drawn than in ordinary life, and the denouement resolved with more finality. There are bad guys and good guys, bad decisions and good decisions. In business "character is destiny", but unlike drama, the good guy rarely wins.

On Sunday Janet's favorite cousin, Emily, an aspiring, driving woman, and her fifty-one-year-old unemployed husband, Sammy, visit us. Sitting over tea in our living room, Emily is impressed with our Oriental rug and original paintings. Sammy is having bad luck, but hopes for something to turn up. It always does, he says—momentarily, no doubt, since I gather he is about to hit me up for a job. Sammy's career strategy has been to succeed through pull and connections instead of hard work and merit. Most of his past jobs, all of which were concluded in bitterness, involved working for a relative. Still, he is personable and warm, rather laid back, only moderately bright, and would make a fair salesman. I like him.

I also feel a certain sympathy for him. At his age he's considered over the hill, useless to most employers and of small value to any company willing to take him on. In other words, most men, having already peaked out by Sammy's age, aren't ever offered another chance. But wouldn't such men truly appreciate, more than their younger rivals, being given one more chance? Wouldn't they work harder and be more reliable? Obviously I don't attribute my bad experience with my neighbor George to his mature age. George's lack of motivation was peculiar to him. If Sammy shows, even at this late date, that he still wants a fresh opportunity to make it, I'm willing to help him. Who is to say when a particular person is finished except himself?

"I'm positive something's bound to turn up," he says, putting a languid smile on his creased moon face.

Sammy, small and round, appears ten years younger than he is, due to a thick shock of salt and pepper hair and lively, humorous eyes.

"Recently, I had a man who didn't work out," I say. "An older man."

"Sorry to hear it," he says, uncomfortably.

"He had ability, but not enough perseverance, will, y'know."

"It's a common complaint, but usually with the young fellas," he says.

"I could use a rep. The trouble is I can't afford to pay much. Not yet, anyway."

"I'm open, Harry."

"If you'd be willing to gamble with me, I'd cover your car expenses and there'd be a small draw—hundred a week. And I'd turn some house accounts over to you right away."

Feeling Janet's disapproving stare, I am puzzled, since it is her relative I'm helping.

"I'll think it over and let you know," he says.

He could taste it already, but I give him credit for not seeming too anxious. After they depart, Janet says I would regret it if he takes the job.

Yesterday he called to say he accepted the position. Janet is sore at me.

"What if he doesn't work out? I'll lose Emily as a friend," she says. "You know they no longer speak to the relatives he used to work for. Hiring him is unnecessary. It troubles me."

"He fully understands the consequences if he doesn't produce," I say annoyed. "He assures me he'd leave with no hard feelings. After all, he appreciates my offer."

"I think you're being naive. We'll see," she says unconvinced.

Sammy succeeded beyond expectations. Among the house accounts assigned to him, I also included our biggest—Perfection Toys—freeing me to spend more time managing and pursuing new business. Sammy performed as George should have, making ten, twelve calls a day, traveling as far away as Long Island. After six months his volume was sufficient to justify doubling his draw. In a year his sales were earning substantial commissions, providing him with a very comfortable income. Consistently in high spirits, he and Emily praised me to their family and friends as a virtual savior. At parties for Janet and me to meet their friends and relatives, we were regarded with a kind of awe. We spent weekends together on Nantucket and talked about how incredibly wonderful things were at Magic. Emily and Janet, and Sammy, too, were in a thrall of wonder. Truly, Sammy was living proof that it's never too late to make it.

"See," I told Janet. "All Sammy needed was the right opportunity to blossom."

"You're just lucky," Janet said.

But luck doesn't last forever.

CHAPTER V

Year Four

1970

Sales: $601,000 (+119%)
Profit: $35,000 (+106%)
Debt: $197,000 (+50%)
Net Worth: $53,000 (+308%)

Thanks to Sammy's hard work, Magic's increasing credibility in the field, and our superior service and quality, growth is perking along at 25 percent. Our old, leaky, wood-frame building is now too small. Though it would require investing substantial capital in special machinery, I suggest to Rob Starr that we move to a larger plant, go for the big market, and manufacture color concentrates.

"Easily done," Rob says. "We'll apply for another SBA loan. The contractor who built my plant will build one for you and we'll lease it."

"Why another loan?" I object, wishing to avoid an increase in my personal obligation, which the SBA would require. "Can't you lend Magic the money?" Not only does Rob possess independent wealth through his wife, but also his businesses appear to be doing well.

"I don't have it," he says. "These days my businesses are a constant drain."

"Are you saying Magic's a drain?"

"I mean except for Magic."

What's the point in arguing? Why do I need Rob Starr if he can't or won't furnish capital? Formerly, in negotiations with the SBA and the bank, Rob's prestige and clout were valuable—yes, essential. No question, his father-in-law being on the bank's board, his line of established credit, and his personal connection with the bank's brass enabled us to secure our previous loans—more than a hundred thousand dollars—without a hitch. If I had gone to the bank on my own, I have no doubt they'd have turned me down. Who was I? Who did I know? What had I done to demonstrate viability? But such questions apply no longer.

My signing a note is risking everything: the company, my house, everything I own in this world. But Rob is risking only a small portion of his wealth. He can afford to be casual about debt. This difference in our point of view is a chronic source of contention.

Although the enormous variance in our financial positions affected our attitudes toward the business, our life philosophies, and even our personal styles, we managed to accommodate each other as long as we prospered. But eventually, during a time of stress, our inequality in wealth had serious consequences.

This month—May—we moved into a new 10,000-foot plant. It is more than three times as large as our old rented shack. After spending months designing the building, researching and acquiring the most advanced equipment available for making concentrates, and devising some innovative processing ideas, I supervised the construction and layout of the facility in every detail.

We've hired several key people away from my old employer, MPI, where disenchantment is spreading among their employees like a contagious disease. Incredibly, even Francis, my old boss who knifed Cal, once bitter because I hadn't cut him in at Magic, even Francis is demoralized and calls to see whether I'd be interested in putting him on. It is an astonishing reversal.

Trite though sayings can be, I ardently subscribe to some: "Never burn your bridges; someday you may wish to cross them again"; "Today's rival, tomorrow's boss, today's underdog, tomorrow's winner."

Francis comes hat in hand, contrite, begging to be my ally, pleading for a chance to exhibit his special genius. He had followed every step of our burgeoning success. Indeed it is evident everywhere as he walks into our glistening new building with its teak-paneled air-conditioned offices, our sleek office furniture, our modern office equipment, and our bustling administrative staff.

"I'm in a straitjacket, Harry. You know how it is with those bastards in New York," he says. "I can't take it anymore."

"I suppose you're way off schedule too."

"I'm sorry. I don't get you. Off schedule?"

"Yeah, a millionaire by the time you're forty. Isn't that your plan?"

"C'mon, Harry," he says meekly.

I can't resist the delicious satisfaction of a dig from the stratosphere of success. I have been at a constant high from the day we committed to build the new plant. Each step, from staking it out on the land to selecting carpeting for the offices, has been an act full of promise. At last I'm having things my way; at last the many small triumphs of the past two years are culminating into total victory.

I had yet to learn there's danger in victory. It was easy to take credit for all my good fortune, for all that serendipity. I grew cocky because I had not yet understood that nothing lasts, no victory is what it seems. The drama of business goes on and on, reversal and success, success and reversal.

I think I am a compassionate man. Sure, there's a side of me that's tough and practical, a side that possesses the will to survive no matter the odds, the side that has brought Magic to its present success. There's also another side that's soft, life-revering and idealistic, believing in the possibility of justice. My yang and yin — they are in constant tension. The tough side inhibits and protects me, the soft side frees me and makes me vulnerable. To have gotten where I am and to keep myself there, I must stay tough. But I can't sustain it. My yearning to believe, to be free, keeps breaking out and ultimately does me in.

I admire Francis for swallowing his pride and having the courage to come to me. I bear him no grudge for my dismissal at MPI. His vendetta toward Cal is more disturbing. But his excellent managerial and sales ability is a fact. He's been a star player in the plastic materials game. Why not use him? Someday I'll need a second in command.

Anticipating my terms, he offers to work on straight commission. A man who expects his income to be solely contingent on his performance is a man who has to believe in himself. Sharing his belief, I assign him northern New England and the opportunity to become sales manager when the sales volume is sufficient.

Janet is making a fuss over my decision to hire him.

"After what he did to you, how can you trust him?" she says.

In addition, she doesn't like his sour wife with whom we used to share a table at MPI Christmas parties. A chronic griper, she would demand that Francis wait on her like a servant. Preferring not to mingle for fear of displeasing her, Francis would spend the entire evening by her side except to replenish her bottomless liquor glass.

"She's an embarrassment to him," Janet would whisper. "What kind of man would put up with that kind of woman?"

Francis's wife and how he is with her is not my concern. But to Janet such behavior can't be ignored, for it reveals the whole man. Our differences over what qualities matter most in people are a recurrent source of argument between us. I make a distinction between a man's personal life and his business life; while Janet sees both as one and the same.

"But I'm not vulnerable," I protest. "I'm the boss this time. He does what I want. And he's a competent guy. He can be a valuable asset to Magic. Can't you see?"

"No, I can't," she says. "I don't understand how one minute someone's your enemy, and the next he's your friend."

"That's because it's business. It isn't personal."

"Of course it's personal. The two are the same. Everything is personal."

I throw up my hands. Is this difference in view confined to Janet and me or is it a fundamental difference between men and women? A soldier kills an enemy soldier even when he's against killing. Janet doesn't understand that business, like war, is serious, concerns survival, and has no connection with one's soul. If business decisions and personal feelings aren't separated, then the soul self-destructs.

Janet and Cal aren't the only ones who find Francis suspect. Old friends from the mid-west—Hal, a Ph.D. psychologist, and his wife—spend a few days visiting with us during their tour of New England. Unable to break away in the midst of our busy season, I invite Hal to spend a day with me at work. He wanders through the plant, fascinated by the various processes in operation, and enjoys talking to the workers about their jobs. Ever the psychologist, he is interested in their attitudes toward the company. In particular, he has a long discussion with Francis, who happens to be spending the afternoon in the office.

On the drive home after work Hal asks, "How long has this Francis been with you?"

"Only a short while," I say. "A very good man."

"I'd suggest you watch out for him. He's going to take over."

"Don't be ridiculous," I say.

I describe our history together at MPI.

"I tell you the man is utterly paranoid," Hal insists. "I'd say he's dangerous. The signs are unmistakable. The world's conspiring against him. He almost thinks he's a second messiah."

"Are you serious? I know the man. I hired him when he had no place to go. And he's grateful for what I've done for him. I don't doubt his loyalty."

"Take my advice, Harry, get rid of him if you don't want to lose your company," he says with conviction.

I shrug. "You're the one who's paranoid, Hal."

He chuckles. "It takes one to know one, eh, my friend?"

Like Sammy, Francis is a clear winner, as expected. Most customers liked his sort of hype, a blend of covert aggressiveness and sophistication and, when necessary, a disarming meekness. Sammy's style is warm, informal, and innocent. My way is that of a friendly problem solver. I flaunt my expertise, seek ways to help, offer suggestions. Customers call me for advice even when their problems have nothing to do with our products. Often they find the answer themselves just by talking about their problem. Realizing that, I have become mostly a listener.

Too bad I couldn't be one with Janet. I suppose I tune her out. But she does the same to me. She and I simply disagree on what's important. To her the family is everything and to me the business is almost everything. The trouble is that neither of us is willing or able to appreciate the other's point of view.

Magic Colorants, whose name I have just changed to one word: MAGICOLOR (catchy, I think), is unstoppable. The spacious new plant, compared with our old cramped quarters, is a pleasure to everyone. We now have fifteen employees, two in the lab, three in the office, seven in the plant, and two salesmen plus myself. And due to the pressure of growth, people troubles plague us.

Jamey, the genius in the lab and a workaholic, has been exhausting himself. Though I have hired him assistants, he works just as hard and refuses to delegate. And, having no patience, he has been harsh with a procession of technicians who can't please him. Since he can't grow in tandem with our growth, I'm compelled to place an experienced manager over him.

I've hired Edgar, the lab manager of a large corporation, as our technical director. After myself, he is the highest salaried man in the company. To no one's surprise, Jamey is roiling and he has come to me complaining that Edgar is incompetent. I urge him to give the new man time, but his intolerance is too much and he gives me an ultimatum: either Edgar goes or he goes. I make the decision on the spot: I choose the organization man over the genius. It hurts to sacrifice a brilliant individual after less than two years for the sake of the team. But we are no longer a small collection of star players. This is the lesson to learn from Jamey's ultimatum. I believe in the organizational concept as a sacred principle.

Why do unhappy events happen in threes? Now it's Jasper, a dedicated fifty-five-year-old man, our supervisor of production. Having once worked for me at MPI, he had been a cooperative and flexible man. As I have heaped more responsibility on him, he has changed, reacting excitably when things don't go right and resisting the slightest alteration. Most damaging, he fights any suggested modification to improve our processes. "Can't be done," he says, or "We never did it that way before," or "I know what I'm doing."

Having my own inner panic to contend with, I can't tolerate Jasper, this Chicken Little. The sky falls too often. His crises become my crises until I can sort out the facts, which takes time. His dumping on me is wearing me down. I hire Phil, a college boy in his late twenties who ran a small local textile mill, to be production manager over Jasper.

Jasper remained in a lesser job, at no reduction in pay, and sulked for eight years; I didn't have the heart to let him go, not at his age. But he never forgave me for hiring Phil. Years later his wife, having had a few drinks too many at our Christmas party, castigated me before everyone for being heartless and cruel. Jasper finally had a stroke. Losing his speech and the partial use of his limbs, he refused to see me when I tried to visit him. I thought I had done the best I could for him under the circumstances. Apparently he thought I could have done more.

Lou is my third problem. It begins the day I hire Cathy, a curvaceous thirty-year-old auburn haired divorcee. Lou had to admit she could no longer handle all the office chores and needed help. But she seethes with resentment toward Cathy. As with Jasper, Lou can't suffer change. She was dejected for weeks after we moved to the new plant. She preferred the intimacy of the creaky shack. The day we moved she cried in my arms and I had to reassure her that it was all for the best. She wasn't convinced.

Cathy's presence deprives Lou of her status as Queen Bee. Not wishing Cathy to get the wrong impression, I no longer allow Lou to massage my shoulders. Furthermore Cathy is a spiffy dresser, uses fancy makeup, and wears gold necklaces and bracelets. Beside her, Lou, plain, with absolutely no taste in clothes, looks and must feel like a bumpkin.

Lou and I finally have a confrontation behind the closed door of my office. She hovers over me accusingly as I sit on my office couch.

"You spend more time with her than you spend with me," she charges. "You take her to lunch but not me."

Her jealousy astonishes me. It's like a child's. I suppose I'm a father figure to some of my employees. They certainly depend on me for their security. As if I were her father, she is venting early anger in raw, infantile form.

"I've invited you but you always refuse, so I stopped asking," I explain.

"And you close the door when she's in your office."

"Don't I close the door when you and I are discussing confidential matters? It's closed now."

"You and I talk about the financial statements. What could she have to say that's confidential?" Her eyes are flashing with resentment.

"Confidential things," I say.

She turns, about to leave, but then swings around and explodes. "I think you're sleeping with her."

"Whether I am or not, it's none of your business, Lou," I say acidly.

When long ago I had made a pass at Lou, she wasn't in the least interested. Now when she suspects I'm hankering after someone else, she asserts a claim on me. Unable to decide how to deal with her, I do nothing. She remains cold and businesslike, which suits me. Soon I learn she is spreading a rumor that Cathy and I are making it together. She no longer distinguishes between my impersonal role as her boss and what I am to her emotionally, whatever it is. Again, as with Janet, it's a confusion of personal and professional attitudes, of injecting her feelings into the protocol of business. I have no choice but to can her, which leads to a painful scene in my office. So ends a once glorious boss/employee relationship, about which I think I'll always feel nostalgic because Lou was irreplaceable and special in the early days of the business.

I confess there's fire behind the smoke that Lou saw. In fact she was ahead of me. Cathy is quite striking, with wide cheekbones and large, soft brown eyes and a demure way. Competent and cool on the job, off the job she doubts herself and is given to migraines. When we have lunch together, she hardly eats. Having divorced her husband five years ago, she is raising two children without his financial help. "I asked for nothing," she said. "I was glad to be rid of him."

The first night I take her to dinner, she confides that I make her nervous. I apologize.

"Oh, please, don't," she says, reaching for my hand and covering it with hers. "It's not your fault. It's just that you give me butterflies. I can't help feeling this way. It's so terribly silly." She smiles, casting her eyes down and fingering the tablecloth. "I'm afraid I'm too attracted to you."

Before I leave her at her house, a three decker in a run-down section of Little Falls, we park with the motor running and the heater on in a dark vacant lot nearby. I kiss her, feeling pleasure and guilt. As I try to pull away her lips press further onto mine.

"You're the first man I've kissed in five years," she says.

"And you're the only woman I've kissed besides my wife since I've been married."

"Actually, the only other man I've ever done this with is my husband. We're both very bad."

"I'd like to take you out again," I say. She stares dreamily into the dark. I wait. "How about tomorrow night?"

"If you'd like," she says with a pixie smile. She is mine and I feel like a teenager again.

Driving home—it's about 11 P.M. and Janet and the kids will be asleep—lulled by the drone of the car, I ponder what I have done. I'm puzzled and beset with pangs of conscience. But I dismiss my confusion, refuse to find answers. I resolve to enjoy life, take whatever comes my way. Why do I feel I'm missing something, that there's more than I've been getting? Why can't I touch it, feel its substance?

My desire for more was new. Until then my expectations had been limited. Until then I had been content with my lot. My wife was a responsible, good mother, my kids were healthy and well behaved, I was my own man and making a decent living. But what was different was the sudden appearance of new possibilities, new options. Suddenly I no longer felt powerless; suddenly I had clout, with employees, vendors, the bank. Suddenly I had a woman on the side who respected me and admired my achievement. Yet, though I had responded to the change, I failed to appreciate its implications.

Except for my home life, I feel good about things. Alleviating Janet's fears, Sammy is performing beyond anyone's expectation, and Francis is content and gradually bringing in solid accounts. Phil is running the plant in a highly professional manner; in the lab Edgar is excited about our innovative digital computer, one of the first in the industry for matching and formulating colors. Three more women have been added to the office staff. Having been assigned to running the crucial task of customer service, Cathy is performing as if she were born for the job. And Rob Starr has visions of Magicolor going public and expanding nationally and beyond. Like God on his seventh day, I am satisfied.

New customers are joining our parade every week. In less than a year after building our new plant (three years after I joined Magic), we are constructing an addition, doubling both manufacturing and office space. We are also borrowing again, but this time directly from the bank (SBA loans are available only to companies who don't merit bank credit) to buy additional equipment, state-of-the-art variety. At existing high inflation rates, borrowing is smart, for it enables us to repay debt with ever cheapening dollars. My salary is now at medium five figures, more than I had ever contemplated earning. We now number twenty-five employees. Every minute of my every day overflows with phone calls from a multitude of business sources, queries from my employees, and informal meetings to deal with small and large random emergencies. These are heady days.

But my job is becoming too much. I've just hired Gary and made him a vice-president of production over Phil. Gary has been production manager of my most successful competitor, one of several that have sprouted since my early days at MPI. While I interview him in the living room of our home, Janet listens in and gives me her unasked-for verdict.

"He's arrogant, a smart aleck shit," she says. "I've heard from people who know his wife that he's a philanderer."

Gary is in his late twenties, dark, small, kinky haired, with a boyish face and an ill-suited Van Dyke beard. Having the self-assured manner of a bright and knowledgeable engineer, he sells me on his intelligence and competence. I am not offended by his veneer of arrogance.

"Most successful young people are fearless," I say. "He's a proven quantity, an engineering background, experienced. We'll be lucky to have him."

"I know, you're impressed with his degree. As long as someone's documented. Just as you believe something has to be true if it's in writing. I'm talking about his character. Doesn't that matter to you?"

"His sex life is none of my business," I say.

As she leaves the room she says irritably, "I don't see why you have to conduct business in our home. Do it at the office next time."

I think that Janet thinks the business soils our family life. Why else does she insist that family and business be kept separate? When she questions why I leave for work very early, at six every morning, I explain, "It's business."

When I can't make it home for dinner, "It's business." When I must go to work on a Saturday instead of spending the day with the kids, "It's business." And now I'm frequently away for a few days at a time, staying overnight, "It's business."

"You place business before me and the children," she charges.

"No I don't, but I know the business feeds us, pays the mortgage, buys us cars every couple of years. It gives us everything we've got. Sure it has to come first. It's a matter of survival."

Maybe she sees the business as her competitor. I suppose she's right. Lately I've been dreading the weekends at home; I'm impatient for Monday morning to come around. I mow the lawn and dig in the garden as if meeting a deadline. Sometimes I hack at the undergrowth in the woods behind the house with a vengeance. In the evening I go to a movie, escape into a story with a sensible ending.

Not all the overnights are on business. Twice a week Cathy and I are sleeping together in motels. At first she fears getting pregnant. "Just hold me," she pleads. Damned by her Catholicism, she agonizes over committing adultery. She stops going to confession and receiving communion; although she had been married for five years and was divorced, she is seeking a church annulment. Torn between guilt and desire, she prays every noon hour at the nearby church to Saint Jude, patron of lost souls.

Soon we settle into a pattern of such passionate, gratifying lovemaking, that it becomes a necessity. After only a few days of abstinence, we are driven again to satisfy our lust for each other. After work we often meet to make love in the backseat of her car or mine in the secluded picnic grounds of a nearby state park or in the solitude of the local cemetery. We meet on Saturday afternoons when the office is empty and make love on my desk. But more often we make love in the one-hundred-room motel across the state line, where our anonymity is assured. Eventually we get to know virtually every room.

We were together last night.

"I feel wonderful. You make me feel wonderful," she says as, our passion spent, we lay side by side in the sweat-soaked bed at midnight in the darkened motel room listening to soft music from an all-night radio station. "I love you, Harry, I love you. Don't you love me? Tell me you love me. You never say you love me."

"Sure I love you," I say.

"Then say it again and again. Keep telling me. I want to hear you say it."

"I love you. You make me feel complete, like the man I am. You calm me. I can be myself with nothing to hide. Sure I love you."

But I know I'm deceiving her. I'm very fond of her, I care for her. I want her to be happy. Love? What is love? I'm not sure I know. I'm not sure I'm capable of truly loving, at least not anymore. Cathy respects me, makes me feel appreciated. I can talk freely about anything, about the business, about my worries, and she listens unshaken. She responds without criticism. What a luxury!

"You're smart," she says. "You handle things so wonderfully. You're so decisive."

We talk about our families, she of her father, who is dying of cancer, and of her two children (her mother takes care of them while she's at work), and of her mother, who tries to run her life, and of her despicable former husband, who used to beat her. She begs me to leave Janet so that we can marry. "She's not a fit wife if she can't satisfy you in bed," she says. "And I can. You know that."

Out of the question, I tell her. I seek no involvement. I like it the way it is. It's ideal.

"Well, do you think it's a game," she asks. "Am I only a plaything?"

"I could never leave Janet, abandon the family," I reply. "You have to be satisfied with the status quo or nothing. Go out with others for your own sake. With me there's no future."

Maybe I'm only using her. It troubles me.

"No," she says, "I'm not in the least interested in meeting others. No one can hold a candle to you, Harry. Don't you love me? Don't you tell me that? Yes, I'll take you on your terms — for now. Don't tell me to be with others."

I can't fathom her sticking by me when I offer so little; it's pathological and my conscience is heavy as a stone.

What in hell am I doing? I feel the pressure of complication. I worry that each of us will get hurt; Cathy, Janet, and myself. But Janet doesn't know — yet. Or does she? How good am I at hiding my infidelity? Really, each of us is deprived. What I give to Cathy, Janet is losing. What Cathy gives to me, her children are losing. What Janet gives to our children, I'm losing. What I give to the business, all of us are losing. The whole mess is smashing me into shards. I am splitting myself, my heart, my loyalty, my trust between two women so that neither has me whole. Worst of all, I am mutilating my marriage vow. I take pride in keeping promises, in being dependable and honest with others. But I'm betraying my principles. What kind of man am I?

I call a psychiatrist in Providence, a pewter-haired, no-nonsense man, and make an appointment. In the very first session, as he leans back in his squeaky chair, placing one leg over the knee of the other, he begins with a reasonable question: "Why are you here?"

"I'm unfaithful to my wife," I answer.

He nods and peers at me.

"What do you expect from me?"

"I want to find out why I'm doing this."

"Most men don't care. And you want to find out?"

"I want to stop."

"Why?"

"Because I don't think what I'm doing is right. I'm losing my self-respect."

"I see," he says. "Okay, we'll see where this leads us. Tell me more."

I soon learn that I'm only part of my problem. Janet should also submit to psychotherapy because it takes two to make a sick relationship. It being early June, I propose that we take a weekend in New Hampshire at a comfortable inn that I saw advertised in *The New Yorker*, the perfect setting for trying to resurrect our marriage, which neither of us has conceded is slowly dying.

Nothing goes right. The inn rambles on a high knoll overlooking a wide swath of tall waving grass beyond which is, according to the advertisement, "an unspoiled cerulean lake." But the lake is temporarily drained, exposing a muddy bottom, an ugly wasteland of ancient tree stumps and gnarled, lifeless branches. We find the tennis court useless due to a cracked and veined macadam surface. At dinner that night, we are the inn's only dining room guests, creating a cold, isolated atmosphere. Somehow it promotes silence. "Let's drive to town and see a movie," I suggest.

We discover only one movie theater and it's showing a hard-core porn film, *The Devil and Miss Jones*. Since neither of us has ever seen this sort of film before, and since we can't believe that a small, staid New Hampshire town would allow a tasteless film to be shown, we go for it. As soon as the movie begins, Janet fastens her eyes to the floor; I watch fascinated in disbelief, until I observe her.

"Do you want to leave?" I ask.

"Unless you want to see it through. I can wait—" she says.

"I'm not a voyeur, either," I say, disappointed.

We drive the fifteen miles back to the inn in silence. The weekend seems doomed. But our room, which during the day gives us a view of a sweeping green panorama, is a success. Furnished in early American decor, and once slept in by Eisenhower, according to the desk clerk, it is cozy. That night I try to make love to Janet in the canopied bed, but she isn't interested. Nor am I really, I suppose.

On the drive home, shattered that our weekend accomplished nothing, I'm angry at Janet for not being more responsive.

"There's someone else," I say, staring ahead over the steering wheel.

She smiles knowingly.

"One of the girls in the office, I suppose."

"That's right."

She knows, she knows.

"Are you sleeping with her?"

"I'm sorry, Janet."

"You are?"

"It isn't what I want."

"Then why in hell are you doing it?"

"I don't know."

"You don't know? I don't believe you don't know. Why are you telling me? You're purposely hurting me."

Yes, I want to hurt her. I want her to make me end the affair. I want her to proclaim her love for me. I want her to tell me she accepts me as I am. I want her to give me her unflagging support. I want her to realize that my struggle in business is for us both. But none of this happens. Instead, mysteriously, she is against me. She sends a silent message of rejection. Both she and I are abandoning our vows to each other.

We are rounding a long downhill curve entering a town on a two-lane secondary road in southern New Hampshire. A twenty-mile-an-hour speed-limit sign appears and, immediately after, a parked police cruiser. The cop motions me to the road shoulder.

"Sir, your license and registration," he says.

"The sign doesn't allow enough time to slow down, officer," I say. Ignoring my protest, he makes out a ticket and hands it to me. I fume for the next hour as Janet sits beside me, sullen. We are prisoners of each other.

CHAPTER VI

Year Five

1971

Sales: $972,000 (+62%)
Profit: $23,000 (-34%)
Debt: $312,000 (+58%)
Net Worth: $85,000 (+60%)

Rob Starr has grand visions. He is motivated by a desire to prove to his wife and her wealthy patrician family that he is worthy of their class. His other businesses, a custom injection molding company and a machine shop that makes molds and dies, have limited potential and cater to local customers. But Magicolor, which is growing by quantum leaps in New England, has seemingly boundless potential in such markets as the New York metropolitan area, Chicago, the expanding Southeast, and the Los Angeles area, which are far larger and growing faster with less competition than the local market. Our new and innovative equipment increases our production capacity to a potential two million dollars in sales. Magicolor is, in Rob Starr's view, his route to fortune and maybe even fame as a successful Massachusetts entrepreneur.

"How about you and your wife spending the weekend with my wife and me at the Hilton in Newport?" he asks out of the blue.

DRIVEN

Rob is a mid-sized, roundish man, red faced due to high blood pressure, so that he always looks as though he's blushing. I am sitting on the sofa in his office telling him how well everything is going, how our bright new production vice-president, Gary, is successfully taking over more of my responsibilities, how sales to our largest account, Perfection Toys, is increasing so fast that we will have to install additional equipment to keep up. Our plant is now operating three shifts around the clock, five and a half days a week. The situation seems phenomenal, breathtaking.

"What's up?" I say, since Rob and I have always avoided socializing.

"Oh, nothing special. I just think it would be a good idea if our wives got to know each other better."

Well, I don't buy that. Rob may be sociable and he may like to have a good time, but his wife dictates and has no ache to mingle with peasants like Janet and me. Something has to be on his mind; of course, I'm curious.

Saturday we play tennis in the afternoon and have a swim in the pool; that evening we dine in the softly lighted, plush-carpeted hotel restaurant. It's a euphoric sort of day, especially for Janet, for whom this is a welcome escape from home chores and children. In fact, that night we make love the way we used to when we were first married.

Not that Janet has forgiven me my trespass. I think she is bent on proving to me—and maybe herself—that she still loves me. Since our New Hampshire trip three months ago, she has shown intermittent periods of devotion amid flashes of bitterness. She has never asked whether I'm still seeing Cathy, which I am. I'm quite able to juggle both relationships—at least so far. How can I give up Cathy? She sustains my spirit. After all, Parisian men have mistresses routinely and get away with it. Why not me?

At Sunday brunch, which begins with shallow chitchat, Rob finally reveals his true motive for inviting us on this weekend. "I'm thinking of becoming more active in Magicolor," he says.

"In what way?" I say innocently.

"Sales," he says. "I think I'd like to handle the sales end."

"Handle the sales end? In what capacity? You mean as a salesman or what?" I'm becoming apprehensive.

"Well, actually, I had sales manager in mind."

"Just a minute, Rob," I say, alarmed. "I think you know I'm basically functioning as sales manager now that Gary's taken over the production end, and I've told you that eventually I'm planning to give Francis the job."

"Isn't he doing pretty good on the road?"

My feet are tapping the floor and I'm fidgeting in my seat.

"Yes, he is, but I promised him the sales manager's job when we need someone full time."

"I say tough shit for him."

"But I made a promise."

"Look, Harry, wise up. He's only an employee. We're owners and we can do anything we want. He has no say in the matter."

Having been someone's employee most of my working life, I have not forgotten the feeling I had then of being alienated, of being a victim perhaps, and I have not since relinquished identifying with the employees. Though my role is reversed, I'm still outraged at the distinction Rob is making. If employees are mostly powerless, I refuse to take advantage. I simply can't endure the kind of attitude Rob's remark implies: that employees are second-class people. Not wanting to start a heated argument between us, I manage to contain myself.

"Christ, Rob, we'll lose him, our top salesman."

"No we won't. We'll just boost his pay a little. Where's he going to find a company as good as us? I know how to deal with him."

But Rob doesn't know Francis, doesn't know his capacity for sly vengeance. I feel like I'm clawing air.

"The fact is, we don't need a sales manager yet, Rob."

"Well, partner, you've got one."

He looks toward his wife, whose eyes are bright with approval. I suspect she is his strategist, the brain behind the brawn. My mind races to envision a scenario with Rob coming aboard.

"What about your other businesses?" I ask.

"I'm putting them up for sale. They've peaked out, but Magicolor has a future. Anyway, they're not doing so hot these days."

"And salary? What did you have in mind?"

"A hundred thousand," he quips like the lash of a whip. I wince.

"Just a minute. That's double my draw."

"Well, I think you should draw the same. We're equal partners, aren't we?"

"I don't agree with that at all," I say indignantly. "We're still loaded with debt. We shouldn't take big salaries until the debt's paid off. I want to sleep nights."

"Harry, Harry, get smart. A company exists for its owners, for you and me, no one else. And Magicolor makes enough to keep us in clover. Don't you realize the bank doesn't ever want to be paid off? OPM, OPM, other people's money. That's the way it's done." He smiled cunningly at his wife. "Anyway, I need a hundred thou to live on."

Do I have a choice? Isn't he a 50 percent owner, which denies me the power to overrule him? Suddenly I understand the fundamental error I made four years ago when I accepted Rob's offer to stay on to save him from going under. Why didn't I demand 51 percent? I didn't realize that I was bargaining from strength; I lacked the self-confidence to capitalize on my advantage. Now, in the clarity of hindsight, I know he would have gone for it. I underestimated the potential of reality; I failed to see the possibility of the impossible.

Before heading home Janet and I drive around Newport, ogling the great old mansions of the first entrepreneurial barons. We amble along the cliff walk and watch the sea slam against the rocks below. Indignant over Rob's audacity, I bemoan my helplessness. But I know I must reconcile myself.

"Maybe he'll work out," I say. "He knows a lot of people."

I am lost in thought as we walk the path in silence. Before Magicolor, I had never known power. Before Magicolor, I operated from weakness. I was condemned, as most men are, to compromise my ideals and to forsake the innocent dreams of boyhood and early manhood. If there was a formula to power, it was a secret I would never know. Though a rebel within, I was resigned to my condition; but it was an acceptance that I could never admit. Now miraculously in midlife I'm on the rise. Now there are unanticipated possibilities. Though I had imagined being in business would give me more control over my life than otherwise, I'm unprepared. I'm uncomfortable with and surprised at the world's reaction to my success.

My employees respect me, believe I am wise and knowledgeable, or at least they seem to. (One rarely knows what an employee really thinks until he or she quits.) The bank invites me to lunch in their private dining room and offers me money that I no longer need. Trade magazines, quoting me on the future of the industry, think I am a prophet. Competitors fear me. My spreading reputation elicits wonder. Those customers who formerly doubted me are now proud to do business with me, proud to have "known me when," to have helped me succeed. A desirable woman gives me total love. I am admired, important, adored, and smiled upon; I'm a force, I'm at the pinnacle, I'm powerful.

Power is so easy to use. If power corrupts, it is also the test of a man's worth. For me the novelty of success has never worn off; I still retain some semblance of my old humility. If I had made it early in life, I might be arrogant, and were I to fail I might not have the resilience to recover. But because I made it late, I don't believe it will last and I'm thankful for each additional day. If I fail I've only lost what I never expected to have anyway.

But knowing the shame—perhaps the horror—of being weak and helpless from my past, I might choose death before failure. Failure amounts to castration. Failure, death, castration: for me they are equivalents. That I want to trust but don't, or can't, is the source of my drive. For survival I am resolved to depend on no one. Though I don't shout it, I have a sense of omnipotence. So I'm always lonely, cloistered in my separateness. Neither do I trust love, in part because I don't believe I deserve love. I would lay down my life for my company, for it and I are the same. I am Magicolor. I am neurotic.

I have mastered the trick of exercising power with a clear conscience. How do I vindicate myself maintaining two women? To Janet I consign the material benefits of my success and withhold love. To Cathy I provide intimacy and withhold commitment. Neither woman is content. I devoutly wish I could give Janet both my heart and my genius. But how? Is my message wrong, or does she hear it wrong? While on the cliff walk, attempting to break through, I ask Janet that question.

"No, you have the problem," she says.

"Can't you see, it's both of us?" I plead. "You're irritable much of the time. I think you're depressed."

"Why not, after what you've done? A husband's infidelity, it's not easy."

"You became this way before I met her, Janet. It's not new; it began some time ago. In therapy—"

"No, I don't think it's a good idea."

"But why? What are you afraid of?"

Holding back tears, her words trickle out. "I'm afraid you'll come to hate me if I see a shrink."

"Hate you? That's ridiculous. Why would I hate you?" I was dumbfounded.

"Because I'm not what you think I am."

"My god, what do you think I think you are?"

"I'm not a good person, Harry. I do have bad thoughts."

As a group of walkers pass on the dirt path, we fall silent. A soft afternoon glow overtakes the day's brilliance. We hear the thud of the Atlantic against the cliff to our left. To our right a greensward of velvet stretches off to the mansions. The air is languid. Can we find peace and understanding? Janet is a good person. I see none of the evil she sees in herself. It is because of her goodness that I love her and hate myself for my transgression. Whatever she would discover about herself is bound to be salutary for our marriage. Janet, bad? Never!

"We have more locked inside us than you can imagine," I say. "How can the truth hurt us? It won't be easy, but you'll be thankful."

"But will you?" she says with a skeptical glance. "Alright, to please you I'll see someone. Remember, I warned you."

On the drive home we are at ease with each other as we talk about Janet's concerns, the children, their school, and our neighbors. There is new hope for us. When the world seems hard, home is sweet. Rob is upsetting my plans for the future, and I'll have to contend with Francis's certain outrage. There's bound to be serious trouble ahead. I'll need Janet by my side.

Janet's psychiatric sessions unleash a pent-up anger toward her deceased father, who had abandoned her (and her sister) to a cruel housekeeper shortly after her mother died, when Janet was four. Rarely home, a womanizer, her father was a traveling salesman for a textile company and occasionally brought strange women home to share his bed. Janet's emerging rage energizes a combative spirit that I haven't seen before. Without telling me, she calls Cathy at the office to invite her to lunch.

"Is it all right, Harry? I didn't think you'd mind," Cathy says, assuming I knew.

"This is ridiculous. What's the point? What's there to talk about?" I say.

I suppose it's flattering to have two women fighting over me. I have to admire Janet's spunk. And maybe Cathy is curious to see for herself what Janet is like. Maybe she can find out what holds me to her.

After the meeting each give me their view of what was said.

"She said she'd never give you up," Cathy reveals. "I told her it was too late. She called me a husband stealer and a whore. A whore, imagine. Well, I said if she was as good in bed as me she wouldn't have to worry about you.

She got so angry she began swearing at me. Words I wouldn't repeat. From the way you talked, Harry, I thought she had class. She's a real bitch. How do you stand her? I was so embarrassed. Then she up and left in a huff and I had to pay the check."

"Here, let me reimburse you," I say taking my wallet from my hip pocket. "How much was it?"

I too felt embarrassed, for both of them, and a little amused. Nothing was settled. The two women's hatred for each other was only reinforced. The episode strikes me as childish. Cathy takes the money.

As soon as I get home that evening, Janet leads me to our bedroom and closes the door behind us.

"I suppose she told you about the lunch," she says, sitting on the bed while I stand.

"Yeah. Her version."

"You've got yourself someone you deserve. She's tough, Harry, a hussy, and I'll bet a real handful. Not a smidgen of class. What in the world do you see in her?"

"Why did you meet her? What in hell did you expect to gain?"

"I'm trying to save my marriage."

"You won't save it this way. The problem is inside us, not out there." I point to the window. "Not because of someone else."

"I wanted to see what she was like, to see how low you've stooped."

"Are you satisfied?"

"No, I want you to fire her."

"I can't do that. She does a good job. What goes on at the business has nothing to do with you and me. You're telling me how to run the business. Don't you dare."

"Well, I never!" She stands and walks to the door. "You fire her or—" Her voice cracks, approaching a scream.

"Or what?" I say.

Opening the door, she storms out.

I now know what the "or what" is. Janet is boycotting me in bed, not that I'm hot for her nowadays. For years I suspect I've made love to her more out of habit than desire. I bury myself in work, and have sex with Cathy three nights a week. At least Cathy appreciates me. Her gift of herself validates my worth. Furthermore my infidelity serves as a way of punishing Janet, albeit secretly.

I've hired and fired three male office managers in the past couple of years. The current one is Gideon — Gid — an accountant who spends most of the day bent over his desk preparing and analyzing our figures. He pores over them like a Roman soothsayer studying entrails. No doubt, Gid has a remarkable ability to find in mere figures the answer to every possible question and to recommend a course of action. But he has no aptitude for dealing with the five women under him. His attitude toward "the girls" is less than casual; he has no interest in their feelings or ideas. When someone is puzzled by or objects to an instruction, he responds, "Do it and don't ask questions."

Cathy has questioned Gid on his changing a procedure I had instituted a couple of years ago. She insists on first consulting me, which in effect is to go over Gid's head. He warns her: "Do what I say or you can leave."

If Gid knows I'm having an affair with Cathy, he is undeterred. I have no illusions that the girls know about Cathy and me, but it's unlikely that the rumor has reached him. Coming to me in tears, Cathy closes the normally open door of my office behind her. I'm at my desk composing a letter.

"I want to do what you want, not what he wants," she pouts, sitting on the couch, dabbing away her tears with a lace handkerchief.

"But he's your boss, Cathy," I say. "He's not always going to do things my way."

"You're my boss."

"No, I'm not your boss."

"You're my lover," she purrs coquettishly.

"Okay, but not your boss. You've got to do what he says. Understand?"

"Why can't I take my orders from you, please, my love?" She stands, presses her breasts against my head, and, bending over me, kisses my lips.

"This is no time. Not here," I say coldly, pushing her away.

"Why not? Don't you love me?" she asks.

"Cathy, stop it. This is business."

"Is that all it is? It's only business between us?"

"You came to me with a problem. I've told you what to do," I say, annoyed. "Now, I'm out of it."

"You mean, you'd let him fire me?"

I hesitate, smelling an ultimatum. "If you won't follow your boss's orders—"

"I don't believe it. I don't believe what I'm hearing."

I swallow hard. "I'm sorry, Cathy."

She walks to the door and without opening it grips the knob, her eyes filling with tears.

"You don't really appreciate me, do you? I'm more loyal to you than anyone. I only do things that are best for you. I give you everything: my heart, everything. No one does as much for you. That nice stereo the office gave you last Christmas, do you know what they really wanted to give you? A piece of junk. They ought to be ashamed of themselves, I told them, a wonderful man like you. And this is the thanks I get. You bastard, you ungrateful bastard."

Her lips form an ugly curl; she is hysterical with rage. "He can't fire me, do you hear? He can't. I quit, I quit." She swings open the door and flees from my office and out of the building.

Obviously, there's more to Cathy's quitting than the incident that prompted it. I know she's been frustrated over my refusal to commit. But she's a free agent. I profess no claim on her. But she wishes I would. It's as if she's in my thrall. Today I let her walk out of my life. I have a sense of relief. Perhaps I can expect more peace from now on. I'm weary of having two women.

Today I fire Gideon. I fire him because of his insensitivity, but I tell him he's overqualified for the job. I don't need a numbers expert to run the office. He shrugs and departs unperturbed. He has been with me less than a year.

I appoint Emma, our receptionist, as manager. She's a fifty-year-old charmer, same age as myself, tall, and full faced with cheerful eyes. My managers express concern because she's inexperienced. In a practical sense, they're right. But I choose her for her exceptional human qualities; she will easily learn the job. She enjoys people yet has no illusions. The worst are not sinners, the best not saints. Informally she has been much more than a receptionist. Though unappointed, she is our counselor, ever ready to listen and encourage. The employees say she mediates disputes, is fair, impartial, honest, and patient. In short, she's a natural ombudsman, a rare find. She stands firm by her principles. Her deficiencies? Only one: Her empathy sometimes goes too far and is better suited to a philanthropic rather than a profit-making enterprise.

Hardly giving me time to remove my jacket, Emma comes to my office this morning complaining that her people aren't earning enough.

"I don't know," I say cautiously. "You realize, of course, that we don't have to pay more than the market. Yes, I'll have to say 'no'. We can get all the girls we want for the wages we're paying."

"So they could earn just as much elsewhere, I assume?"

"Yes, I suppose you could say that."

"Well, then, why not give them an incentive to stay? I mean, they're trained in our ways and procedures, so aren't they worth more to us?"

"Well, that's true," I say, impressed with her dogged logic. "What are you doing about a replacement for Cathy?"

"One of the girls is handling the job quite adequately," she says proudly.

"Temporarily, you mean."

"No, Harry. If you'll agree to the increase, I won't hire a replacement. I'm confident things will run smoothly."

She has me. Her argument is irrefutable. As a businessman I can't resist getting more for less. I grant the wage increase, including one for herself, which she refuses "for now, until I have proven myself". But I insist upon it.

A business is like an old worn-out automobile: Solve one problem, another pops up. The most difficult problems involve people—myself included—whereas the technical problems and machinery failures are readily solvable. Were I granted one wish, it would be the robotization of Magicolor. But how boring it would be. After all, when things are smooth, I get antsy.

Rob Starr has renovated the empty office next to mine with teak paneling and deep pile carpeting and furnished it in French Provincial. When Francis learns that Rob will occupy the new office, he asks why. Ever perceptive, Francis knows our staff is adequate. Rob will surely be redundant. When Francis asks what Rob's job will be, I break the unhappy news as he sits on the couch in my office, a sheet of paper containing a tally of his record-breaking month's sales in his hand.

"Sales manager," I say.

"Did I hear you right? You said sales manager?"

"That's right," I say weakly.

"What about me? Where do I fit in?"

"I'm sorry, Fran, damn sorry."

He sits silently for a while letting his fuse sputter, then says, "I thought we had a deal, Harry."

"We did. I know." I feel helpless against his rightness.

"I've done what I said I'd do." He tosses his tally onto my desk. "I won't take this. Now it's your turn to deliver."

No question, he has surpassed expectations. I don't like his intimidating, conspiratorial style, but it works with most customers.

"Fran, I'm sick about it. I fought like a tiger for you, but Rob wouldn't listen and—"

"You're the president of this outfit, aren't you?"

His tone and manner are commanding, reminiscent of our MPI days, and I feel uncomfortably like the employee again being given notice.

"Hell, I can't tell Rob what to do," I say defensively.

"So you let him tell you what to do. Is that it?"

"No, but it's a fact of life that he owns fifty percent of this business. He has an equal say. Can't you understand my position?"

"Do you understand mine? I'm the one who's injured."

I feel a surge of hate toward Rob. Shafting Francis is bad enough, but he has caused me to break my word, which strikes at my integrity. Francis can't know that I too am injured.

"I'm helpless to do anything, Fran. As I say, I'm sorry."

"Rob doesn't know the first damned thing about the business," Francis says. "He can't tell me what to do."

"So, he'll learn fast. He's no dummy. Help him," I say, foolishly, knowing I'm asking too much.

Francis stares at me with a leer, as if to ask, Are you kidding?

"Give it time, Fran. See what happens. Rob has a short attention span. Who knows? He may tire of the job. You know how he is with his big ideas. He wants plants across the country, a dreamer. He's not for gut work. But the way we're growing, you'll get your chance. And I'll see to it."

"Shit," says Francis. He lunges for my desk and the paper containing his record sales tally, retrieves it, and departs my office, leaving me wondering what he will do next. I suspect, that he hasn't the slightest idea himself.

CHAPTER VII

Year Six
1972

Sales: $1,514,000 (+56%)
Profit: $74,000 (+222%)
Debt: $389,000 (+25%)
Net Worth: $131,000 (+54%)

My sixth year in business has been a good year on the surface: Sales are growing by more than 50 percent; the plant is operating around the clock five and a half days a week; and month by month profits are increasing dramatically (despite Rob's and my exorbitant salaries). I doubled our manufacturing space in April, and in October I shall complete additions to the lab and office, bringing the total facility to twenty-five thousand square feet—two and a half times the original size. It has been like gliding on ice; may it never melt.

"You're my hottest client these days," says my trusted accountant, Julius Hillman, whose firm, after working gratis for three years, has been steadily raising the fee with each year's success. At the end of each quarter Julius sequesters himself for a day or two in one of our corner offices to "do the books," after which he sits down with me to review the rough first figures. After June 30, the end of our fiscal year, we take a long look together.

"We're operating at 110 percent now," I say.

"I expected you to succeed, Harry, but I confess not at this dizzying rate."

"Y'know, Julie, I'm as surprised as you. I have to pinch myself. Never in a hundred years did I think we'd get so big and make this kind of money. I would have been content with just making a good living, y'know, enough to take care of the family comfortably, send the kids to college. That's all a man needs to do. But this—" Tears well up in my eyes. "Just between us, I have this feeling I don't deserve it."

"If anyone did, the way you've worked, Harry—"

"I know, I know, but other guys work too. My father worked sixteen hours a day for years through the Depression—in his small market all day, then at night managing the local Postal Telegraph office. They kept cutting his pay. He hated the big corporations. "You can't trust them," he'd say. You know he believed in Roosevelt more than he believed in God. He was one of the lucky ones: He worked. None of us starved; we got new clothes when the old ones wore out. But he never owned his own house, he never had much money in the bank, and he was afraid to take time off.

"I look around, look at the guys in the plant, some my own age and, y'know, they've got no security. I worry about that. Everybody seems to think I'm a genius, like I'm privy to a kind of superior wisdom. But I'm the same guy I've always been. Until I got into business, no one thought I was smarter than anyone else. What happened? You know what happened? Luck, and that's all that happened."

I can confide in Julius. Most of his clients are people like me. He knows how we are—what starts our engines. Knowing him is a pleasure.

"You don't give yourself enough credit," he says. "You were clever to perceive an opportunity when things seemed dismal. What about your courage to take a risk, your determination to win, your ability to make others believe in you, your employees, the bank, me?"

I can hear the commotion of the outer office, the phones buzzing, the murmur of zealous voices, the sounds of business.

Julie's become a good friend, therefore he's prejudiced. He believes he serves a rational, purposeful entity and not one formed by blind chance. His work is important. He thinks he tells me where my business has gone so that I can direct where it will go. He believes I can create destiny.

"Opportunity? Look, Julie, I was over forty when I began. It was then or never; this is the only business I knew. Courage? No, foolhardiness. I ask myself, given what I now know, would I do it over again? I'm not sure. My marriage is a wreck. The people who believe in me have to be nuts. They think I can't make mistakes. But I know better. I know I'm not in control. More happens than I can make happen — in this business, in this life. I've shed my illusions."

Julius snorts, "Are you saying you have no role in Magicolor's success?"

"Sure I've got a role. I'm here. That's my role. I react. I make plans — next month, next year, five years from now — but they're useless fictions. All I do is react. A machine breaks down, a key employee quits, a customer goes elsewhere, interest rates go up — I react."

"Of course, but more often than not you react correctly. That's my point. So if you don't appreciate what you've accomplished, just as well. Does a great artist recognize his masterpiece in the making? Only the world can say what it is, what it's worth."

"Hell, Julie, this is no masterpiece. It's just an ordinary business."

"It's your masterpiece, Harry, regardless of what you think." Julie raised his finger in emphasis. "And it's all there is."

My masterpiece! Certainly Magicolor is the product of my style, my ideas, my principles, my honesty, my dishonesty, my self-deception, my hope, my despair, my reality, my dream. As with an artist's work, it is no more or less than its creator. It is myself.

"Y'know, Julie, I love it all, love it, love it. There's not a boring split second. I wouldn't swap what I'm doing for anything."

"No kidding! What do you know!" He patted my hand and laughed.

Enough talk. Now to business.

"We've got to add another production line to keep up with Perfection's orders. But a quarter million bucks is a lot of money."

"You've got the business. Why hesitate?"

"Well, old Howard Carl sold his company to a conglomerate and he's managing it for them, but it's not the same. I guess it's my father's voice. I don't trust big outfits. Their managers are afraid to make mistakes. They try to protect their own skins first. I'd rather take a chance with entrepreneurs who expect to screw up once in awhile and pay for it. I worry that Perfection makes up fifteen percent of our sales. It's a dangerous situation."

"To be sure. Still, you're gaining new accounts and the old ones are growing. Business is strong."

"Rob's pushing for another plant out west, Chicago area."

Julie listens without further comment and my phone buzzes. Cathy, whom I haven't talked to since she quit three months ago, is on the line. Sobbing, she says, "I need you, I need you." I tell her I'm busy, and I'll call her back as soon as I'm free. Reshuffling my mind back to business, I tell Julie I see no reason for another plant. We are big enough already; my salary is more money than I can spend and I have enough to keep myself occupied and interested. Furthermore it's easy enough for Rob to want a second plant, since he'll not have to lift a finger to make it go. I find there's an enormous vacuum between what Rob wants and what he's willing to work for. In his first few months as sales manager he has shown little aptitude for the job, to put it euphemistically. Actually, he's incompetent.

"Only you know your limits," says Julie.

"I've reached them, at least for now," I say, terminating our conversation.

At the beginning Rob traveled with the salesmen, meeting the customers, taking them out to lunch, showing off his charm. After this phase was over, he sat in the office wondering what to do, and for good reason, because it was obvious there was nothing. I had all tasks assigned, everything well under control. I suggested he try his hand at selling, go out on the road himself, go after the wire and cable trade, a specialized market in which we do negligible business. Good idea, he said, reminding himself of several social contacts he has in that industry.

After a couple of months with little to show for his effort, he begins spending more time in his office reading *The Wall Street Journal*. I point out that it will take at least a year of calling on prospects to break into the market; however, expecting instant results, he has given up and tries no further. I think of George, my next-door neighbor, who had also thrown in the towel. Both men lack determination, a willingness to go against odds. In a sense they're like spoiled children seeking immediate gratification or none at all.

Rob comes into my office one day with a cup of coffee in hand and sits down on the couch. "I'd like to take over the quoting," Rob demands, a task that I have always assumed because it affects our profitability directly. From my point of view, he may as well be asking for the key to our safe.

The aim of quoting is to attain the highest possible price, not leave anything on the table, as they say, without losing the order. To achieve this requires an intuitive feel for the market, the customer, the application, and the competition. Due to Rob's limited experience and his loose nature, I don't believe he is capable of assessing such a complex mix of factors, or parameters, as highfalutin executives might call them. But quoting is rightly a sales manager's function and I don't stop him.

"If you do it, I want to review the prices before they're sent out," I say.

"Harry, I'm no kid."

"I'm only saying you don't know the business well enough yet. If you quote wrong, well, you know what that can cost us."

He goes along with me. It's hard to give up quoting, or to relinquish control of any function that I consider essential to our success.

As it turns out my fear is justified: After months of practice Rob shows no judgment, no shrewdness, no perception of the subtleties in quoting.

While I am away on vacation or on a sales trip, his quotes are not subjected to my review. Only months later after running a customer's order quoted during my prior absence do I discover from our job costing that we have lost money due to Rob's below-cost quote.

"How could you do this?" I demand, storming into his office and brandishing the file copy of the quote and cost sheet in his face as he sits behind his desk. We have just lost thousands on an order due to a misplaced decimal point.

"Damnit, you should have known. Common sense should have told you that the price had to be wrong. Any ninny would know it was ridiculously low. But you don't think, do you?"

"I'm sorry," he says, slowly raising his remorseful eyes to mine. "I'll watch out from now on."

"I was afraid this would happen. Damn you, Rob."

"Harry, take it easy. Calm down. Don't get so excited. I said I'd be careful."

"But you don't know what in hell you're doing," I say. "I doubt if you ever will."

"Maybe if you'd stop looking over my shoulder—"

"I have to. You don't think or you don't care. Which is it?"

"Sure, I care," he says defiantly. "What are you so panicky about? We're making money, aren't we?"

Rob has a point. Why am I making such a fuss? We can afford some mistakes. I regret my explosion, a futile over-reaction. Yes, we're making money; it certainly forgives much. But if we weren't—a circumstance not hard to contemplate—how would I cope with him? What drives me to such terrible perfection? Why is every mistake such a fatal threat? Small errors are dangerous but triumphs don't count. Magic is now so finely tuned, I fear the slightest error. I hang suspended by a spider's strand.

Cathy is also worried. When she quit out of pique she had no job to go to; in searching, she found nothing that could compare with what she had. I paid her well, gave her the freedom to organize and perfect her tasks, and, during most of her employment, acknowledged her competence. Undeniably, sleeping with the boss is a special and favored status. Though that status could be matched by some other boss, Cathy finds the idea unacceptable, for she is not promiscuous and I am the one she loves. Though she hadn't fully realized it until now, leaving her job at Magic also meant leaving me, depriving her not only of her specialness and my protection, but also, it seemed, worst of all, my love.

"Please take me back," she pleads amid sobs when I return her call that had interrupted my meeting with Julie. "There aren't any decent jobs around. Everything is menial office work and it pays nothing. I've made a terrible mistake, Harry. Take me back; please take me back."

"It's not up to me, Cathy. Gideon fired you and — "

"That's not true. I quit."

"Well, whatever, it has to be final. Look, it's better this way: you'll be on your own, no complications. It's cleaner, easier for both of us."

"But I've lost you," she pouts.

Before returning Cathy's call, I close my office door and commune with myself. What does Cathy really mean to me? Here's an opportunity to give her up and to tell her so. Do I want that? I have already informed Janet that Cathy is gone. Of course, she's relieved, but, surprisingly, so am I. Balancing Janet and Cathy was a hard act to sustain, for I saw that I was deceiving both women. So Cathy's departure served to clear my conscience.

Yet, when Cathy finally calls, I don't seem able to turn her away any more than I can abandon Janet. I believe my primary role in the world is that of protector and provider for my wife, my children, my mistress, and my employees. I believe every man's duty in life is to take on dependents and to care for them to the best of his ability. Is this not really a man's mission? Do not my wife, my children, my mistress, and my employees expect me to fulfill that mission? It's an ancient, primitive, and valid one. I also believe most men willingly meet their responsibilities as a function of their self-esteem, although each man sets different limits. My limits include all who depend on me for material support in any form. But some men's limits, such as Rob Starr's, end with family.

"You haven't lost me," I assure Cathy.

"Say you love me, Harry."

"I do."

"Say it."

"Of course, I love you."

"My darling."

"Cathy, are you free for lunch?"

DRIVEN

I see Cathy and sleep with her as long as she needs me. At last she has found a job as a buyer for a small women's clothing chain. A tasteful dresser, Cathy knows clothes. We continue to hang onto each other which, for my part, is acceptable because now it's easier than when we faced each other at work and pretended we had nothing going. In a sense, my infidelity is less demanding. She's not there every day to remind me of it.

We hang on also because of what I call the conspiracy factor. Cathy and I share a secret life together. Neither our children nor our parents nor our friends know of it. If some of our employees do, it is only speculative. We are therefore joined in a common rebellion against the proper and conventional, against society's prohibition. It seems we need to rebel to be free. Specifically, Cathy is betraying the church and her parents, and I, of course, my wife. It is the glue to our love. Somehow our secret is an affirmation of a precious part of ourselves that is strictly our own and must never be shared with others.

I presume Janet has no inkling that I still see Cathy. What is our marriage? I suppose it's a kind of truce, barren of affection but not without devotion. Ask do I love Janet, I would have to say yes. It's a caring, a remnant of passion spent. The glue is our duty to our children and each other. Anyone watching Janet and me together would mistake our marriage for the real thing. Whereas Cathy and I defy the world, Janet and I deceive it.

By why is it this way? It's not what I want.

My therapist says, "Life has played a dirty trick on both of you. You changed as you began to succeed in your business—becoming more confident, more powerful, no longer needing your wife as you did while you were struggling and feeling helpless. And she, needing you to need her—her insurance policy, so to speak, feels abandoned and unprotected. You've cheated her of the man she once knew—a dirty, low-down trick. And I suspect she's mighty angry."

"So here I am carrying things a step further by being unfaithful and withholding most of myself from her. I despise what I'm doing."

"You blame her for your predicament?" asks the therapist, a blunt-speaking, sixtyish, graying man, resting back in his desk chair.

"No, I don't."

"Yet you acknowledge the abandonment."

"I'll always stand by her; I'll never truly leave her. I couldn't bear us to split."

"Well, isn't that nice?" he says. "Be advised, the trick is on you as well."

Although my marriage is like a shipwreck, my business is like a great ocean liner ploughing proudly through the waves. Its momentum is so powerful that nothing can stop it, not even Rob's costly mistakes. Nothing that we do wrong seems capable of deflecting us from our glorious course.

Good fortune often causes ordinary men to feel infallible. Rob has a mystical belief in himself; he believes that his life is somehow charmed and that Magic owes its success mostly to him, simply because he is Rob Starr. No other reason is necessary. He is convinced that any venture he tries will succeed, even when at its bleakest. That his other businesses have not done well does not challenge his belief. After all, he unloaded them profitably. The proof lies in the final result. His earlier business ventures were merely preparatory to the big one. Magicolor's soaring success confirms his predetermined destiny.

"The only way to expand is geographically—build more plants," Rob speculates as we are having lunch together. "A satellite in Chicago, then maybe New York, down south—Atlanta or Charlotte—and eventually on the West coast, L.A. Someday, Toronto. The Canadian market is still virgin. Then overseas, the Common Market, maybe Paris. Have an apartment there. Nice, huh?"

Rob's strategy for growth by satellites is correct. Service is important to customers in the plastics business. Since delivery time is a factor, our optimum shipping range is no more than five hundred miles. Frequently a customer demands shipping overnight or next day because he has inadvertently run out of a color which could mean lost production time. And since most colors are custom-made, we must be ready and willing to move swiftly.

"I think one plant is enough for now," I insist.

Rob's a mad dreamer. Cover the entire country, then the world! But who's going to perform all the necessary work? Not Rob. The adventure of it is certainly appealing. But with Rob it's mostly ego; bigger is better by his definition. To be bigger qualifies him to join his wife's family's league. I'm wary of Rob's rampant ambition.

The restaurant near the plant is crowded with office workers. Rob and I are seated across a crimson formica table in a red plastic-upholstered booth. We are more fortunate than most of the people seated around us who are wage earners and must return to their offices. No doubt, Rob and I are beneficiaries of more worldly luck than they. How many are so fortunate to be their own masters? How many receive enormous reward for their efforts, as Rob and I do? I know their plight and empathize. Rob has no idea how it is and is contemptuous. He ignores them. Our small booth is the seat of the only important action; the area and people around us are an insignificant blurred backdrop.

"Why keep the lid on if there's nothing to stop us?" he asks. "There's a whole world out there—"

"Don't we have enough, Rob?"

Clicking his tongue, he gazes at me piteously.

"What are you afraid of, Harry? Becoming rich? We're small time now, but real success, big success, is ours for the taking. And you don't want it. My God."

"It's not that easy; it's risky."

"Not with Rob Starr, not the way I have it figured."

He expounds a daring proposal. He has a friend, the president of a cash-rich local coatings manufacturing firm, who is seeking to join forces with an up-and-coming outfit like Magicolor. Their market is declining as their customers find it cheaper to make coatings in-house. Rob and the president explored the idea (without consulting me) of merging our two companies in a start-up color concentrate venture in the Midwest. The coatings company would furnish cash; we would furnish technical expertise and management staff. Ultimately the two companies would completely merge through a stock swap.

Though Rob's proposal is unlike anything I would have envisioned for Magic, I'm intrigued. He reveals his concealed purpose.

"In a year we'll end up the major stockholders in the merged company. You can bet on it."

"Don't you think that's stretching it?" I say, though I'm impressed with his Machiavellian imagination. "After all, you say they're five, six times larger than we are."

"Doesn't matter, Harry. The ownership is fractured. They're fed up with the present management. Between you and me we'd have control, especially after we show their board what we can do in the joint venture. Then we kick out the dead wood, get rid of the president."

"You mean your friend?"

"Well, business is business. He's a nice guy but that's his trouble."

Rob's scenario is rife with unknowns. Who knows how successful a new venture will be? Can we be sure that we will win over the other stockholders? What are the politics of the situation? Will the existing president take his ouster lying down? Furthermore, operating with a secret strategy in mind is not my style. I'm open and direct and attain my goals by dint of hard work and ingenuity. Any other way makes me uncomfortable.

"You'd be president," Rob says.

I'm president of Magicolor clear and simple, my own man in my own place, with no possible threat of being unseated. If sometimes I choke on Rob, I still manage to get him down. But being president of the merged entity would be another matter. At Magicolor my position is earned, the harvest of my storm and stress. In the new position I would be no more than a pretender.

"If we're going to expand, I'd rather we do it on our own," I say. "Outsiders will only complicate things."

"We're talking about geometric growth, Harry. They're there, ready for the plucking. It'll be a cinch to pull off. What's the harm in just talking?"

"Just talking," I say.

We meet with their tall, patrician president and his sleek, tanned vice-president at their place and talk, and they meet at our place and talk, and the more we talk, the more we become mired in their muscle-bound thinking. They leave no detail to chance. Every eventuality must be anticipated with a plan of action. Risk must be reduced to a virtual zero. Their manner, strangely cozy and laid back, as if we were at a club chatting, belies their anxiety. The talk is incessant and Rob has fun.

Nothing comes of it; nothing could come of it because they know any rescue effort will render them superfluous. Their sun had set before we met. Only months later their board fired them.

During the lengthy negotiation, however, I get used to the idea of opening another facility. I'm not without my share of ambition. I enjoy the thrill of a challenge. After all, things are going fairly smoothly now. Unperturbed by the breakdown of negotiations, Rob begins researching a start-up venture in Chicago, with my consent. I forget I was against it in the first place.

I find business exciting for two reasons: (1) a number of deliberate simultaneous events are always in progress; (2) there's no knowing what will happen next. In the former instance I make the events happen, I'm in control; in the latter quite the opposite is true. The contrast, the tension, between running things and having things run me is the source of the thrill. As for the unexpected, the news may be either good or bad, of course, but in either case you deal with it, like God, and try to turn it to your advantage. You may have to punish or reward someone, you may have to take a risk or make sure there is none, you may have to spend or sell, you may try to win but lose, you may have to perform contrary, opposing acts at the same time, but in the end all you need do is survive.

According to the bible, even God exerts negligible control over his creatures. He's a victim of his creation, but were it otherwise, how bored He would be. Had I precise and total control over what happens at Magic, I'd sell out. So I'm like the god of Magic, the world of my creation, a mini-god, perhaps benevolent, certainly fallible. And I must deal with Francis, my one creature now out of control.

Rob complains that Francis is avoiding him by not calling him every day from the road, as is customary, and by dealing directly with the various departments rather than through him. As a matter of policy the salesmen are prohibited from contacting people in production and the lab to prevent the favoring of one salesman's projects over another. It seems Francis refuses even to acknowledge Rob's functional existence. I beg Francis to cooperate for the sake of the company. He fails to see how he's causing any damage. Then cooperate for the sake of our friendship, I plead. He's not sure there's any left between us.

Francis is on slippery ground with Rob. He seems not to appreciate that Rob has authority, that the issue is now between two egos. No matter Rob's incompetence, he won't tolerate recalcitrance for long. Sure enough, one evening Rob calls him at home and tells him not to come to work—for good.

The next morning when I arrive Francis is seated at my desk adding up his monthly sales figures on my calculator. As he rises, I motion him to stay put while I sit on the couch, spreading my arms across the back. It's a drenching, gray day outside, matching the gloom on his face. He assumes I know of Rob's call; when I deny that I do, he refuses to believe me despite my surprise and outrage.

"I'm your best salesman, Harry. How can you let him do this?"

Francis knows which of my strings to pluck. He knows that performance, not mutual compatibility, is the principal criterion I go by in judging an employee. He knows we have employees whose personalities I cannot abide but whose jobs are nevertheless secure. Apparently Rob operates on the reverse principle. Firing Francis will hurt Magic. Firing him without first consulting me hurts me. I'm prepared for a first serious confrontation with Rob. He can't get away with this.

"Forget what Rob says, Fran. I say you're still employed here. I'm boss, goddamnit, and what I say goes."

Not true, of course, and Fran knows it. Rob has the power of his veto, which, if used (and neither he nor I have used it to date), can lead to a stalemate. And he has the family money connections, which as we expand are as essential as ever.

"He'll destroy you yet, Harry. That bastard doesn't give a damn about Magicolor. What kind of future do I have with him around? Better forget about me."

"Look, Fran, we're old friends. We've had some rocky times between us, but we respect each other. Don't you agree?"

"Yes, I sure do."

"Well, I want you—I want you to stick it out."

"I won't work for him, Harry."

"You won't have to. You report to me. Okay?"

"In that case—"

"Then it's done. You're staying."

Francis rises from my desk chair, waves me into it with a flourish, and leaves.

My confrontation with Rob turns out to be a minor deal. Bursting into his office, I blurt: "I just hired Fran back. Next time you plan to do something like this, you'd better let me in on it."

He blinks. "Okay, but he's your man. You deal with him. I think you're making a big mistake. I don't like him and I think he's dangerous."

Why does Francis turn off so many people? Cal, not without cause, despises him; Janet distrusts him; my friend the psychologist says he's paranoid; Rob thinks he's our nemesis. But Francis is my friend who has twice fallen. As my friend he merits my support. Why would he ever wish to harm me? Nor can he, since on my bus I'm the driver.

CHAPTER VIII
Year Seven

1973

Sales: $2,600,000 (+73%)
Profit: $54,000 (-27%)
Debt: $791,000 (+103%)
Net Worth: $183,000 (+40%)

PVC Corporation is a good-sized outfit that polymerizes and compounds polyvinyl chloride—a material used in making shower curtains, for example. The plant is located in the smoggy portion of north central New Jersey. Billy Bangs is PVC's production manager. I find him highly likeable as I get to know him in day-to-day business dealings over the phone. Francis, who calls on him and buys him off with elegant dinners and tickets to football games, suggests he would be a suitable choice for manager of our new Chicago plant. Moreover, Billy has been signaling that the New Jersey smog is getting to him.

Not that Chicago smog would be any improvement; obviously smog is only his excuse. According to Francis, Billy knows that he has progressed as far as he can at PVC. Actually he may have gone too far and fears his days there are numbered. Having always wanted "his own show," as he says, (indeed he has failed twice in the restaurant business) he thinks running a satellite plant, independent of headquarters and operating under minimum scrutiny, would fill the bill.

"Francis tells me you're interested in us," I say in my initial approach on the phone.

"That I am. Sure. I can run your Chicago operation hands down. Long as it's worth my while."

"I'm concerned that you've worked mostly in vinyl. Your experience may be too narrow, because we deal in a wide range of plastic materials. This could be over your head."

"No problem, Harry, no problem. I've dabbled in most plastics—polyethylene and styrene, for instance. Hell, I can do anything. I've been around, y'know. Ha, ha."

"I see. Why don't you send me a resume?"

"Well, sure, if that's what you want." He pauses, then adds, "How about my coming up there so we can look each other over, see if we connect?"

"I suppose—I guess that would be alright."

"When? Ha, ha."

We set a time for two days hence. At my suggestion, he makes the four-and-a-half-hour drive to Massachusetts the evening before and spends the night in a motel near the plant at our expense. On that hot August morning he appears at the door in jeans and T-shirt at 9:30 A.M., a half hour late. Accompanying him is a young woman and her five-year-old child.

"Figured I'd take a little vacation while I'm at it," he explains, smiling merrily as I greet him in the lobby. Of medium height, his physique is slight; a mop of unkempt sandy hair falls over his forehead.

"Your wife?" I ask. I think bringing her along is a smart idea.

"Hell, no, a friend," he says. "Haven't lived with my wife for years."

"I see."

"Yeah, this is Monica. This is Mr. Simon, Monica." We nod to each other. "And this is our boy, Tom. Now say hi to Mr. Simon." I take Tom's timid hand.

DRIVEN

We leave Monica and Tom in the lobby and I lead Billy through the maze of desks in the outer office to my office, where he immediately plops on the couch and assumes a spread-eagle position.

"Tell me what you've got here, Harry, and I'll tell you what I can do for you." He maintains a steady grin.

Billy is hard to define. Is he customer or applicant? I can't decide and neither, I think, can he. Is what he can do for me the correct question? Who is in greater need? Maybe it's better to ask what I can do for him?

"Tell me about yourself, Billy. Your personal history, a verbal resume."

"Well, it's a long story, Harry."

No question Billy has been around—and around. Though he assures me every move he's made was to better himself, I have the notion he peaked out several jobs ago. Now, at forty-five, he's an obsolete walrus fighting to hold his place in the pack. There's a looseness about him that concerns me, yet I find his brashness original and attractive. Throughout the interview my first impression sticks: He's a renegade.

I introduce Rob to Billy, and the two get along like old chums talking golf and baseball. Rob asks Billy nothing about his qualifications.

"That guy's a lot of fun," Rob says after Billy has gone.

"He's technically qualified but will he make a good manager?" I wonder.

"Why not? Business is fun, Harry."

We could argue indefinitely. Actually business is a matter of life or death but Rob obviously doesn't see it that way. I'm not surprised that Billy is his kind of man. Thank God the choice is mine, not Rob's, to make.

Billy is one of two applicants I'm considering. Jeb Hanson, also a customer, is the other. For the past ten years he has managed the production department of a large manufacturer of plastic sheet. Having a wife and eight children to support, he's serious and industrious and loyal. But he's stuck, taken for granted by his employer, who, needing Jeb's hands-on expertise, won't move him up. Ironically, Jeb's very excellence and his leadership ability have impeded his progress. Some employers exploit rather than develop their people. In the years I've dealt with Jeb, I've found him open and honest, thorough, decisive, and fair—an admirable man deserving respect. But is he daring? Does he have the necessary imagination? Is he, in short, entrepreneurial? These are the qualities our Chicago manager must have. I delay making a choice.

Janet and I and the children take a week off and rent a cottage on the southern Rhode Island shore. We sail our dinghy in the salt ponds and cavort in the surf and grill hotdogs on the lawn while I ponder. My mind never leaves the business, never stops trying to figure out how to deal with Rob's incompetence and how to assuage Francis's frustration. It dwells on the countless details of starting up a Chicago operation. It can't rest while Rob's in charge. Who knows what mistakes will be made and go uncorrected without my oversight? I decide Jeb's the best man for Chicago.

Janet, the martyred wife, has no patience with my constant preoccupation.

"When are you going to pay some attention to me? At least spend time with your children. We're on vacation, for God's sake."

For God's sake, give me credit for being here. Doesn't she understand after all these years the business is my life? To please her I refrain from calling the plant until midweek. Francis, visiting the office, is on the line.

"I thought I'd drop by to see how your partner is screwing things up," he informs me.

I'm pleased that Francis cares, a sign that he's accepted our arrangement without misgivings.

"I see you hired Billy for Chicago," he says.

"What do you mean? I've hired no one—yet."

"That's not what I hear."

Do I dare think what I'm thinking? "Who told you he's hired?"

"Oh, he's definitely hired. Rob hired him."

"You've got it wrong. Rob can't hire him." My voice cracks out of control.

"He did, Harry." There's a hint of delight in his voice. "Did he cross you, Harry?"

"Where is he? I've got to talk to him, the sonofabitch. Never mind, I'll come in."

"He's already gone for the day—gone sailing."

That night I lie awake roiling. Still awake at 5:30 A.M., I dress while the family sleeps and take off for the plant in my Mercedes. As I tear along the highway through the morning mist, I rehearse the upcoming confrontation with Rob. I rehearse controlling my anger. In Providence on the expressway, I'm caught in the morning rush on its way to the 7:00 A.M. shift.

Usually I welcome the quiet of early morning, before the office begins to hum. When I arrive this morning I speculate on why Rob has crossed the border into my territory. Is it an innocent trespass? Is it simply another facet of his incompetence? Or is it a calculated attempt to take over? Two office women, taking advantage of our flexible work schedule, arrive shortly after I do. (See Appendix A: Magicolor's Management Methods.)

Rob walks into his office at 10:15 A.M. and I walk into his office at 10:16 exactly. He complains that he had to drop off his wife's Jaguar at the dealer to be repaired. It is the fourth time in as many weeks.

"What are you doing here?" he asks as it dawns on him that I should still be on vacation. "Everything's fine."

"Tell me you didn't hire Billy," I challenge.

"I didn't."

"That's a relief."

"YOU did."

"Hell, I did."

"He called to learn your decision and—"

"So you hired him," I yell.

"Just a minute, Harry. You told me he was qualified. So—"

"I said he was *technically* qualified."

"Well, right. I think he's an ideal man for the job—perfect for Chicago."

"I don't care what you think. It's not your place to make that decision." My voice is shaking as I try to moderate my anger. "His technical ability isn't the only consideration. In fact it may be the least important. He's unstable—a wild man. I had decided not to hire him."

Rob reddens and searches for a reply. "I thought... well, if you don't want him, you tell him."

"I intend to." I reach for the phone.

"The trouble is, Harry, he's given PVC notice."

I fling the phone back into its cradle. "What do you mean he's given notice?"

"I told him he was hired, so... I'd say we're committed."

I stare at the phone simmering in silence. I'm unable to release the futile rage I feel. Can I possibly renege on Rob's word? If I do, the man will be without a job. Like any businessman, I should have the callousness to pay him off and tell him to look for another job. But I can't do that. I have no choice but to take a chance and live with Rob's blunder. So even before Chicago starts, I have a problem: The key man is the wrong man.

My rage is also a problem. I don't handle it well. When it's justified I don't use it. Instead it slips out in subtle ways, mostly in the form of impatience, against innocent people who can't fight back.

Magicolor was organized into four departments: Production, the heart of the company, Gary's responsibility; Administration, the nervous system, run by Emma; Sales, the stomach, ostensibly Rob's baby; and the Laboratory, the brain, under Edgar.

When one department became disabled, all the others were adversely affected. Usually at any given time, one or another department was weaker than the rest. Throughout Magicolor's history, the lab was the sick organ most of the time. Not that the other departments weren't beset with illness from time to time. But the lab, our brain, had a neurotic predisposition and often caused us misery.

The reason for this is unclear. However, the person who headed the lab, the technical director, was usually a prima donna. Of the many technical directors who ran the lab, all believed they played the starring role in the company, and the rest of us were merely bit players.

I call Edgar, our technical director, to my office one day, and ask that he shut the door behind him—a signal that everyone understands to mean that unpleasant matters are about to be discussed.

"I see you've hired your wife for the lab," I comment.

"Well, yes. The lab is falling behind. We agreed that I needed more help. Or did I misunderstand you, Harry?"

"True, but I didn't have your wife in mind. Don't you think we should have someone with more hands-on experience?"

"Well, she picks things up fast. In no time at all she'll handle the job. Believe me I would never have put her on otherwise. Actually, I demand more of her than I do of anyone else."

"I notice she gets quite a lot of overtime."

"Well, until she has the job under her belt. She's still slow and you know how big the backlog is." His legs are vibrating and his hands fidgeting.

"I see. But on principle I think it's a bad idea to hire relatives, especially one's spouse."

After pondering my statement, he stammers: "Are you telling me to let her go?"

"Yes. But I have nothing against her, mind you."

"Sure, sure. I know that."

"It's okay to keep her until you find someone else — someone more experienced. You understand?"

"Yes, sir."

Though Edgar knows that a relative of mine, Sammy, works at Magicolor, he doesn't have the courage to mention my hypocrisy.

Edgar is a typical technical director in subtle ways. He's soft-spoken and self-effacing; he's smoothly manipulative, politically spineless, and obviously very intelligent. I am never sure of his loyalty despite having no particular reason to doubt it. His thinning hair, the dark pouches surrounding his eyes, and his innocent expression conspire to make him appear innocuous. Yet he arouses the distrust and intense dislike of many in the company.

Jamey, our former technical director and resident genius, whom Edgar replaced, refused to work under him.

Jamey accused Edgar of incompetence, of taking personal credit for the ideas and achievements of his people, and of blaming others for his own mistakes. But Jamey gave me no concrete evidence to support his allegations.

Many employees in other departments refuse to cooperate with Edgar. Some are concerned enough to warn me that he is a threat to the company. Again I must argue that I have no basis for such concern. No one offers proof, only impressions.

I tell people that to dislike someone is not cause for dismissal. Everyone must be judged by performance alone. It is a sacred precept, one that I must repeat often. If I found that I hired the devil by accident and he was doing the job, I would not fire him. I have no particular fondness for Edgar, yet I won't dismiss him. I liked Cal, but I ousted him. I'm fond of Rob, but I'd get rid of him if I could.

Edgar has been using a computer to formulate colors—his idea. Being only the second outfit in the industry to have such a setup in-house, we thought we were leading the way and beating our competitors. But after a year of debugging, the computer is still inept, actually reducing the lab's output. Contrary to Edgar's expectations and assurances, we are burdened with a fifty-thousand-dollar nonproductive addition to lab overhead.

Edgar is the only one who understands the device, which places him in the indispensable position of specialist. Disappointed in the computer, I'm even more so in Edgar. Has he deliberately deceived us? He must have known that in being, as he pointed out, at "the cutting edge of color matching" we were taking an expensive gamble. Early on he had posted a sign on the face of the computer (The machine is as large as a refrigerator.), which reads: "The difference between men and boys is the price of their toys," suggesting that he had secret doubts about it.

Meanwhile, the computer has lent us unexpected prestige. It's useful as a public relations gimmick. Our brochures and magazine ads tout the advantage of making high-tech formulations that are more accurate and less expensive than those of our competitors (though not necessarily so). According to our advertising agency, our brochure's cover photo of a beautiful blond female "technician" seated at the computer keyboard is supposed to arouse interest.

Edgar has hired Earnest, a man from Bombay. True to lab tradition, Earnest is talented, cranky, self-aggrandizing and convinced that he is better than his co-workers, better than his boss, Edgar. Indeed he describes himself as the best color technician in the world. In short, he's impossible but very likely accurate about his professional ability. Learning to swallow hard, Edgar keeps him on because after only a few weeks he restores the lab to grace.

How often people I've forgotten resurface. I believe that we should never burn our bridges. When I make an enemy, I'm foreclosing a future option.

Though I forced Cal to sell me his portion of Magicolor, a strand of our friendship survives. He doesn't entirely blame me. Men don't blame others for acting out of self-interest in business. This rationale is understood. If raw self-interest is mean and tough to take, that's business—just a more vivid form of life. Janet is repelled because the ways of business ignore feelings and inflict wounds. Is she typical of most women? But put a woman in a business role and she can abandon her inclination to nurture and even outdo her male counterpart in acting out of self-interest.

After eventually selling the marina to his Mafia-connected partner, Cal went into the business of buying, selling, coloring, and reconditioning off-grade and scrap plastic materials. Consequently he began placing orders with us for color concentrates.

He drops by the office, the first time I've seen him since we were partners almost five years ago. Thinner now, wearing a full beard, he speaks wearily.

"I heard you were doing great, Harry; now I see what they mean. Quite a place."

We have a great bustle in progress, for sure: the construction of a second addition to the office, doubling its size, and a new air-conditioned laboratory, tripling its size. The foundation of a vast new warehouse is also being poured. Magic's building is expanding to forty thousand square feet from its first small addition and original ten thousand square feet.

"It's a shame you're not with us," I say, implicitly bragging.

But I remind myself I may be bragging too soon. Despite our exponential sales growth over the past six years, the memory of Magic's early losses still haunts me. The Chicago start-up will drag down our profits for an indefinite period of time. We are in a wild and daring phase: debt has doubled, the future is a giant gamble. No, it's too soon for kudos; not all the innings have been played.

"Yeah, well I'm doing okay," Cal says. "I always said you'd make it big, Harry." He forces a grin. "I know I made a mistake selling out. Everything's clear afterward, but how do you know beforehand?"

"You knew, Cal, you knew."

Suddenly I felt a fresh surge of anger, a hangover of that moment long ago when I begged him to fulfill his commitment to the partnership. He had refused. If he had been so sure of our success, why hadn't he stuck it out and worked for it?

"Well, as I say, I'm doing okay now," he says.

"Good," I say, knowing that his D & B (Dun and Bradstreet report) shows a sick balance sheet.

Doing business with him is risky but, after all, he's still a friend.

"Where should we live when I retire?" I ask Janet rhetorically.

"You, retire? Are you serious?"

"I'm fifty now. We should be thinking ten, fifteen years down the line."

"You'll never retire, Harry. You wouldn't know how."

"Why do you say that?"

"Because the business is your glue. Without it you'll fall apart."

She knows what it means to me, after all. But she doesn't know it's slowly becoming less than everything. I don't know why. Things couldn't be better, yet there are days at the office when I feel something is still missing. I don't know what.

My father died on the job. It struck me as sad—he never got to be free. But he needed to work. That's all he knew. My generation expects more.

"Let's build a place at the Cape now," I say, "near the water so I can sail, with enough land for a garden."

"Fine," she says. "I'd like that too."

When I mention retirement to Cathy, she says she doesn't want to think of the day I retire because on that day she'll lose me. I say, why worry now when I have so many more years to go?

DRIVEN

I'm impatient with my car despite its comfort and its superb road-hugging capability. I don't need the prestige of a Mercedes and its burnished wood dashboard. Were it not for Rob I'd still have my trusty Buick. But Rob insists we have cars befitting our positions in the company and our status in the community. In any case, no matter what I want to do, he, or rather the company, buys one for him. But I can tolerate that. It's when he, or rather the company, also bought a Jaguar for his wife that I'm ready for war.

"Go ahead, buy a Jag for Janet, too," he says. "She'll love it."

"Damnit, Rob, it's illegal."

"C'mon, Harry. Wise up. I haven't been audited by the IRS in twenty years."

I'll be damned if I'll allow him to receive more of Magic's largess than I do. I too bought my Mercedes but that's all. Janet is perfectly happy with her Chevy station wagon.

For a couple of years Rob and I have been each drawing salaries of $100,000 a year. Although my contribution to Magicolor's success is far greater than his—it's obvious that he's a liability—I don't mind his equal draw. The company can afford it. Moreover, since we would have never made it without Rob's credit at the bank, a large salary is his just reward. But I scream when he proposes boosting our draw to $150,000. We are in my office, the door open.

"This is madness. The company must reduce its debt before we take out that kind of money," I rant. "Anyway neither of us needs it."

"Just a minute, Harry, it's not a matter of need. It's what's due us as owners, as risk takers. Without you and me there'd be no Magicolor. It exists strictly for us. Get it?"

"No, I don't. That's a pretty narrow view of what being in business is all about."

Since our voices are rising, I walk from my desk to close the door of the office.

"Money, Harry, money—that's what business is about," Rob says, his round red face turning redder. "What else is there?"

"What about the employees?" I say. "What about the customers, the town—even the country? Sure, we make Magic possible, but it exists for more than you and me."

"Do you actually believe that crap? Nobody's that noble. I don't buy it. I see your drive. You're in it for the money just as much as I am. Level with yourself, Harry."

"Wait a minute, Rob, just wait a minute. Don't tell me what I believe."

"Maybe you shouldn't be in business."

"You only give a damn about yourself. To hell with the rest of us," I say, slamming my desk drawer closed.

"My family matters, that's where it stops and I'm not apologizing for it," Rob says.

"Well, I can't stop there. That's how I am."

"Okay, Harry, I'll take the 150 G's and you do what you want."

Damned if I'll let him take more than my share. We'll both draw $150,000, two-thirds of which I'll just bank away. Who knows, I may yet need it if, because of it, we go bust.

With inflation increasing, Magicolor's debt was actually far from burdensome. We prospered and grew on the cheap by borrowing ever depreciating dollars. Thus the more we owed, the larger our future. My moral conservatism contravened our long-term interest, and Rob's "irresponsibility" was on the mark.

Seeing the world as a mindless place and blinded by a noble purpose, I tried to minimize risk and manipulate our destiny. I hadn't yet learned to step back and take a wider look. I was a ridiculous, moralistic dreamer to Rob; to me Rob was a selfish, immoral exploiter.

CHAPTER IX

Year Eight

1974

Sales: $3,600,000 (+38%)
Profit: $159,000 (+194%)
Debt: $789,000 (-.25%)
Net Worth: $369,000 (+102%)

Cathy is my ally. She offers me a steady flow of love and respect and approval, filling the void left by Janet. Not that Janet hasn't some cause for hostility. She gets only a part of me, the part that protects her from the world, and I get only a part of her, the part that provides a secure place to come home to. To make up for what she doesn't get, she gathers comfort from our children. Whenever my spirit is wasted by the battering of business, Cathy is my fix. Our time together is like a retreat, an island of love, giving us security and uninhibited freedom for a few rapturous hours.

Of course we are most discreet. Fearing discovery, we frequent only remote motels and restaurants. We perhaps delude ourselves into believing that as long as no one knows, we are harming no one. But in fact we are. We are damaging ourselves and those who love us. Cathy betrays her God and cheats Him of the love she gives me. And I deprive Janet of the love and attention I give Cathy.

Often my infidelity overwhelms my conscience. How do Frenchmen do it? Often, I realize my marriage is fake, a performance, and I resolve to end it with Cathy. So she sadly steps aside, realizing that it's impossible for me to leave my family. For six months maybe, or a year, we may have no contact, not a letter, not a phone call. Then one of us, either from loneliness or from the burden of our lives, breaks the silence. That's enough to start us all over again. Our hunger for each other is unremitting. Each of us craves caring for the other and being cared for. Each of us yearns to be both parent and child to the other, if only for a few hours now and then. The cycle is renewed.

"Your wife should thank me. I keep your marriage alive," Cathy says. "If it weren't for me I think you'd leave her."

I don't wish to put her claim to the test.

My other source of happiness is the business, which I find, for the most part, emotionally rewarding. It's a place to be every day, a place with seventy dependable souls striving toward a common goal. I'm as sensitive to their smiles and frowns as a mother. They are my other family, my children, who give me loyalty and respect, in return for which I take responsibility for their welfare. Sometimes I think they are all I have.

The staff of the Chicago operation are my children away from home. Each day Billy reports what he wants me to know. Like a true renegade, he locates manufacturing space by driving around Cook County in his pickup truck and inquiring over his CB for leads. The CB'ers offer a flood of suggestions. I fly out to inspect the six most eligible buildings and choose one to rent in a Chicago suburb.

On the same trip I screen several salesmen applicants for the Chicago area. Rob hires one of them, Helmut Miller, on my recommendation. A tub of a man, shaped like the nose of a rocket from the neck up, Miller speaks with sincerity and authority. He is subtly aggressive and has a keen grasp of reality.

In the back of my mind I see Miller as Billy's possible replacement. Billy's erratic style and his distorted reports on what's happening are trying my patience. Enormous entertainment expenses, an outrageous inventory buildup, and enough overtime to justify hiring two more employees are showing up in the monthly P & L's. At this rate we could lose as much as $40,000 by year's end. I'm also frustrated by not being able to reach him no matter what time of day I call.

"Where were you when I called yesterday?" I ask.

"I was out to lunch."

"At eleven o'clock?"

"Well, I got hungry early."

"But you never seem to be there, Billy. Do you have lunch at four in the afternoon?"

"When was that?"

"One day last week."

"Shit, Harry, I don't remember that far back."

"How about returning my calls?"

"Sure, if I get the message."

"Well, you better get the goddamn message," I say.

Billy is unable to take problems seriously. He runs the business as if he were playing a game of dime poker. Yet I hesitate to fire him until he's had more time to disprove himself. Who knows? Maybe he'll reform with enough guidance.

I agonize over letting people go. A suspicion I may be committing an injustice nags at me. Not that I don't always have rational reasons for sacking someone. I procrastinate, tolerate poor performance too long. It's my most serious management error. Only after firing someone do I see how foolish and damaging my delay was. Yet I have to keep learning the lesson over and over.

DRIVEN

Looking for ways to reduce Billy's costs, I decide to dispense with salesman Miller, whose salary, car, and expenses have been substantial and whose efforts after more than a year have hardly increased sales, though a year is not really enough time to tell. Rob goes along, but not for my reasons. Rob thinks that Miller is too technical, too original in his thinking, too particular about detail, too demanding that things be done right. After Rob sacks him over the phone, Miller calls me.

"What am I doing wrong, Harry? I can't get a straight answer out of Rob."

"Nothing," I say. "I think you're a good man. But we can't afford to keep you on. The operation is losing money. It's as simple as that."

"I feel I was just getting somewhere, and then you cut me off. A whole year wasted."

"For us too, Miller. I'm sorry. We've got to be realistic."

"Damn." He pauses and I can hear his anxious breathing. "Well, if you change your mind, you know where to reach me."

"You can use me for a reference. I'll give you the best."

"Yeah. Thanks."

As I hang up I'm relieved that the dirty deed is over. I feel the usual ache of conscience. In this instance we are sacking an innocent man. Am I refusing to face Billy's incompetence?

But it isn't over. That very night Miller calls me at home while I'm watching TV.

"I've been thinking," he says. "I have some ideas. Maybe I can change your mind."

"Look, Miller, once we make a decision, we stick with it. We didn't let you go lightly, I assure you."

Trying to take in the TV program while I'm talking, I'm becoming increasingly annoyed with Miller for not accepting his dismissal as final.

"I don't doubt it, Harry, but what can you lose by hearing me out?"

"Okay. Speak."

"Not over the phone. I want to meet with you."

"I see. I know it's tough for you, Miller. Well, I'm supposed to be in Chicago next week. How about getting together on—"

"Wait a minute, Harry, what about tonight?"

"Tonight? What do you mean, tonight?"

"I'm here at the airport in Boston—at my expense."

"You're here?"

"I can be at your place in an hour."

Any man so determined deserves my attention, and my respect. Renting a car at the airport, he drives to my house thirty miles southwest of Boston and starts selling me. But even before he begins I'm already on his side. "Get rid of Billy Bangs before he sinks the operation," Miller says. He offers to reduce his salary to barely enough to pay his mortgage and feed his family. He'll bag his lunches, plan his trips to avoid stayovers at motels. He says he believes in Magicolor, in me, in the way we do business: "You run a clean setup, Harry, and you make it exciting." He believes in the future of the Chicago operation, Billy Bangs notwithstanding.

Janet prepares a bed in one of the children's rooms for Miller and he stays the night. I reverse my decision: I'll keep him on. Over breakfast in our kitchen I ask how he'd feel about running the Chicago operation.

"I'm only a salesman," he says, reminding me of my reply years ago when Cal offered me a similar opportunity at MPI.

"Think about it," I say. "When the time comes we'll talk again."

Miller's the kind of man I need.

At this stage in Magicolor's development, we have three salesmen working out of New England: Francis, of course; Sammy, Janet's relative; and Larry, in upstate New York, a steady young man who has persevered for years without causing a ripple. Two salesmen contribute to Chicago: one, Miller, in the metropolitan area, and Hank, who serves both facilities covering western Michigan, Ohio, and Indiana. Recently I've added two independent reps on straight commission—one in Chattanooga and one in Detroit—who also handle related lines for other firms. (See Appendix B: More on Magicolor's Management Methods.)

As vice-president of production, Gary presides over manufacturing from an office next to mine. I hired him despite Janet's objection—"a little shit," she called him— after deciding not to advance Phil, the young production manager then in charge. Gary is a smart engineer, trained by a reputable competitor, expert in cost containment, which is one of my pet concerns. In time I have realized that although he is extremely competent and thorough, good at managing things, he's cold, a zero at motivating people. To get results he adopts a subtle dictatorial style, issuing demands softly but without explanation or consultation or seeking consensus. He disallows his subordinates their free expression by imposing his own will first. A quiet tyrant, perhaps.

Gary's style isn't working, nor is it consistent with the company's. I had installed him as an extra layer of management in order to share some of my responsibilities and to improve our production efficiency. He has improved nothing; in fact, having brought politics into the organization, he may actually be making things worse. Gary has become a complication. Before his arrival a spirit of cooperation was pervasive among us but he tries to polarize us into opposing groups.

I speak to him about it in his office. A mechanical calculator sits on his desk, center stage.

"You know, Gary, we're one company."

"I'm aware of that, Harry."

"And you know that production's important, but it can't function without sales or the lab or the office."

"Certainly."

"Well, I think you ought to always keep that in mind."

"What's your point? Are you saying I don't?"

"I hear from the other departments that you expect them to kiss your ass."

"They really function to support production, don't they? Production is where we make the money, isn't it?"

"Yeah, but it doesn't make money by itself."

He raises his peanut eyes to the ceiling.

"So just remember, you need them. Okay?" I repeat.

"Sure thing, Harry."

I leave his office feeling I failed to reach him. But could I ever? He is always so certain of his rightness, so positive that his is the only way. He's never willing to examine another point of view and change his mind. I have encountered this mentality time after time in business—among my own people and others, among vendors and customers.

Is it blindness to what is beyond one's ego, to a goal larger than one's own petty purposes? It is inherently destructive. It doesn't entertain respect for the mind of another. It is anti-idealistic and pretends to omnipotence.

But there are souls willing to open up and risk their egos. How refreshing to deal with them! As Magicolor has prospered and grown, now with more than a hundred employees, many have been hired and fired for countless reasons, poor performance being only one of them. An employee with a strictly "me" rather than an "us" point of view doesn't last here. Since the "us" view is required of management as well as worker, sackings are frequent at higher levels too. Building an organization of open, self-critical minds is an ongoing process, but gradually I'm accumulating the kind of people who think in the "us" mode, who have no preconceived mind-set and who seek excitement.

Late Friday night the plane from Chicago lands in a raging summer storm. Irritated and exhausted, driving home the thirty miles from Boston through a battering torrent, I am in no mood to deal with Janet's confrontation.

She is sitting in bed propped up on her pillow knitting like a dervish.

"I can't live like this," she says not raising her eyes from the knitting.

"Live like what?" I say truly innocent.

"That bitch," she says.

"What bitch?"

From my hip pocket I remove my wallet, my change, my keys, and place them with my wristwatch in a box that Janet had hand finished and presented to me on my last birthday.

"Get her out of our lives," she demands. "I know you're still sleeping with her."

I undress, slide naked beneath the covers like a sword into its sheath, and hang onto my edge of the mattress.

Janet wears a nightgown—she always wears a nightgown. Skin to skin is anathema to her. Sex must always be performed clothed.

"Either she goes, or you go," she says.

"I'm tired, too tired to talk now," I say.

"And I'm tired of talking."

Leaving the bed, she slips into her robe and goes to the kitchen.

Despite my tiredness I'm unable to sleep. My mind is steeped in thoughts not of Janet's unhappiness but of the business. Unprecedented events are occurring in the greater world that seriously affect it.

The oil embargo is on. Since plastic and pigment raw materials are petrochemicals derived from oil, severe shortages develop. Prices skyrocket, changing so frequently that published price lists are immediately obsolete. We are lucky to buy raw materials at any price; even then, terms are cash on delivery, replacing the traditional payment terms of thirty or sixty days.

Thanks to my compulsion to pay bills on time, Magic's credit standing is solid. With its cash position sufficient and its relationship with vendors congenial, our sources of raw materials keep us adequately supplied under generous allocations. Magic in turn meets its customers' needs, of course at a nice profit. The question is never price but rather can I have it? Thus Magic's unprecedented profit—$159,000 that year—was no mystery and due more to favorable circumstances than genius.

Rob finds it tempting to utilize Magic's buying capability to make an easy buck—to buy, say, titanium dioxide, a white pigment, at 75 cents a pound and sell it with great ease to a less fortunate competitor for $1.25— earning more than if we had converted the pigment into manufactured goods.

"No," I protest, pounding my desk before Rob finishes his sentence. "What you want to do is immoral and it's shortsighted."

"Hell, it's business," Rob counters. "C'mon, Harry, we're not a religious order. We're here to make money. What's dishonest about buying cheap and selling dear?"

"I didn't say it was dishonest. But we have an obligation to keep our customers supplied as best we can."

"They won't complain, Harry. Why should they? They know there are shortages. They expect us to limit them."

"Yeah, what about our suppliers? We're on allocation, a generous one; I think we also have an obligation not to take advantage of the vendors."

"Christ, how will the vendors know what we do with the stuff?"

"They won't, but I will," I shout, pounding my desk and causing my pen to roll and drop onto the floor.

"To hell with the vendors," Rob declares.

"My answer is NO. I'm drawing the line," I pronounce, stabbing space.

Money and profit, profit and money. For Rob it was enough simply to make it. For me, how we made it was as important as making it. Rob's bottom line required few rules. My bottom line was burdened with a mine field of restrictions. His greed collided with my moral idealism. The fundamental distance between the lines Rob and I drew tore at me. Sooner or later there was bound to be a cataclysm.

Yet at year end things were going well. Indeed, Billy was finally doing the job; Chicago was redeeming itself, actually turning around in its second year and making the small but significant profit of $16,000. Total company *profit tripled—$159,000—Magic's highest to date. Though I couldn't know the hardship that Magic was yet to endure—it would be another nine years before attaining such profits again—I had a premonition that things were going only artificially well.*

CHAPTER X

Year Eight
(Continued)

1974

Janet and I drive to her psychiatrist's office in separate cars, since I plan to go directly to the plant after our joint therapy session. Like strangers on a subway we sit in the waiting room silently reading ten-week-old *Time* magazines. After about ten minutes a perturbed woman, her eyes fastened to the floor, emerges from the inner office followed by the doctor—a middle-aged man with a silver splattered beard, sleepy eyes, and floppy gray hair. Weakly smiling, he solemnly ushers us in, shakes my hand with a rubbery grip, and motions us to sit side by side in slippery synthetic leather chairs as he sits back in a lounge chair facing us.

He nods and Janet begins, with a complaint: "He's still seeing that woman."

The doctor looks at me for comment.

"That's true," I say.

"And do you intend to keep seeing her in spite of the pain it causes Janet?"

"No." Sorrow creeps over me. I want Janet. I want us to be happy. I want my family to be whole. They come first. Nothing is more important. But I want Cathy. I want her to be happy too, yet I know I have to end it. There's a higher need than strictly my own.

"You say no?" the doctor says.

"I don't care; it's too late," Janet states firmly. "I've had enough, Doctor. He's done nothing but hurt me. My feelings are—well, they mean nothing to him." Her voice is measured, a package of rage tied with a bow.

"I said, no, Janet. I mean I won't see her."

"I heard you. It's not the first time, Doctor. He's promised before."

"Please, Janet. I love you. No matter what I've done, I still love you."

"I don't believe you. I've given you everything. I trusted you, placed you first, and for this you've hurt me."

"Then for the kids' sake. Forget about us."

"It's over. There's nothing more to say."

"Wait a minute," the doctor says reaching to pat Janet's hand. "Don't be hasty. Why not give him another chance? He seems contrite. It's obvious he doesn't want to leave."

I nod, grateful for his support.

"Do you think it will do any good, really?"

"What have you got to lose? He says he loves you. Let him prove it."

"I do love you, Janet," I say resolutely and turn imploringly to the doctor. "I can't abandon them, Doctor."

I'm unequivocal. I will give up a degree of personal happiness for my family. Isn't it a man's duty, my duty, to provide for my dependents, to sacrifice for them if necessary? How else can I live with myself? After all, my children are innocents. Though not Janet. I don't understand her; I don't understand myself. Anyway, if the going gets rough, at least I have the business. At least I have a source of satisfaction.

"It will take time but perhaps you could try to forgive him," the doctor says.

"You know how much I've given, Doctor. All of myself. It's the way I am. How can I ever forget what he's done to me? How can I?" Janet pleads.

"You can't," he replies. "Nothing in the past is ever truly forgotten. You can only forgive." Turning to me he asks, "Are you willing to accept her conditions?"

"You mean to end the affair?"

"That and her not forgetting."

"Well—"

"Yes, I think I can forgive you," says Janet, her eyes softening, "if you'll promise—"

"That's enough for me," I say. "You don't have to worry. Having an affair isn't all it's cracked up to be."

As with all bad memories, time would probably wear away the sting of my infidelity. We'd have a fresh beginning. But whatever is wrong between us is unaddressed. How would that go away? We'd bury it. We'd hide it from the children, our friends, ourselves. That's what we'd do.

Driving to the plant content that the trouble at home has been resolved, I ponder a problem that hasn't yet occurred: Things are too good to last. Those skyrocketing prices, our incredible profits, a volatile economy based on shortages and the whims of foreign oil producers, add up to a dangerous situation. But Rob insists nothing's wrong.

"Since early summer I've been reading economic reports that say we're in a recession," I tell him.

"There you go—gloom and doom again. Business has never been better, our profits are off the chart, and you're worried. It's ridiculous. Why can't you enjoy success, Harry? What's wrong with you?"

"Nothing's wrong with me. You're wearing blinders. You don't want to see. I'm telling you what the experts are saying. They have statistics to go by. So I listen; I'm not waiting until disaster hits us."

I close the door to Rob's office as I pace in front of his desk, my tie loosened. He balances himself backward in his desk chair.

"What recession?" he demands. "Who are they talking about? Maybe someone else's recession; maybe coal or steel, but not ours. We're in the plastics business, Harry. Remember? There's never been a recession in our industry. And there never will be, not in our lifetime."

My argument is futile. From June until October, I send Rob copies of reports by various economists in which I underline crucial paragraphs that describe the dire conditions developing.

In October the phones virtually stop ringing. The women in the office sit polishing their fingernails and gossiping among themselves. All month with no new orders coming in we manufacture unneeded product to inventory just to keep the production workers busy until business turns, which is "just around the corner" according to Rob. The laboratory staff waxes the floor and paints the walls; the lab glows as it never has before. But a clean lab is a dead lab. Calling on the trade in a tenacious panic, the salesmen hear the same complaint everywhere: The phones have stopped ringing, the orders have stopped coming in. Their visits are now little more than social calls.

Our bottom line by the end of the month is a frightening $50,000 loss.

In mid-afternoon only moments after I get the profit and loss statement from the bookkeeper, I call Rob at his home. Knowing that he's supposed to be on the road selling, I leave a message with his wife to have him phone me as soon as he returns. But he's not on the road, she explains. Rather he's out sailing, his last sail of the season before he hauls the boat. I'm irate: the world is crashing down on us and my partner is out on a lark. Typical. Goddamnit.

Ignoring my message, Rob wanders into the office the next morning about ten. I challenge him with the disastrous news. He shrugs. "What are you worried about? It's only a month."

"That's your only comment?"

"Well, it's not a quarter, or a year. A month means nothing."

"Are you saying a loss of $50,000 is nothing?"

"Of course not. But next month we could make $50,000."

"How? The phones have stopped ringing."

"Just give it time. Relax. We're in the plastics business."

"I'm not waiting; we have to do something now." I'm irritated at his calmness.

"Like what?" He reaches for a letter opener and nervously slashes open his mail, giving it his full attention.

"I have a plan."

"Oh, yeah?"

"To cut expenses. We can't keep losing like this."

"For crying out loud, one bad month and the damn sky's falling in."

"First I want to let Gary go. We don't need a vice-president of production—not now. With the warehouse bursting with finished goods, it's time we laid off all the workers except for a small skeleton crew. The foremen and the production supervisor can man the machines too. We can leave the lab and office as is for the time being, pare them back later. You and I must cut our salaries in half; it's a big chunk of cash. Then we'll give the sales staff a pep talk, tell them the score and offer them an extra bonus for bringing in new accounts."

Raising his eyes from the letter he just opened, Rob stares at me as if I had regressed into babbling idiocy.

"You're out of your mind. I've got mail to read." He returns to his letter, dismissing me.

My fear is genuine and powerful. Like a person who fears heights, I must avoid the terrible edge. Even the anticipation frightens me. What do I fear? I fear falling. I fear failure.

Although my fear for Magicolor's security was justified, the strain of panic that underlay my need to act stemmed from an earlier time.

During the first five years of my marriage I couldn't hold down a job. Usually I didn't get along with the boss; I wouldn't "suck up to him." Or I would become impatient with my progress and quit. When friends would ask, "What are you doing now?" I felt ashamed. I was simply going no place. As a result I felt I was not meeting my responsibility as a father and husband. I told Janet she deserved someone better than me and urged her to leave. Feeling a failure as a man, I became sexually impotent.

But Janet could only think of sticking by me. She empathized and shared my suffering. Her nobility and love and self-sacrifice sustained me and I felt indebted to her. My luck turned for the better when I landed the sales job at Majestic Plastics Industries, working under Cal. In his loose style he gave me enough leash to be my own man. With the memory of those humiliating pre-Majestic days still haunting me, I resolved that I would never fail again. I would make sure that Janet and the children would never be denied the best things in life.

Naturally my fear of failure turned Rob off—Rob who had never known failure, who would never have acknowledged failure anyway. He saw life as a fortuitous series of lucky events. "I always land on my feet no matter what," he would say.

Of course the financial status of Magicolor was the other major difference between us. I had invested all I had in the company. My entire net worth was on the line to the bank. As for Rob, Magicolor could go down the drain and he'd hardly feel it. Like a pilot wearing a parachute need not fear crashing, Rob was immune to risk; he didn't need Magicolor for survival.

I don't have the nerve to flout Rob and fire Gary, the vice-president of production. But I call Gary into my office and inform him of our need to cut back.

"Work up a plan to lay off the production workers and use the foremen and supervisors in direct production," I tell him.

A little man with black curly hair, he caresses his Van Dyke beard thoughtfully.

"Do you think it's really a good idea?"

"Why so?"

"They're highly trained; we might lose them to competitors."

"Maybe," I said. "But if we're slow, the competition must be slow too. Jobs won't be easy to find."

"I think you're making a mistake, Harry."

"Look, Gary, I hate having to do this as much as you. Some of these guys have been with us for a long time. But they won't go hungry; they can collect unemployment insurance."

"Suppose business picks up—say, next week."

"Then we'll bring them back."

Pulling on his beard nervously, he is agitated and squints.

"I don't think we should disrupt the organization like this."

"What's the choice? You know the bottom line; you know what's happening. What do you suggest as an alternative?" I ask poking the air with my index finger for emphasis.

He doesn't answer.

Why is he opposing me? Perhaps with a reduced crew to manage he fears he'll become superfluous, or along with his team I'll assign him to the bench. But I have too mundane an imagination to guess the hidden motives of one so clever as Gary.

After a week my instructions to Gary are ignored. I summon him to my office again.

"Why aren't you doing what I asked you to do?" I inquire.

Again fingering his beard, he thinks awhile then informs me, "Rob says to forget it."

"What do you mean, Rob says? You report to me, not Rob."

"I'm caught in the middle, Harry."

"No, you're not. Production's my bailiwick. You know that. You don't listen to anyone but me."

"Well, Rob owns half the company."

In a flash I pick up the phone and dial Rob's number. "We've got a problem here. Will you come into my office?"

Spotting Gary's downcast face as he enters Rob speaks before I have a chance. "I told Gary—"

"I know what you told him," I say icily.

"Well, he wanted my opinion and I—"

"You've gone over the line, Rob," I shout. "And you better remember who's your boss," I say, turning to Gary. "What unmitigated chutzpah you've got. You're no better than a child who plays one parent off against the other." My anger feeds on itself. "Get out of my sight. Maybe you should work elsewhere. Clean out your desk. This minute! Now!"

Rob merely shrugs as Gary looks to him for support. Gary sees that Rob is not one to put himself out, that his loyalty is as thin as toilet paper.

I discover later from Emma that Rob previously had instructed her to increase Gary's pay, this after Gary asked me for a raise and I explained, that due to bad business conditions, he'd have to wait. Another instance of getting from Rob what he couldn't get from me. I am well rid of this man. It would be better if I were rid of Rob too. Yes, more than just an irritation, he's become an obstacle and a threat to our survival. But buying out Rob would take more money than I could ever raise without giving up autonomy. What's happened to my daring? Probably that I have more to lose now. I'm still a victim of a timid imagination.

My task now is to devise a scheme that would force Rob to deal with the economic situation. He needs a taste of real responsibility. Why not let him run the show and experience the consequences of inaction? Let him try to keep the production crew, the lab gang, and the office staff from twiddling their thumbs. Let him experience the silent phones and the mounting losses. Let him hold the hands of our salesmen when they call in crying the blues. I'll go on strike like labor does when it doesn't get what it wants. Though the idea involves inaction, it's really action. It's a brilliant idea. I'm absolutely invigorated.

Arriving home from work that evening I walk into the kitchen where Janet is preparing supper for the family and announce, "As of now and for at least the next two weeks I'm incommunicado."

"You're in what?"

"Incommunicado. I'm not answering the phone and you don't know where I am if anyone asks. Just pretend I've dropped off the face of the Earth."

I explain how Rob and I are at loggerheads and that by going on strike I expect to get him to cooperate. Janet is intrigued. The kids are rapturous that their daddy, who is usually gone before they awake in the morning, will be around all day. And how wonderful that daddy, their weekend daddy, will be there every day to play with them, to wrestle with them on the living room carpet and dance when they get home from school.

"Now you can't say you're too tired," says my son.

"And you can tell us stories," say my daughters.

It's a plus I hadn't thought of—spending time with the children who haven't seen much of me since I've been in business.

Janet, however, is skeptical. It's a cold December and I'll be confined indoors.

"What are you going to do with yourself?" she wonders aloud.

"Read, listen to music, tape concerts. I'll get a taste of the retired life."

"Forget it," she muses. "I'll give you less than a week before you go crazy, like you do on vacation. You can't stay away from the business. Aren't you afraid that Rob will cause more problems than you've already got?"

"How much damage can he do in two weeks? Anyway, whether I'm there or not makes no difference. We're already in trouble."

"Well, I hope having you underfoot won't get on my nerves."

Why do I feel as though I'm intruding on Janet's domain. Does she see our home as more hers than mine, our children as more hers than mine? Does she think my commitment to the business is an abdication of my commitment to my family? My god, does she? I don't pursue the question.

DRIVEN

I spend my time reading a couple of novels, finishing for the first time in years the Sunday *New York Times*, and when the weather is good taking long walks alone. I tape selected music off the FM radio. I imagine that each time I play a piece, it will remind me of my two-week revolt.

When Rob phones looking for me, Janet tells him that I'm away and can't be reached nor does she know when I'll return. He calls twice the first week, three times the second. Appearing at the office on the third Monday, I whiz through to shocked stares and knowing smiles. I seclude myself in my office behind a closed door to study the prior two weeks' production and cost reports stacked in my basket. The slide toward disaster has continued, indeed has worsened.

Hearing that I've arrived, Rob enters my office and closes the door behind him.

"Where in hell have you been?" he asks in a quavering voice, hovering over me as I sit at my desk with a report in hand.

"On vacation," I say.

"What vacation? You never told me about a vacation. What kind of game are you playing, Harry? It's been hell around here."

"I take it you haven't been leaving at two in the afternoon."

"How could I? For chrissakes, Harry, don't ever do that again. I can't run this place single-handed. We've got problems."

"From these figures, I see you've had a few troubles," I say, tossing the report onto my desk.

"Troubles! Christ, machine breakdowns, emergency orders, can't get raw materials, power failures, trying to keep everyone busy—you don't know what it's been like." His eyes water. "Christ, Harry, don't ever do that again."

Taking a handkerchief from his pants hip pocket, he wipes away tears and blows his nose.

"Well, I just dropped by to see how you're doing and I think you're handling things fine, Rob. So I won't be sticking around."

"Whaddya mean?" he demands in outraged panic.

"My vacation isn't over. But I'll be back one of these days."

"Just a minute, Harry. Look, it's your show. I'm only the sales manager. Remember?"

"The hell you are," I say, rising and meeting him eye to eye. "You're everything. You make policy, you tell my people what to do, you give them raises we can't afford, you poke your nose into my business as if I don't exist, you watch the losses build and you sit and wait. No, Rob, it's your show. That's what you've been wanting, so do it, goddamnit. You make all the decisions, and you take the responsibility for them."

My outpouring is a marvelous release.

He closes his eyes, a dam of tears bursting beneath the lids, and embraces me.

"I'm sorry, Harry, really sorry. I didn't realize you were sore. I didn't realize."

Returning the embrace, I feel sorry for him. He's suddenly a child begging for forgiveness.

"Then let's try it my way for a change," I say.

"Sure, sure, Harry."

I'm victorious, but for how long? Our differences are rooted in our irreconcilable natures. Have I won the battle but am destined to lose the war?

I cut Rob's salary and mine in half, reluctantly lay off most of our trained workers, ask everyone to work harder for the common good, and appeal to our salaried people to accept a temporary 20 percent pay cut, which I promise to make up when business improves. "You have my word the cut will only be deferred," I explain. "We need the money to help cash flow. The company will owe it to you."

The foremen and supervisors readily agree to "go on the bench," a heartening sign of their faith in the company and in me. But Janet's cousin Sammy—taken in seven years ago when unemployed, then in his mid-fifties, presently our top commission earner—refuses to go along. He complains that with his commissions down, he's already sacrificing.

"But, Sammy," I say, "even with the cut in pay, yours will be the highest salary in the company after Rob and me."

"It's purely voluntary, right?"

"Right," I reply.

"Well, I'm not volunteering. I'm working harder than ever and you're asking me to take less. It's not right."

"Okay, Sammy, if that's your decision," I say stiffly, holding in my resentment.

"It is."

His pay cut would only be a token sacrifice because of its temporary nature. After so many years I'm surprised to learn how untrusting and self-centered Sammy is. Why haven't I spotted it before? Sure as hell I'll not forget it. Sometimes it takes a crisis to learn the truth, to learn who are the real stars in the dark night.

The new measures do help reduce our losses in Massachusetts, but they aren't sufficient to stanch the severe bleeding in Chicago. Since we'll still lose money, but less, I suggest we close down the Chicago operation. Rob disagrees. It's not in his nature to retreat. He can't imagine cutting off a wasted limb to save a life.

I no longer listen to Rob; I ignore his suggestions whether good or bad. I pretend he doesn't exist. We now make decisions independently of each other, an intolerable state of affairs. I detest my tyranny over him but I see no other way. I dread his incompetence, a hindering force I resent having to contend with in these difficult enough times.

The employees are now fully aware that the partners are at war, but they are uncertain who will win, who holds the most power. Both Rob and I, subtly testing their sympathies, try to marshall key allies among them. Finally three camps form: those who support Rob, those who support me, and those who remain neutral, the latter including those I most despise.

In numbers I have the most supporters, but the uncommitted carry most of the weight and are pivotal in their importance to the company. Sammy declares himself on my side despite our clash over a pay cut—a case, as they say, of blood being thicker than water. Edgar, our technical director, offers his support, but I suspect he has made the same offer to Rob. Emma, the office manager, rises above it all and for this I respect her. Earle, our brilliant lab technician, stands squarely with Rob. Phil, our production manager, is inscrutable. He may resent having to go "on the bench."

Our salesmen are split down the middle: Helmut Miller, in Chicago, is neutral, a disappointment after the opportunity I gave him when he pleaded that I keep him on. Francis, my former boss at MPI, a friend whom I hired when he was desperate and whom I defended against Rob, the one whom I was sure I could count on as an ally, shocks me when he refuses to take sides. The rest, waiting to see who wins, are undeclared.

We trudge on daily through a dismal swamp of distrust and insecurity. It is deadly and will only hasten our demise. It must stop. I see only one solution:

DRIVEN

Somehow Rob and I must find a way to terminate our partnership before it terminates us.

The effects of the oil embargo struck us in October 1974; I struck in December. Now with January over we have endured a third consecutive month of losses despite our cost-saving measures. Refusing to acknowledge that conditions are unlike anything we've experienced before, Rob still forecasts an early economic rebound and insists that "it's only an inventory adjustment." Since I hesitate to combat him on the issue of closing down Chicago for fear that he'll do something foolhardy I expect inevitable disaster.

It's hard to keep my troubles to myself. Upon revealing them to Janet, she comments, "I can't get involved with the business. Anyway, material things don't matter very much to me."

"If Magicolor goes down the drain, we're finished. It could happen. Don't you understand?"

"I think you're exaggerating, Harry. You'll find a way. You always do."

If Janet has faith in me, she offers no solace. But as my anxiety increases, as I worry more, she becomes calmer, less demanding, almost solicitous. Often I hear her humming contentedly to herself. Strangely, she seems to thrive while my fear mounts. Typically, things are good either at the business or at home, never at both simultaneously.

As conditions worsen, I resume seeing Cathy. I have no one else to talk to, no one who can empathize with me. I know she will be my ready ally again. Sure enough, she understands my frustration and my concern.

"What an awful man your partner is," she steams as we lie side by side in a motel room after making love. "You've got to get rid of him, my love. He's bad for you.

Come into my arms, my sweet. Let me hold you. Tell me how much you love me."

Cathy is generous of herself and gives me glimpses of heaven. When I show weakness she believes I am still strong; when I show toughness she believes I am soft; when I weep she urges me to let myself go and weep still more; when I'm wrong she stands by me; when I feel lost she makes me feel safe. Yet I hold back. I can only give part of myself. My duty to my family is a restriction. I can't betray Janet all the way. I must reserve a part for her. Being loyal to neither woman, I'm suspended in a state of loneliness. I'm only a fraction of a person at any given time.

"Either Rob or I has to buy the other one out," I explain to Cathy. "It's the only way out of the mess."

"You don't mean you'd give up the company, darling?"

"It's the last thing I want," I answer desolately.

"Oh, my sweet, come let's make love. Come into me again. Let me make you happy."

CHAPTER XI
Year Nine
1975

Sales: $3,800,000 (+6%)
Profit: $68,000 (-57%)
Debt: $622,000 (-21%)
Net Worth: $417,000 (+13%)

"This can't go on. One of us has got to buy the other out," I say, standing before Rob's desk one morning in early February after waiting three hours for his late arrival, as usual.

Without a hint of surprise, almost as if he had come to the same conclusion as I did—for a change—he declares, "I'll buy you out."

I gasp. It hasn't occurred to me that he'd want the business, especially after his unhappy experience running things during my absence in December.

"Alright," I say. "Magicolor is yours. We've already agreed on the price. Is that still okay with you?"

I was referring to a written agreement that we signed at the end of each fiscal year. It established the value of the company for the purpose of eliminating any dispute between our surviving spouses in the event of the death of either principal.

"Sure," Rob says.

"I assume then you'll draw up a purchase and sale agreement." I guessed that he'd need a week or more before presenting a proposal outlining the terms.

"Well, it's quite simple, Harry. I figure the company would give you a note with interest at prime payable in equal installments over the next ten years."

Astonished at his preparedness, I sit stunned for a few moments before responding: "Not a note from the company, Rob. Not on your life. You'd have to personally guarantee the note and back it up with solid collateral, nothing less than your own personal assets."

"Well, OK, my company stock."

"No way, no way."

He stares into me silently as I continue. "Under your management, I'd give Magicolor a year, maybe two before it goes under. The stock is a doomed asset as far as I'm concerned."

"Well, that's my best offer," he says with cool finality.

"I'd buy you out if—" I begin.

"Hah, you buy me out! With what? What guarantee? Not with Magicolor's stock. If it isn't good enough for you, it's not good enough for me either."

"I think the company would have a better future under my direction," I say weakly, cognizant that emotion has entered the discussion.

"So that's what you think."

"I'm a proven quantity," I argue.

"Not to me," Rob says bitterly.

I realize that our debate has deteriorated; reason has flown. We have lost the chance to agree.

"Then the only thing left is to sell out to a third party," I venture.

"That's OK with me. You find one."

"I will," I say, my anger burgeoning. "I'll find one if it's the last thing I do."

Immediately I contact several business brokers in New York and Chicago who specialize in bringing parties together to effect the purchase and sale of small companies. Some work for a fee up front, others are compensated according to a formula based on the size of the transaction and contingent upon a sale. After sending their representatives to look us over, the brokers each compose a lengthy written presentation of Magicolor's phenomenal history, a description of the present situation, an analysis of the industry's shining long-term climate, and an exaggerated projection of Magicolor's "certain" prosperous future, all between fancy covers.

"Don't you think you're being a bit over-optimistic about us?" I say to one exuberant young lady who flew up from New York.

"We're simply aiming to stir a buyer's interest," she says. "It's like advertising."

"Well don't expect me to back up your claims," I warn. "For one thing I don't believe we can double sales in three years as you indicate."

"We base that projection on your partner's statements."

"He's full of baloney."

"Don't worry, Mr. Simon, whoever looks at you will come to their own independent conclusions."

But I think she hopes not. She hopes they'll want us enough to believe the hype I despise. Haven't I learned that business abounds with small deceptions that are usually found out sooner or later?

A half-dozen clients show interest of whom all but one prove to be short-lived. That one, Insulmark, a company from Norway, explores us diligently. Insulmark owns a score of operations around the world, some in plastics, none in the United States. A flurry of correspondence with Thor Peterson, their "Managing Director of New Business Development," precedes our first meeting. In late February Thor writes:

"I have received information about your interest in taking up discussions with us concerning a possible acquisition of your company. With this letter I just want to express our interest and willingness to go into direct and deeper discussions with you in this respect. For some time we have been looking for an entry into this field of business where you so successfully have been developing your company.

"As the personal contact and impressions from our point of view play such an important role, I propose that we try to meet as soon as we have had an opportunity to penetrate your ideas and figures about your company's coming five years."

Although written in awkward English, Thor's initial letter is clear and direct, and I respond with guarded enthusiasm.

"We shall be most pleased to enter into discussion with you. Based on what we have learned about Insulmark thus far, it would appear that our company and all parties involved could benefit from the injection of your many resources. There is no question that sooner or later the principals here will have to forsake independence in order to solve the problems inherent in a closely held corporation. We look forward to meeting you shortly."

Though I present no specifics on our reasons for selling, I nevertheless feel obliged to hint that not all is well between the partners.

Rob can't wait. He hastily decides on a Scandinavian vacation with his wife — at company expense, of course — and arranges to meet Thor on Insulmark's home turf. Before Rob returns I receive the following note from Thor:

> "Yesterday I had the pleasure of meeting with your Mr. Rob Starr. Through a most stimulating discussion I got the impression that we have a lot of points in common. I am really looking forward to meeting with you."

Now what in the world did Rob tell him? Certainly it was in his interest to present a positive picture. No doubt he laid the political foundation for his own advancement exclusive of mine. Rob returns home with nothing of substance, only stories of Thor's congeniality and raves about Insulmark's "unlimited resources" and their sincerest intentions. I write Thor as follows:

> "Mr. Starr has informed me of your excellent discussion (especially since it included sailboats) and I too look forward to meeting you."

For the past month Thor has written several short letters apologizing for the delay in visiting Magicolor. I suspect he's stalling while sizing up our competitors, who have undoubtedly heard rumors through our common vendors that a Scandinavian company is "out there on a fishing expedition." Finally in late March, one month after Rob's visit to Oslo, Thor comes to Magicolor and the three of us meet in my office.

Thor Peterson, wearing an eye patch, is a hulking, athletic, thick-necked, handsome blond man in his early forties. Unlike his strangely written letters, he speaks a surprisingly colloquial English with barely a trace of an accent. Squinting his one eye, he quietly probes Rob and me with deceptively salient questions.

"My good friend, how do you account for these losses? I'm sure there's an easy explanation, but—"

"Nothing to worry about, Thor," Rob interrupts, his tone assuming intimacy. "The oil embargo—you know what it's doing to everybody. But it's only temporary."

"Of course, of course," says Thor, shaking his head.

"I think we've stanched most of the losses with cutbacks," I chime in.

"Temporary cutbacks, only temporary," says Rob flashing a dark look in my direction. "The U.S. plastics industry is nowhere near a mature stage. And we're at the cutting edge, dealing with new materials and the latest processing technology."

"Of course, we are well aware of this or we wouldn't be interested," says Thor, "but what precisely do you mean by temporary?"

"At most a few months. I think our overall record tells the story, not what's happening now," Rob points out smoothly.

I have to hand it to Rob. He knows how to lay it on. For the first time since he became actively involved in Magic, we aren't adversaries. We have a common goal: sell the company.

"Tell me, gentlemen. It's an obvious question, of course, but with the future so positive, why do you want to sell?" Thor asks apparently in pure innocence.

Rob and I stare at each other, suddenly realizing we have never discussed how to address such a question and therefore run the risk of crossed signals. I nod for him to lead off. I can see in his eyes the busy machinations of his mind as he concocts the answer.

"The best time to sell is when you're riding high. Last year was our best sales and profit year ever, and I say we're going to do it again this year. A few bad months don't make a bad year."

Good answer, I think. Convincing. Apparently honest. Thor seems satisfied.

He also interviews us separately, much to my consternation, because I doubt that our independent answers will be consistent. But consistency doesn't seem to be a serious factor, for soon enough Thor perceives the difference in our styles and attributes to it our variant views.

Two weeks later after returning home, he writes:

> "As I mentioned at our meeting I am prepared to go back to the U.S. very soon again provided that you feel that it is possible for us to mutually agree upon a form for future cooperation.
>
> "Enclosed I return a very interesting article about basic approach to acquisition management planning, which I hope we will have the possibility to discuss further when we meet again."

Since Thor seems anxious to move now, I decide, without consulting Rob, to be contrary and play coy. I fire back the following message:

> "Please bear in mind that several options are available to Magicolor in the U.S. market, some of which tap our value not only as a profit center but also for what we can contribute managerially. Indeed two solidly based competitors have approached us to consider merging forces. In view of such possibilities, Magicolor could quickly prove to be a more significant factor in the industry than at present, bringing with it weight as well as vitality and keenness to a joint effort in Europe.

"Our impression of Insulmark is only favorable, leading us also to seek a formula for working with you."

Except that I laid it on a bit, there was a wisp of truth in my reference to competitors. Indeed two had put out tentative feelers. But I quickly nixed the idea of joining forces with them for fear that competitors might not have genuine intentions and would only be seeking confidential information. Still, why not use them to whet Thor's appetite, letting him think that he isn't the only suitor? Isn't it human nature to want more what someone else values? Without delay Thor replies:

"We have just acquired the market leader of colour concentrates in northern Europe. America is now our target. I am planning to go over to the States on April 10 and will stay for one week if necessary. Could it be possible for us to meet during the weekend as well?"

"We've got him by the balls," says Rob.

"Maybe it's the other way around," I say.

"Whaddya mean?"

"I wouldn't frame our last quarter's P&L and hang it on the wall," I explain. "Wait 'til he sees it."

"We've got nothing to worry about. He needs us, Harry. He can taste us. He wants entry into the largest market in the world, right here, the U.S. of A. And we're the way in. A few months of losses don't mean a thing to big outfits once they make up their minds. They think long term."

Making the most of the perks his job provides, Thor stays at the posh Ritz-Carlton in Boston where the movie stars bed when in town. He frequents only prestigious restaurants, mostly French, and private clubs, the sort of places Rob also enjoys and which very quickly they enjoy together. Rob introduces Thor to similar spots in his own backyard, such as his country club, with its ninth hole on the shore of Narragansett Bay; the Brown University Club; his exclusive men's club downtown, (in which women are only lately allowed but only as waitresses); and the picturesque northern Italian restaurants, with their old-time mustachioed waiters in black bow ties and lavender cummerbunds, at which Rob — and the Mafia — are graciously greeted and have charge accounts. Rob's easygoing, high living style is far more appealing to Thor than my lean and parsimonious ways. It's no surprise that Thor would lose his impartiality: Rob's words sound more promising, are what he wants to hear.

At the same time, Rob is infatuated with Thor's worldly ease, his smooth confidence, his comfortable way with money and power. Rob announces that after the sale he wishes to remain with Magicolor as an Insulmark employee. In fact he's enthusiastic about the prospect. If Thor is blind to Rob's fluff, his incompetence, why should I dispel his erroneous impression? On the contrary, at every opportunity I praise Rob. If even falsely he adds extra value to the deal, all the better.

Though I don't intend to stay on myself, I lead Thor to assume I will. He'd prefer to keep the existing management intact, at least in the early stages. But I'm aware that I could not tolerate reporting to a higher authority, not after being in charge and making independent decisions for the past eight years, not after the agonizing price I've paid to be autonomous. Thus neither party is honest or trusting with the other; only the figures, perhaps the least troublesome ingredient in our negotiations, are honest.

On the last day of Thor's visit he presents us with a "Draft for an Agreement between the Shareholders of Magicolor, Inc. and Insulmark":

For 100% of Magicolor, Inc., Insulmark will pay:
1. $1,000,000 at the closing.
2. Messrs. Harry Simon and Rob Starr, in addition to competitive salaries, will each receive $40,000 per year for ten years guaranteed by Insulmark. This payment will be predicated upon achieving certain minimum after-tax earnings level which are the following:

Year	One	Two	Three	Four	Five
After tax earnings (thousand)	$230	$280	$330	$380	$430

3. Insulmark will pay an additional $1,200,000 according to the following schedule: $200,000 upon reaching $600,000 after tax profits in year 3; $400,000 upon reaching $1,370,000 in year 4; and $600,000 upon reaching $1,700,000 in year 5.

The above is subject to Insulmark's conducting a detailed analysis of the company, subject to the approval of the Board of Directors of Insulmark, and subject to the approval of the Norwegian National Bank.

My immediate reaction is extreme disappointment. I consider the proposal insulting and Thor nothing less than a Norwegian robber baron.

"Take your time. I don't expect a definitive answer today," says Thor. "But before I leave, possibly you could tell me if it's doable—say, within range."

Rob and I go into a huddle in his office while Thor sits in mine on the couch perusing a trade magazine. Rob is enthusiastic over the proposal.

"It's basically a $3,000,000 deal," says Rob.

"Hell it is," I counter. "It's only a $1,000,000 deal."

"How do you figure that?"

"Everything over the $1,000,000 at closing is contingent upon performance."

"That's right. So?"

"The most profit we ever had was last year, $160,000, and that's pretax. It's unlikely we'd make his projected earnings figures."

"Sure we can. They're our figures. They're the ones we gave him."

"You gave him, Rob. They're your figures, not mine. Do you actually believe they're attainable? Thor's calling our bluff. He's saying, if you believe what you're telling us about the future, then put your money where your mouth is."

"Well, with Insulmark's bucks behind us, with their prestige and reputation, I think it'll be duck soup. Don't forget, they're buying us for growth. You can bet they'll pour money into us."

"Oh, yeah," I say. "Not me. When I sell, I want it clean. I'm not interested in gambling. If I have to bet, I'll bet on myself, not on some impersonal corporate giant that's pulling the strings—from a foreign country yet."

How intriguing that our contrasting personalities bring us to interpret the same proposal so differently. Rob—trusting, positive, a gambler, confident that things always turn out for the best—was a believer in his own happy lies and I—cautious, distrustful, fearing the possibility of the worst, comfortable only when depending on my own resources—insist on the raw bone truth. I don't doubt which of us gets the most out of life, the most satisfaction from our unique states of being. I am sure that I do. My so-called purity, my compulsive morality, my sense of high purpose, my dedication to the larger universe, my idealism—are not these the requisites for a superior existence? Or is Rob, who so casually casts himself adrift into the ocean of life, is he finding the voyage more exciting and richer? These questions are only barely discernible, and I am not ready for answers.

I can't abide Rob's style any longer. It's either him or me, and since he's set to stay on, has cultivated Thor's friendship, and is mesmerized by the multinational corporate scene, I have no choice but to leave. There's no room for the two of us. Sad though I feel—after all, I'm relinquishing the offspring of my intelligence and accumulated wisdom, of my consuming labor, and, in a sense, the essence of my personality in its material form—I am ready to move on to a clean start, where I can apply the lessons I have learned at Magicolor. I feel like a parent leaving a child to a foster home, a loss I must endure for my own sake as well as the child's. I feel sad that it will be over after so many years, yet I am happy at the prospect of starting over. I'll have a chance to experience once again the rapture of those early days in the old place with the leaky roof and the dirt floor. The plastics industry in southern California is still young. I'll join millions of others who have migrated there to be born again.

So that afternoon Rob and I negotiate with Thor separately. Rob accepts the proposal essentially as it's presented. Oh, he got Thor to up his contingent salary by

$10,000 and to reduce the earnings threshold by $50,000 for the first two years. Big deal—there's hardly a chance that either will be realized.

I confess to Thor that I have no wish to stay on, explaining that I'm too entrepreneurial to work for anyone but myself. Applying a persuasive frankness, he points out that I would be given substantial freedom to make decisions.

"Like spending money? Taking risks?" I ask.

"Within certain limits, of course," he replies.

"Then I wouldn't be really free."

"Your constraints wouldn't be very restrictive. Anyway, I don't think you're a big risk taker. I gather you are a cautious and thoughtful man."

"Maybe. No matter. I must be on my own, in control. It's the way I am."

"I see. Well, you are perhaps right. We could not make you happy."

We bargain for about a half hour and settle on $850,000 cash for my Magicolor shares. But Thor is concerned that I might compete with Magicolor after leaving (a no-compete agreement is obviously essential) and he wants to know of my future plans.

"I'm planning to start a similar operation on the West Coast," I say, "probably L.A. The market is young and growing out there."

"Of course, we'll have to restrict you, Harry, you realize."

"Certainly, I understand that."

"Let's say," he says, focusing his single eye into middle space, "you can't do business east of the Rocky Mountains, no further than Denver."

"That's okay with me."

We study a road map of the United States which I retrieve from my desk, and decide on a line west of Interstate 25.

"And what are you doing for financing?" he inquires.

"I haven't got that far. But I don't expect a problem, especially with my share of the proceeds from Magicolor as seed money."

"No, I doubt that it will be a problem." He narrows his eye, a characteristic signal of his intention to advance a telling idea. Like a baseball pitcher trying to catch a runner off base, he suddenly flings it at me. "Would you be interested in having Insulmark participate?"

Jolted, caught off guard, I rebound quickly. "Sure, I guess — well, I'd have no objection but..." I pause, remembering well my error in underestimating my strength negotiating with Rob eight years earlier, in which I sought only 50 percent of the company rather than control.

"Under one condition," I continue.

"Ah, yes, and your condition?"

"Insulmark would have only a minority interest. It has to be my show."

He laughs. "Certainly. We would have no problem with that, Harry, just so long as we own a seat on your board. We hold similar positions in several companies and they have gone smoothly. Of course, we would want the right of first refusal on your stock if and when you decide to retire or sell."

We shake hands. Thor will now return to Oslo headquarters to get the approval of his board, which he assures us is "only a formality." He will then draw up the deal we had all agreed to, and return in a few weeks for a closing.

Everything seems to be moving along without a hitch. The selling price is settled. Rob will manage the new subsidiary. I will be far away on my own, with Insulmark as my minority partner. All parties seem satisfied, the sign of a successful negotiation. A deal appears inevitable.

"Now that everything's sewed up," says Rob, "and I'll be in charge, how about stepping aside, letting me run the place my way?"

With the prospect of money and power behind him, what amazing courage Rob now shows. Does he imagine that he will make fewer mistakes than before, or that miraculously their consequences will be somehow muted? He has a bulldozer mentality: power is forgiving. Like America in Vietnam.

Still, his request seems reasonable. I withdraw, and for the next two months only occasionally show up at the office to appraise current conditions. In the meantime, to keep busy, Jane and I arrange to have a home designed and built near the ocean on Cape Cod. Even though we plan to permanently settle in Southern California, Jane wishes to spend her summers in the East, and I know I can never completely forsake my geographic roots. We agree that after I retire, the East is where we want to be. We want to die on old familiar ground, be there for eternity.

With so much time off I have the opportunity to attend a three-week executive program (part of a nine-week course) for small company presidents at the Harvard Business School. It requires that I live in a dorm and have no contact with my company. Many of the other students also have partnership problems or are seeking to sell out. Expecting to acquire new management insights, instead I get no more from the courses than a rationally sophisticated conceptualization of what I have been doing by gut feeling for the last eight years. The instructors are an arrogant, in-grown lot, immersed in themselves, willing to offer all-knowing advice. Indeed one, Professor Hoyt Strong, a gangly, friendly, controlled, and intense man, thinks that Magicolor is an excellent candidate for a B School case study.

The rationality I learn at Harvard, the techniques of gathering and interpreting information essential to making correct judgments, both impress and intimidate me. Humbled, I wonder how I ever succeeded using mostly my intuition and hunches. Has my success been merely an accident, a product of sheer chutzpah that may just as easily have led to failure? Have I simply blundered into the heights I've reached?

The business of business is far more complex than those neatly described cases we analyze at Harvard. With all the school's smart tools and methodology, many of its students still fail in the harsher world off-campus. Harvard hasn't taught them how to accept muddle, only how to correct it with cold certainty. The human factor is missing. Only a dedicated, constantly learning, forever self-correcting human mind hell-bent for independent survival is capable of coping with all the ramifications of being in business. Such ability to cope is beyond being taught. It is rooted in distrust.

When the course at Harvard is over, building the house proves to be a salutary distraction. I have no time to get bored. The architect is ingenious and exciting to work with; the builder is honest and conscientious, and has become a friend. The financing proves easy at a favorable 8 1/2 percent rate through the bank I use in the business. As they say, "Them's that have gits." The biggest problem, imposed by the continuing oil embargo, is finding enough gas to get us to the construction site on Cape Cod and back home again.

The "few" weeks during which Thor is to draw up Magicolor's purchase and sale agreement has grown to six, then eight with no word forthcoming. As agreed, we sent him the figures for each passing month. Attempting to sweeten continuing bad news, Rob writes:

> "We are enclosing statements covering April and May as requested.
> "In regard to an up-to-date or revised projection, if you delete our present fiscal year from the projection, we feel that the original projection is still valid. It will just take an extra year to achieve the end results."

What kind of naive fool does Rob take Thor for? Insulmark will never buy such an optimistic view of our worsening bottom line. Still it's likely Rob is not quite being insincere. He always sees what he wants to see: a happy ending. Meanwhile I haven't examined the statements, nor do I want to, for fear they will so disturb me as to impair my ability to remain uninvolved.

On June 15, a memorable day, Thor's letter arrives, which makes clear his reason for stalling.

> "The bad economic conditions in U.S. have now come to Europe. Therefore Insulmark's president has instructed me to delay all negotiations on acquisitions for the time being. I believe after we see how the economy develops in the fall, we can start our negotiations again.
> "I note that Magicolor's profits have not improved. The cause may be only temporary, but I must be sure that a changing market or a bad competitive situation is not contributing to your poor

performance. However I believe this is not the case and that we are sure to make a deal in the future, but I must convince our board.

"Thank-you for your excellent hospitality. Good luck."

I take this as the death knell to the verbal deal we had made in April.

"California's out," I say to Janet.

"Just as well. I'm happy here. But you know I'll go wherever you go."

"Good," I say. "I just don't know what's going to happen. I was counting on the Norwegians. Now we've got a second house—a big mortgage—and in the fall a college tuition. It's going to be tight for us if business doesn't improve."

"But you always find a way, and you will this time," she says confidently.

"That's true. I always do," I comment, hardly letting on, especially to myself, how worried I am.

CHAPTER XII

Year Nine
(Continued)

1975

"It's over, Rob. Insulmark has its own troubles. We can't afford to sit by and wait for things to change. You've got to face up to the fact that the oil embargo is screwing up the world and things won't get back to normal for some time."

Hesitantly Rob nods. "Well, do you have any ideas?"

"Yup. I'd like to buy you out." After waiting briefly for him to absorb my words, I add, "But I'll need some time."

Sitting impassively across my desk, he blinks, his jaw slackens, and he waits for me to go on. He seems depressed, beaten. I feel pity for him. Events are belying his optimism and his self-confidence is unraveling.

"I have some ideas," I continue. "I made some contacts at Harvard."

"Look, Harry, can't we try to get along?" he begs.

"We're incompatible, Rob. You're miserable and so am I."

"I'm not complaining," he says. "I think we've got a good thing going. Tell me what you want me to do. Just tell me and I'll cooperate."

"We've been through that," I say. "We're simply not for each other."

"For God sakes, we're not married, Harry."

"Oh, but we are. We're very much married and I want a divorce. So I'm asking you to step aside as I did for you when we thought we had a deal with Insulmark."

"I see. So that's what it's come to."

"Christ, why do you act surprised?"

His jaw tightening, he agrees, "Okay, goddamnit, but I can't give you forever, y'know. You got three months."

"That's not much time."

"As I said, I can't give you forever."

"Six months."

"No. No way. And I'm staying on as sales manager until you raise the cash — if you can."

My mind is already working. I know I'll have to offer no less than I had demanded of him. If I have to I'll do it in three months.

At my invitation, Professor Hoyt Strong of the Harvard Business School agrees to join Magicolor's board of directors, no doubt in part because we would make an interesting case study to present to his students. Certainly we have problems galore: partnership problems, management problems, problems of declining sales amid inflating costs, problems of material shortages, cash flow and rising interest rate problems, employee morale problems, and problems in the marketplace due to increasing competition in a maturing industry. Magic offers him an outstanding opportunity to witness failure firsthand, disaster as it happens with all the concomitant causes blaring — great stuff for the classes at Harvard to study and arrogantly judge with the benefit of hindsight. Learn from the mistakes of others. Learn how to do from how not to do. But how would they do, not in the comfortable air-conditioned lecture room making up a list of my mistakes on the blackboard, but in the very thick of it as I am?

Well, I'll fool Professor Strong; I'll turn this thing around if it's the last thing I do. I'll make us a model case, an exceptional experience for the students to emulate.

"Don't you think it would be well to delineate the problems?" Professor Strong urges in that coolly confident, incisive, analytical, Harvard B School way. "Then lay out a comprehensive strategy for dealing with them simultaneously—in detail mind you. Uh huh."

Rob Starr could be an obstacle to my adopting Professor Strong's recommended procedures. Seeking to win over his cooperation, I write him a memo based on logic and common sense, realizing that such an approach might have doubtful appeal to his way of thinking.

> To: Rob Starr
> From: Harry Simon
> Subject: Recommendations for Preserving Magicolor's
> Financial Health

> REVIEW OF THE PAST SIX MONTHS

> Last November, Magicolor experienced its first significant decline in sales and profits in seven years. In view of signs from leading statistical indicators, from authoritative economic advisory services to which we subscribe, and from the atypical dip in sales during a traditionally strong month, it is obvious that Magicolor is caught up in the effects of a serious recession.

Though in the past Rob had not agreed that what had happened was happening, I hope now, six months later, that he's ready to admit a recession is in progress. I continue:

> At that time it was [I] suggested that the company prepare for a protracted decline in sales and profits

by devising a plan for overhead reduction and eliminating weak and unprofitable aspects of the total operation.

Indeed in December I initiated our first layoff of workers but held back on going further because of Rob's opposition. I go on:

> But little was done due to lack of consensus. [The two of us had disagreed, resulting in a stalemate.] One argument [Rob's] against taking action was based on the expectation that an inventory adjustment was taking place and would be swiftly over, leading to a sudden business turnaround. Another argument [Rob's] was based on the belief that the plastics industry was historically immune from the downswings that prevail throughout the rest of the economy. Thus there was no recognition of [Rob did not acknowledge] the fact that this recession was deeper than any since the Great Depression and had engulfed the plastics industry as well. It was [Rob had] also not understood that the enormous buildup in inventories during the oil embargo coupled with an overreaction of buyers toward extreme caution would lead to a delayed revival.
>
> As [I] predicted last November, so long as complacency would be the rule, Magicolor has continued to endure losses.

Then after detailing the mounting losses and especially the fragile condition of the Chicago operation, I state that the company has experienced a serious $94,000 reduction in working capital, adding, "Clearly, while late in the day, we should take a more conservative stance and institute proper remedial action to stanch the outflow of working capital."

RECOMMENDATIONS ON ACTION TO BE TAKEN

To preserve and ultimately enhance its cash-flow position, the company must earn an after-tax sum of $25,000 to meet its long-term debt repayment schedule each quarter for the next three years. The company should also strive to reduce the length of time during which it resorts to short-term borrowing in order to have it more readily available for emergencies, to smooth out cash-flow crunches, and to take advantage of opportunities that can lead to swifter profits.

Admittedly I am proposing a highly conservative approach, which I know Rob will find absurd. But I believe it is what any experienced and successful businessman must do in our situation. The underlying assumption guiding all businessmen is not, as is commonly thought, to grow bigger or to increase profits, but to reduce risk. In short, the first order of business is to survive; only after the odds for survival seem favorable are other goals considered. But the odds are constantly changing in this threatening world, so that the businessman, like a shark that forever keeps swimming to stay alive, must never stop at improving the odds against failure. He must deal with the possibility of his company's disablement, perhaps death, when he makes a decision, even a seemingly innocent minor decision. If he is insensitive to his environment, ignores it, as I fear Rob is doing, he is doomed.

After saying this, I confess my personal preference for survival is more compulsive than rational. Seeing "death" in every threat, in every risk and decline (and some are imagined perhaps), I respond swiftly to ward it off to the best of my ability. In view of my tendency to overreact, to keep my sanity I devote considerable energy in trying to contain my fears and stay on a reasonable course. I must remind myself that I will survive; I am not doomed; and that the business has a sound foundation and possesses a certain stamina.

To extinguish our losses I list five well-considered specifics:

(1) As recommended last December, the position of Director of Manufacturing should be eliminated. This was recently accomplished [when I sacked Gary], yielding a savings of over $3,000 per month.

(2) As earlier recommended, the salaries of the president [myself] and treasurer [Rob] should be reduced by one half to save over $8,000 a month. [I expect a bitter argument against this one.]

(3) Although the Chicago operation has lost over $5,000 per month during the past six months and will probably continue to do so during the coming summer months, we can expect a pickup in the third quarter. In the meantime I propose reducing its staff to the barest minimum: lay off two workers, attempt to sub-lease half the space we occupy, eliminate the office staff, and transfer the paperwork to Massachusetts headquarters. These steps will save over $2,000 per month. If sales fall below $20,000 per month [the break-even level] the operation should be shut down, placed in mothballs, and revived when business conditions warrant. By mothballing, our losses would be reduced by more than one-third to only $1,500 per month. The Massachusetts plant would take over servicing Chicago sales.

I plainly don't have the courage to propose what I intuitively wish to do with Chicago: eliminate it completely. If retreat was acceptable, the admission of failure wasn't.

(4) As recommended previously, we should reduce by 10 percent the salaries of all employees earning over

$10,000 per year. If done tactfully with adequate explanation and in the form of an appeal with the promise to resume the original salaries after profits rebound, most employees should cooperate. There is little danger of losing key people under existing poor economic conditions. This step will yield about $2,000 per month.

(5) Transfer one technician from the lab to production, for a savings of $1,000 per month.

Were all the above recommendations followed, Magicolor would save approximately $16,000 per month, about $48,000 per quarter, sufficient to yield a steady cash flow of after-tax funds and eliminate all present losses. Should profits exceed this projection, and the economic trend change for the better, some or all emergency measures may be abandoned.

Not to adopt this program will most certainly result in severe hardship and cause great risk to all concerned, both those within the company and to others [the bank and creditors] who play a supportive role. Your comment is most welcome.

Rob's comment is not to comment: Silence, as if my recommendations were not worthy even of acknowledgment. Though I'm not surprised, I'm boiling angry. Does Rob think our problems will go away by themselves? Is his contrariness a form of plain vengeance? Though he agreed to my taking over, he has conceded nothing else. Distrusting him, fearing his destructiveness, I am aware of a deepening hate within me.

Under Rob's brief aegis, Magicolor has sunk deeper into a mire. Only our remaining line of credit saves us from going under. Rob has wasted a large portion of that reserve. The unanswered question is how will the bank react when they see the new quarterly statement listing our persistent losses.

I then write the following memo:

To: Rob Starr
From: Harry Simon
Subject: Delineation of Responsibilities

During the last quarter I turned over the reins of
Magicolor to your administration, allowing, at your
request, the middle management structure to remain
intact. This was done in order to present an
interested buyer of my shares in the company a viable
and undisturbed organization.

It is now clear that we do not have a buyer for
Magicolor and that I must now resume my former
role as president. We have agreed that your
responsibility will be sales and ...

I spell out his duties in precise detail. In so doing I
hope that, should he overstep his authority, as he has
done in the past, I can apply this memo, something in
writing, to bring him back in line. I then outline my
responsibilities as well and list the department heads who
would report to me, not to him.

We have also agreed that each of us will generally
work a full eight-hour day, five days a week. In the
event we miss a day, take time off, each must notify
the other, advise the pertinent employees, and
arrange for responsible coverage among those
reporting to us.

There will be no more casualness on the job. It is not
a hobby. There will be no more arriving at 10:00 A.M.
and leaving at 3:00 P.M. [As if dealing with an
immature spoiled teenager, I insist that he behave
responsibly.]

As president I have instructed Emma [our office
manager] to process no expenditures, including
accounts payable and wages and salaries, without my
approval.

I predict that this, my control over Rob's salary, will stir him to protest. Unfortunately, having equal power to sign checks, he then writes his own. As in the earlier crisis, he refuses to cut his salary still further even in the face of possible disaster.

A ship cannot have two captains. Hopefully, this clear delineation of responsibilities will prevent the sort of conflict that has arisen before. It will also clarify for all employees where they stand and to whom they are responsible.

Copies of the memo are distributed to all key employees. Their response is silence.

In contrast to the tensions at Magicolor, at home my life is calm and routine. Evenings I read the paper, have supper with Janet and the children, watch TV, and read *The New Yorker* or a biography of a successful person before falling asleep. My sleep is restless. Weekends I mow the lawn, go to movies, dine out with friends, and walk the neighborhood. Janet seems content. She gives me the normalcy I need. I rarely see Cathy. I'm too preoccupied with "divorcing" Rob to meet her demand for love. I also need an easy conscience. Trouble in business, peace at home; trouble at home, peace in business.

I make a formal offer to Rob to purchase his entire stock interest in the corporation and the real estate, in part by the corporation and in part by me individually for $780,000, of which $125,000 is payable at closing, with three annual payments of $50,000 followed by three annual payments of $83,333 each and 5 percent interest on outstanding balances. I would also pay him $50,000 a year for three years and provide medical and other fringe benefits in return for a six-year no-compete agreement.

The company would maintain life insurance on my life to guarantee the deal in case of my death. Rob's stock would be held in escrow and released in proportion to payments made. I reserved the right of pre-payment after six months. In the first year he would receive almost $250,000.

I further stipulate that the closing would be set for ninety days after the sale agreement was executed. The agreement would be subject to the condition that satisfactory financing could be obtained by me and/or the corporation.

Where I would get the money is a big mystery to me and obviously a bigger one to Rob, but my bravado compels him to take the offer seriously.

"I'll think about it," he comments after skimming it.

"Take your time," I respond.

And I don't mean that casually. What I most need now is time. To me the deal seems fair, even generous, and it's consistent with our private understanding of the company's worth. I think he'll go for it.

After delegating most of my day-to-day functions to employees, I concentrate on raising the capital to buy out Rob. First I go to the local bank with whom Magic has been dealing since our beginning. In the early days the bank extended credit based on Rob's prestige and credibility. Now, after almost ten years, having proved my capability to the loan officers, I carry some clout in my own right. But the initial meeting is discouraging.

"You barely have enough assets to cover a loan of that size, Harry. The equipment and inventory are already assigned. There are the receivables, of course. Well, you know we can only value them at fifty cents on the dollar," explains the bank's lending officer.

"They're good receivables, one hundred percent collectible," I insist.

"Sorry, Harry, I don't make the rules."

I feel I'm caught in a trap of Rob's making. Because of the recent half year's losses due to his profligacy, our debt has mushroomed and now lives on to haunt me. Had we reacted earlier and held down debt, as I recommended, the bank would have found the buyout less risky. The sonofabitch. And I castigate myself for not having been more insistent on holding the line.

"Well, take the receivables, then."

"Of course there's also your earnings problem," the lending officer points out.

"What earnings problem? We haven't had a loss year, and my projections—"

"Your projections are very encouraging, but we must remember they're only projections."

"I realize—"

"Let's take the worst case scenario. Let's suppose you don't make the projections. Will you have enough profits to cover your interest expense?"

Why in hell doesn't he just say no? Why in hell does he string me along?

"I think the profits will be there," I insist.

"Of course you think so. I think they will too. You've proven you can do the job. But the loan committee will never buy it, Harry. No, they'll never buy it. Sorry, my friend."

I try other banks in Massachusetts and out of state—Providence, Hartford, even New York—with the same result. They say the company is already too highly leveraged, its profit history too erratic.

Julius Hillman, our reliable accountant and respected sage, puts me in touch with a prominent, old bank ensconced in a brand-new glass building in Springfield, Massachusetts. They are willing to finance the deal after collateralizing all Magicolor's assets and charging 20 percent interest. Under those circumstances I figure they'd be hardly less than my employer. Anyway they stall and stall, ignoring my calls, and after three weeks they finally say only that I must be patient. Although they're sure they'll go for it, the committee hasn't made up its mind. I say to myself, "let them go to hell" and I say to them "forget it."

Meaning well in making the connection for me, Julius is surprised at "the crude way they handled me." Money is money no matter the prestige or the trappings. And people are people; even dignified people don't always level.

I consult with Professor Hoyt Strong, who with his Harvard connections arranges for me to meet with several investment groups in Cambridge. They are all alike, consisting of a swift bunch of young MBAs who talk figures in terms of percentages and ratios (quick ratio, liquidity ratio, asset ratio) and use a specialized lingo (goodwill, tangible net worth, asset versus stock purchase, investment payback) with which I'm unfamiliar. They derive their results from complex analyses of Magic's financial statements, which their computers spew out like a waterfall in springtime. After awhile I get lost. Despite my bewilderment, I suspect they know what they're doing, but the fact remains we speak on different wavelengths. They seem unaware that people, not ratios, constitute the essence of our company, that the smooth running of our machinery, the innovativeness of our ideas, and the fine quality of our products depend upon the devotion and conscientiousness of our employees. Since figures are everything to them, are all they go by, they turn me off.

"The name of the game is ROI," the MBAs say. ROI—return on investment—dominates, a simple, hard, uncompromising ratio. Emperor ROI. And for them Magic's ROI doesn't come up right.

"According to our analysis you're paying your partner too much for his shares. Talk him into settling for a half less and we'd be interested."

I leave their office with its array of electronics, dizzy and depressed. Hoyt Strong is surprised. He has been upbeat about the many opportunities for raising cash among his former students, now youthful Cambridge investment warriors noted for their daring.

"Maybe they're right; the deal's impossible to put together," I say.

"Don't get discouraged," Hoyt consoles. "You haven't exhausted all possibilities. You should try the insurance companies and some SBICs [small business investment corporations] and there are individuals who would give their eye teeth to participate."

Hoyt is right. They're out there aching to find vehicles like mine, only they want control. Some are ex-corporate executives who for one reason or another have been separated from their companies at too young an age to retire. Gnashing to get back into the fray, any fray, they talk of parlaying Magic into a giant. Their grandiose ambition strikes me as visionary and absurd. Some are doctors who, weary of their profession and ridiculously unsophisticated about business, seek not only ownership but also direct involvement. It is soon obvious that our balance sheet is no more comprehensible to them than a column of hieroglyphics. As I see it, their ignorance may be a potential problem, and after my experience with Rob I certainly don't need another unrealistic active partner.

As always Julius Hillman is my trusty sounding board.

"The only guys willing to come in are impossible dreamers or they don't know the score. The smart ones turn me down. Give it to me straight, Julie: Am I paying Rob too much? Am I screwing myself?"

"You may be." He pauses, allowing me to absorb his brutal frankness.

So my dream of buying control of Magic is ridiculous after all, nothing but sheer audacity. I'm no more realistic than the frustrated doctor entrepreneurs for whom I have a certain contempt.

"But not necessarily," he continues. "Isn't Magicolor worth a lot more to you than to someone else?"

"It's my life, Julie."

"I know that. Now ask yourself the next question. Do you think you can make it while you're paying off Rob?"

"I know I can. It won't be a cinch but I don't doubt it for a minute," I say unhesitatingly.

"Well?" He grins. "You know it's worth it—as you say, it's your very life—and you know you can do it."

"But I don't know how to put it all together. I feel beaten."

"You'll find a way, Harry. You always have." He winks as he retrieves his wallet from his suit jacket. "Wanna bet?"

CHAPTER XIII

Year Nine
(Continued)

1975

During the weeks I try to raise capital, Rob and I resume our war, a war of silence. He ignores recommendations that would solve Magic's problems. He makes no sign that he is even considering my offer. Although our offices are adjacent to each other, we have no verbal communication. When passing by his office in the morning, I refuse to acknowledge his very presence. We avoid each other like creatures of different species. Our mutual hostility once again permeates the usually relaxed office atmosphere. The staff also grows serious and silent.

Rob is my enemy whom I see as evil and destructive. He threatens the survival of Magic, and Magic is me. His inherent selfishness and gross blundering have upset the subtle balance that provides everyone a comfortable feeling of security. He is ruining the fine-tuning that has taken me years to establish; he is cheapening our striving for excellence and damaging our sense of a common purpose. I am discovering how enormous is my capacity to hate. How could I have ever liked him? Yet for years, especially the early years, I raved to Janet about his good nature and charmingly easy ways.

Each of us seeks allies among our employees. Not knowing who will win, most prefer to remain neutral.

Some, like children of a deteriorating marriage, refusing to acknowledge the culpability of either party, listen sympathetically to both. A few gamble and take sides. I conclude that anyone who doesn't expressly support me is probably against me. So in addition to distrusting Rob, I also distrust many of the employees, perhaps justifiably.

I am too busy searching for capital and repairing the damage that Rob has done to notice a plot developing.

Chicago is hemorrhaging. I fly there immediately notifying no one, and am shocked at what I find. As I walk into the plant at ten o'clock in the morning, I'm greeted by Mrs. Slocum, our wispy, fiftyish woman office manager, whom I thought to be capable and conscientious ever since I interviewed her when she was hired.

"How good to see you, Mr. Simon."

"It has been a long time."

"Much too long," she says in a way that makes me start.

Touring the plant, I'm surprised to see only part of the crew working and one of the three production lines idle. Since the chatter of the machines is too loud to permit conversation with employees we wave to each other as I pass through. At the time clock I peruse the time cards to see who is missing. But according to the cards, no one is: All are punched in as present. Baffled I return to the office.

"Where's Billy," I ask Mrs. Slocum.

"Oh, yes, I'm afraid he's out somewhere." She sighs.

"Is he ill?"

"Oh, no, he was here. He opened up."

"You mean he's gone on a business errand?"

"I don't know. He doesn't say." Her words are clipped.

"Well, when do you expect him back?"

"Not until five." She eyes me expectantly.

I flush with anger. "What's going on, Mrs. Slocum?"

"Let me tell you, Mr Simon. I'm so relieved you asked."

She explains that Billy would show up in the morning, punch in the time cards of certain absent workers, then disappear until five, when he'd return to punch out the cards.

"From what I've overheard, I believe Billy gets a cut from their wages," she says, her voice cracking. "I told Gary what was going on when he visited us from Massachusetts last month. I—I really thought you knew."

"You mean Gary knew?"

Though controlled, my anger heightens. Gary, my star production manager, my designated alter ego, had said nothing to me. My having fired him is now doubly vindicated.

"Oh, yes. I hoped he'd do something about it, but nothing happened."

The revelations continue. While Billy was on the premises he spent most of his time on the phone handling personal matters or indulging in small talk with Mrs. Slocum, which prevented her from doing her daily tasks. He falsified production reports to show more favorable figures. Suddenly I understand the inconsistency between the monthly losses appearing on the profit and loss statements and the excellent daily production results. I tended to distrust the P & Ls, never dreaming that what I am discovering is possible. Once again reality outclasses my imagination.

There is more to shock me. Billy and Gary were having lengthy phone conversations long distance not only during the business day but also from their homes at night. Mrs. Slocum volunteers that she thought "they seemed to be hatching something, like a sort of conspiracy." She also states that Billy had bragged that he knew Rob's salary and mine and revealed the figures.

"What did he say my salary is?" I ask.

Her reply is uncomfortably accurate. I feel myself blanche, remembering that months earlier, after inadvertently leaving the keys to the file safe on our bookkeeper's desk overnight, she had complained the next morning that she found the records "not as I had left them." Gary must have satisfied his curiosity.

Mrs. Slocum goes on. Billy had cautioned her to keep confidential whatever she observed, or else he'd fire her.

"After he said that, I did just the opposite and called Mr. Starr and told him everything."

"What?" I scream. "You say you called Rob Starr?"

"That's right, Mr. Simon, and he said he'd take care of it, but from what I can tell—well, it's still going on."

"Why in hell didn't you call me?" I demand, unable to quell my outrage.

"I didn't want to bother you—the president. Isn't Mr. Starr an owner? Anyway, you were away and he was in charge."

Of course, already I forget I had stepped aside. I apologize, thank her for her loyalty, and assure her that her identity as a source of information will not be disclosed.

After immediately ordering the half dozen workers present to shut down the plant, I meet with them in Billy's office. I sit on his desk with my legs dangling down the front while they lean against the walls or sit on the floor.

"What's happening here?" I begin. "And please, I want you to be honest, give it to me straight."

They vent a chorus of disgust.

"It's poor management, Mr. Simon," one says.

"No one's on top of things," says another.

DRIVEN

"This used to be a good company to work for. Now I hate coming to work in the morning," someone else says.

One of the older respected workers, a man whom I know to be intelligent and responsible, speaks. "Y'know, Mr. Simon, there are times I wake up in the middle of the night and say to my wife, I ought to call Mr. Simon and tell him what's goin' on."

"I wish you had," I say dejectedly.

Why had life dealt this man such a minor position? On my past visits, he and I often had rewarding conversations during his coffee break. He was content with his lot, his job, his fine family, proud of having sent four children through college. "I appreciate everything I've got," he had said, and I knew he didn't mean in a material sense. Why do I envy him? Have I the courage to emulate him? No, it would be giving up too much. But too much of what?

"Well, my wife said I should mind my own business. I don't agree, but I heard that you were leaving the company so I figured there was no point."

"I'm not leaving," I promise him. "I'm going to clean house as of now, this minute. We'll be one team again. You'll be proud to work here."

Being too late in the day to restart the equipment, I promise everyone a full day's pay and send them home. Then I instruct Mrs. Slocum to make up final paychecks for the absentees whose time cards are dishonestly punched in. When Billy shows up near five o'clock he is shocked to find himself summarily fired and paid off on the spot. It's swift and clean. The incident is prosaic. Knowing what he has done, he doesn't argue and leaves with a weak mutter. I call Helmut Miller's home and leave a message with his wife instructing him to cancel his next day's plans and to be at the office at eight. I remember Cal's similar call years before, which started me on my career in the plastics color field and eventually led to owning my own business with all its pain and pleasure.

I write Rob a memo outlining what I have discovered, ending it with the following paragraph:

> The Chicago operation is now in metamorphosis, undergoing a regeneration of spirit with Helmut Miller as manager, accountable only to me. At the request of all Chicago's employees, I shall visit the facility at least once monthly. However I shall maintain operation of the facility only so long as it makes a contribution to company profits. If it fails to make that contribution, I intend to temporarily shut it down until sufficient area sales are generated to justify its resumption.

In his capacity as sales manager, which I agreed to let him hold, Rob maintains his old routine and as usual ignores my reminders that he tend to business. The war between us intensifies as my anger over his negligence mounts. I attack him with a series of daily memos.

One, entitled "Leadership and Sales Management," criticizes his performance, pointing out that the salesmen and staff are complaining that he is not giving them direction or support. In factual fashion I enumerate his deficiencies: his failure to visit our largest customer or to spend any time with our salesmen and commission reps in the field; due to his long lunches and early afternoon departures, the salesmen can't reach him during call-ins at the end of their day; he isn't filling out the proper forms to facilitate administrative procedures; he has incorrectly delegated a portion of his responsibility to Edgar, our technical director who doesn't even report to him. In conclusion I write, "I would be happy to recommend to you or receive your suggestions on how you may become more effective. Let me repeat: I have written this memorandum at the urging of several people in our organization." Such a veiled expression of my rage certainly doesn't zip past his antenna.

Next day another memo gripes about his exorbitant entertainment expenses and donations. "I intend to oversee such expenses closely and disallow any that do not meet IRS requirements. Donations also require my consent. You have the same right to review my expenses and donations, which I would welcome."

To Rob worrying about the IRS is like betting that a plane you're on will crash. "The odds against an audit are negligible, so it's a good gamble," he has said. He has ignored Julius Hillman's advice that we not take such enormous salaries, which are unjustifiable in a company of our size. He has ignored Julius's warning against expensing his wife's car, and his fifty-five-foot sailboat, parties at home, personal dining out, and home repairs. Fool I may have been playing it straight, for we are not audited while he is my partner. Forever a man of rigid principle, I can't escape myself and take advantage of questionable or shady opportunities; I pay all my own personal expenses and refuse to admit that I envy Rob his freedom from conscience and his ability to break rules with impunity.

Emma, ever conscientious Emma, walks into my office in the early morning and reports desperately that a feeling of insecurity has beset everyone in the company.

"I think some are planning to leave," she confesses.

"Who do you mean?" I ask, not surprised.

"Well, I can't say because no one has actually said so. It's just a feeling I have."

"C'mon, Emma. You know more than that."

"Not really, Harry. Some people have confided in me and I—"

"Sure, sure. I understand."

"I think everyone would like to know what's going on—some kind of statement."

"There's nothing to worry about," I assure her, avoiding her eyes.

"Forgive my bluntness, Harry. Are you leaving us?"

"Certainly not."

"Then why not tell us that you're not?"

Her suggestion hangs suspended in space for a moment. What has happened to my belief in the benefits of communication? I wasn't sure that anyone cared anymore.

"Good idea," I say, snapping out of it. "I'll post an announcement on the bulletin board."

"And include it in everyone's paycheck envelope too."

"Right."

Emma is the unofficial company confidante and counselor to whom everyone at one time or another unloads both their personal and on-the-job problems. Thus her value far exceeds her formal position as office manager. Lucky is the organization blessed with such an empathetic soul, a born ombudsman. By simply listening, she is an outlet for our frustrations and thus a creator of harmony. Often when I'm muddled I use her myself.

ANNOUNCEMENT
TO ALL EMPLOYEES

I understand there is concern among you about my intentions with respect to Magicolor.

Let me assure you that for better or worse I intend to remain president. My personal interests coincide with yours in seeing that Magicolor remains a thriving, progressive, profitable organization for all. My stock ownership is not for sale and I have so informed those who have expressed an interest in acquiring it.

I shall strive to preserve our financial strength through the current recession and restore our old vitality so that we can build an even better company upon the sound foundation we have created together over the past nine years.

Your president,
Harry Simon

As usual Rob Starr has responded neither to my buy-out offer nor to my memo campaign asserting my presidential authority. Not that Rob would ultimately ignore the offer or take my attacks lying down. His way, though typically non-confrontational, is never passive. When he finally reacts on June 21, he sent me a letter bomb registered mail.

To Harry Simon:

I find your proposal unacceptable. The buyout would be from funds generated by the company itself and, unless the whole price were firmly guaranteed, I would have to take the risk that the company, which is already highly leveraged, could support the additional burden.

In the meantime, because of the actions that you have taken during the past week, you leave me no alternative but to bring this matter to a head by some action in addition to an exchange of recriminatory memos. Accordingly, I have instructed my attorney to file a petition in the superior court asking for a dissolution of the corporation on the grounds that the two major stockholders are divided and there is such internal dissension that serious harm to the business of the corporation is threatened. The only condition on which I will cancel these instructions would be if you and I can agree to make sealed bids for each other's stock with the highest bidder buying the stock of the other and also the interest of the other in the real estate. The terms would be an immediate transfer for a certified check and the consummation of this alternative within a period of thirty days.

Unless you agree to the alternative of sealed bids outlined above, I have instructed my attorney to proceed with the petition for dissolution one week from the date hereof.

The letter stunned me. "Dissolution," "petition," "superior court," "sealed bids,"—these are alien words whose meanings are outside my realm of experience. I close the door to my office, slump on the couch, and sink my face into trembling hands. Not since being under fire as a young soldier have I been so full of fear. As my shaking gradually subsides I try to make sense of Rob's threat.

Obviously it's an ultimatum: Either I agree to blindly gamble my share of the business or he'll bring the whole enterprise down on our heads. My God, what vindictiveness! What destructiveness! But isn't it psychologically brilliant? He knows well my natural caution, my propensity for only partial or strictly calculated gambles. He knows that laying it all on one chance bid is to me the equivalent of Russian roulette. But to him, it's a way of life, even fun. To me, losing is death; to Rob, losing isn't even a consideration. He knows precisely how to get at me to get what he wants.

Our opposite views of life are a reflection of his almost mystical faith that only the best will happen, versus my need to play it safe lest the worst happen. Rob trusts life, trusts that he will always come out a winner even when struck by adversity. From his point of view bad luck is only temporary. Events make it right. I see life as not being on my side. I have to reckon with it every second, make it into a positive force by my own effort. Adversity will endure forever if I don't wrestle it to the ground and make it say die.

At home, I hide my panic from Janet and the children. By sheer will it is contained within the writhing pit of my bloated, flatulent stomach. I hardly see Cathy anymore for fear that she will discover my frailty.

Our employees are conscious of Rob's exquisite power over fate, his uncannily consistent good luck. He has the world convinced that he is a born winner. One day an executive who had formerly worked for Rob in his old company meets me by accident in a local fast food restaurant and joins me for lunch.

Hearing of our struggle for power, he warns, "Rob can't lose, y'know. Somehow he'll beat you. The gods are always on his side. You'll see."

Such talk unnerves me. I too have observed that even when Rob seems to fail, he is more like the apparently doomed hero in an old tale who, at the climax of a series of reversals, manages to extricate himself and bring his fate to a happy conclusion. Suspecting that my battle with Rob is a battle against cryptic forces that extend beyond ordinary mortality, I develop a new frame of mind, a kind of reconciliation with fate: I would probably not win, but all that really matters is the fight. If I lose, so what? At least I will have joined the battle. At least I will feel proud and have my self-respect. In this way, losing can actually be a form of winning. I am beginning to feel unafraid.

For a week after sending his ultimatum, Rob fails to show up at the office. He is giving me time to stew. In the meantime Thor Petersen suddenly phones from Norway.

"I hear you're trying to buy out Rob's share," he says.

"Where did you hear that?" I ask, astonished.

"And I gather the two of you aren't getting along."

"I s'pose you can say that," I admit cozily. "You are exceptionally well informed. Is Rob your pipeline?"

"Maybe we can be of some help."

"How so? It's really between Rob and me."

"Well, if you wish to stay on, why not let us be your partner."

I listen hard; my mind whirls with a potentially new concept of coping with Rob.

"Would you pay as much for Rob's shares as I'm willing to pay?" I ask.

"And how much is that?"

"Definitely more than your offer before you took it off the table."

"I see. Allow me to say you're paying too much, Harry."

"Don't you think it's all in the way you look at it?"

"We'd pay more for, well, say 55 or 60 percent of the stock."

"I need control, Thor. You know I'll accept nothing less."

"It looks like we can't do business—yet."

Thor's "yet" slices through me. He must know the whole story. Rob must be in touch with him, engineering something.

"I'm afraid you're right."

"I hope you'll think it over. Call me collect anytime."

"Tell me, Thor, have you talked to Rob?"

"You can say there's been some communication."

"Then you know what he's trying to do."

"What do you mean?"

"The threat of auction, the sealed bids."

"I've heard something to that effect."

"I'd appreciate your frankness. If that were to happen, if Magic goes to auction, do you plan to participate?"

"Well, Harry, that's—you know, well—I don't think I'm in a position to answer that—"

Instantly losing control, I shout, "You conniving sonofabitch."

"Now, Harry, do not be hasty. We've just offered you—we'd rather avoid such an eventuality. It need not come to that."

"Goddamn you and Rob, Thor. Goddamn you both." I slam the receiver down so hard it bounces off its cradle.

A divorced friend of mine says that the law exists for judges and lawyers, not for ordinary people like him and me. Ever since I've been in business I've managed to avoid lawyers. In the few times I've had to deal with them, I found they made simple issues complicated, assumed an unnecessarily adversarial stance toward the other side and under the premise of protecting their client indulged in overkill. But now, despite my reservations, I am ready to consult a lawyer. I phone the company's secretary, a local attorney, who has been a member of our board for several years and who has faithfully attended the board meetings. His minutes, always submitted promptly after the meetings, are usually accurate and succinct.

I read him Rob's letter.

"What recourse do I have?" I ask.

"I'm sort of in the middle here, Harry. I can't advise you against Rob."

"Then don't advise me. Just tell me whether he can do what he's threatening."

"I can't tell you that either."

"Why not?"

"Because I helped him draft the letter."

Et tu Brute. The world is leaking like a sieve. Rob is getting around with uncharacteristic efficiency.

I then call the lawyer who years before prepared the papers on the purchase of my home.

"It's not my specialty, Harry," he says. "But I'll see what I can do. I take it you're a Massachusetts corporation?"

"I think so. I never noticed."

"You mean —"

"Legal stuff bores me, Dan."

"I'll find out at the State House, unless you have a copy of your charter handy. In any case I'll search the Massachusetts statutes on what your partner is proposing and I'll get back to you."

Five minutes later he calls. "From what I read, it takes a majority of the shareholders to sue for dissolution of the company. You say your partner holds only 50 percent of the stock?"

"That's right."

"He has to be bluffing, Harry."

So Rob, as usual, is still a balloon of hot air. And I, boy oh boy, am again feeling as sharp as a tack.

CHAPTER XIV
Year Nine
(Continued)
1975

Anything goes in love and war, they say. Make it a triad: add business. What love, war, and business have in common is desperation. They are activities in which humans invariably react with passion when our position is threatened. Morality becomes thin or nonexistent. As a moral person, which I try to be, I have trouble acknowledging Rob's unconscionable tactics. Should I return his fire? Can I? I mean, can I put aside my interior rules? I know at least intellectually anything should go, and I know I'm desperate.

On guard, Rob. I have, Dan, my lawyer, send Rob a letter which reads in part: "Mr. Simon is gravely concerned over the survival of the Corporation if the two principal officers continue to draw salaries and bonus payments when the Corporation is losing money and has large loans outstanding.

"If Mr. Simon is unsuccessful in obtaining a prompt reduction in these salary and bonus payments, it is his intention to seek relief by a stockholder's suit."

A copy of the letter is also sent to the bank.

Whether Rob is truly bluffing or whether he is simply uninformed remains a mystery. I assume that his ultimatum is empty and he has found my offering price right, requiring only a guarantee. So I tell him I'll definitely provide one—still having no idea how. Am I acquiring his mystical belief in life that things will somehow work out? Ever since the day I read his ultimatum and hit rock bottom, I've been climbing inch by inch towards hope. Now I no longer expect defeat.

Convinced that Rob has conspired with Insulmark, and fearing that they will devise some new twist to wrest my shares from me, I pursue sources of capital with fresh zeal. Suddenly a new twist unfolds during a phone conversation with Professor Strong.

"Why don't you look into an ESOP?" he suggests.

"What in hell's an ESOP?" I ask, thinking that Hoyt is spouting typical Harvard B School surrealism.

"It stands for Employee Stock Ownership Plan. A very new concept. Congress just passed a law a few months ago that enables the employees to own stock by providing tax advantages to a corporation."

"That won't work, Hoyt. Where are the employees going to get the money?"

"From the corporation," says Hoyt, patiently. "The company can contribute up to 15 percent of the company's gross payroll to the plan and deduct it from profits; the plan in turn invests it in the company's stock."

Ah, I see fireworks; rockets are ricocheting across my brain.

"In other words, being in the 50 percent tax bracket, the company in effect contributes fifty-cent dollars to the employees, who in turn buy the stock with hundred-cent dollars?"

"You've got it, Harry."

"And it doesn't cost them a dime."

"Right."

"Yet it gives us the bucks to buy back Rob's shares."

"And all the while you retain control, Harry."

Immediately my mind machine calculates that each year I could conceivably contribute as much as $90,000 to

$100,000 to the ESOP, the equivalent of 15 percent of Magicolor's annual payroll, quite enough to liquidate the debt to Rob. Wouldn't this then satisfy the bank, which has been fearful that Magicolor's after-tax profits might be insufficient to meet the installment payments due over the term of the proposed agreement? Under an ESOP, in which the payback would be achieved with pre-tax dollars, the rules have vitally changed.

"This is damned exciting. Y'know, Hoyt, I always liked the idea of my employees being my partners."

"Apparently so does Congress. But understand, you'll be subject to strict IRS oversight, and the company's statements must be open to all the employees. You've got to mind your p's and q's, no hanky-panky."

"Hey, that doesn't bother me. Rob would never put up with disclosure, but this won't concern him. I prefer to operate openly. Let our people see that running a business is no joyride; maybe they'll try harder. And if we make it big, why not let everyone share in it? This whole concept gets me going. Y'know, Hoyt, I never gave a damn about—well, I'll put it this way. Magicolor is much more than making money to me. It's people. People creating, innovating, trying to win as a team. Sounds corny, I s'pose, but doing it together rather than alone would give me the greatest satisfaction of all. We'll be like a family, committed to each other."

As I hear myself, I realize that Magic is more than just a means of making a living, more than a serious game of competition and ingenuity, more than a source of ego satisfaction or a way of gaining society's respect and approval. Magic is the family I miss not having at home with Janet and "her" children. It may even be the family I missed belonging to as a boy.

Armed with five years of revised cash-flow projections based on Magic adopting an ESOP, I return to the bank with whom we've been doing business since our inception, the very bank that has already turned down my earlier request to fund the buyout.

The first question that the loan officer asks is no surprise: "ESOP. What in the world is an ESOP?" asks Greg, a balding, slender man with bulging eyes.

"I'll tell you," I reply.

And I do, after which he says, "In other words, you could fund the buyout with fifty-cent dollars."

"Right. On that basis my projections—and they're realistic, I assure you—show that the buyout becomes feasible. Take a look."

"Intriguing, very intriguing." He squints, placing the sheet bearing the projections on his desk. "Yup, maybe I can sell it to the committee. Maybe they'll go for it. I like the concept, Harry, but our legal department will—"

"They'll find it's all legal, Greg. Twist the committee's arms for me. Now look at these projections. It's a whole new ball game."

(See Appendix C for a shortened version of what I handed him.)

In simple words I predict a 10 percent annual growth in sales, a consequent increase in profits and sufficient cash generated to pay off Rob and the interest on the bank debt, all this assuming no ESOP. By means of the ESOP, taxes would be reduced by at least $90,000 a year, which upon flowing into the ESOP would purchase Magic's stock on behalf of the employees. In effect the U.S. government would subsidize the buyout and would get its cut only when the employees cashed in their shares upon retirement or leaving the company.

But who can know the future? Certainly not me, not the bank, not even God, as far as I'm concerned. The projections are a game, a what-if game, a presumptive fiction that everyone concerned pretends to take seriously. But it's mandatory, a part of the ritual, in order for things to happen. Nor does this fiction have to be very close to reality, because no one can really know future reality. The bank obviously wants to keep me in charge or, more to the truth, being wise to Rob's inadequacies, they don't want him running things.

As it turns out, my fictitious numbers, the ones I show the bank, bear no resemblance to what finally happens. And their correspondence with reality begins going awry right away.

When I hand Rob my revised offer designed to meet his objections, he says, "I don't think you can deliver. I doubt any bank would go along. And I'm not changing the deadline."

"Read the offer. Is it acceptable or not?" I say. "I'll worry about the financing."

"I told you I need guarantees," he argues still holding the paper containing the offer.

"You've got them."

The offer I hand to Rob is essentially mine alone. It is designed to give me the breather I expect to need during the first years of the payback—time to recover from the weak condition we're in. I bounced my figures off Julius and he offered some valuable minor suggestions. The lawyer, Dan, took my basic instructions and merely reformulated them into legalese, throwing in a slice of protective boilerplate here and there. I have no doubt that I know my own interest better than anyone else. I depend on no one for essential input. In this matter I prefer to be alone.

The critical ingredient of my offer to Rob consists of a $750,000 note payable as follows:

Date	Principal
At Closing	$200,000
Year One	25,000
Two	25,000
Three	100,000
Four	100,000
Five	100,000
Six	100,000
Seven	100,000
	$750,000

Unpaid balances would bear interest due quarterly at the published prime bank rate but would not be less than 6 percent nor more than 8 percent.

The first $100,000 of the note would be guaranteed by a letter of credit from the bank. Although subsequent payment of installments would be subordinated to secured notes of the bank, I would personally guarantee the note to Rob. The bank would hold Rob's stock in escrow and release it to Magic as principal payments to Rob were made. The bank would also hold my stock in escrow and return it only after I had performed under the agreement.

The killer clause, the one that lingers in my consciousness daily, spells out what would happen in the event of default. Let me quote the cold words: "In the event of default by the Buyer [me], the escrow agent shall give prompt notice to the Buyer that if default is not cured within ninety (90) days from the date of such notice, the escrow agent shall transfer and deliver to the Seller [Rob] the remaining shares held by it, both of the Seller's stock and the Buyer's stock."

In other words, should I fail to pay (the technical word is "default"), I lose all and Rob gains total control of Magicolor. The stakes therefore are hardly less than my very life, for I wonder what my life will be worth to myself in the face of such a failure and loss.

The agreement also stipulates that Rob receive a consultant's fee of $4,166.67 per month ($50,000 per year) for fifty-four months, which is simply a way of Magic paying more for his shares on a tax-deductible basis. Of course, I hardly expect to ever consult with Rob after he is gone.

As for the real estate, the factory building, which Rob and I personally own together and which is worth several hundred thousand dollars but highly mortgaged, I agree to purchase his share for a mere $25,000. Although I'm willing to maintain that partnership if he wishes, he refuses, preferring to sever all connection with me.

Years later, that decision would become an amazingly fortuitous one—a veritable life saver.

"How'd you do it?" Rob asks after he peruses the deal, which amounts in total to more than a million dollars.

Enjoying his bewilderment, I smile with unrestrained triumph. "Can't tell you. Not yet." I know even if he hallucinated he'd never guess.

"Is there a chance you'll change your mind, Harry? We can get along. We've built a fine company together." His eyes grow teary. "I'm willing to do things your way."

A familiar refrain. He can no more give up his way of doing things than a salmon can stop fighting his way upstream to spawn.

"You made that promise before, Rob. It won't work."

"I—I can't believe this is happening."

Apparently he has convinced himself that I couldn't put together a satisfactory deal. Not Harry Simon, not that "poor" fellow, a man without resources, strictly small time, without connections, without the prestige of old family ties. Rob knows that his price is too high, Magic's profits too lean, and my credibility too questionable to effectuate what is now occurring.

"I'm sorry, Rob. We're just incompatible. You won't change; I won't change. It's over."

I don't tell him that I can't tolerate his incompetence. I am sad that he is losing what little of his heart and soul he has invested in Magic's promise. Our break resembles a divorce, and as in a divorce, as the rejected one he denies that it's over. He can't accept what's happened, not yet. And the full force of his anger takes awhile to erupt.

That opportunity comes after Francis, our star salesman, sheepishly enters my office and announces late on a Friday afternoon that he's quitting.

"But why? Just when things are sorting out," I say, dismayed. "You'll get what you've wanted. Rob will be gone and then you'll be sales manager, as I promised. It'll be a great opportunity, a new start for you and me, for all of us."

"I think you're dreaming. I don't believe you can do the buyout," he says.

"Of course I can. I've found a way. You've got my word."

"You've given your word before, Harry, and look what it got me," he says, his voice thickening with controlled anger. "I've been sucking hind teat ever since."

"I thought you understood I had limits. But not anymore. No one can interfere this time."

"Well, it's too late. My plans have gone too far," he says with finality.

"Even if you owned a piece of the action?"

"I'm not interested."

I take a deep breath. There's more to this than I'm grasping.

"Damnit, Fran, when you came to me hat in hand I took you in; I went to bat for you when Rob fired you. Is this your thanks?"

"I don't owe you a goddamned thing, Harry."

"I see," I say, nodding. "You're not very long on gratitude, are you? I'm disappointed."

I surmise he arrived at his decision months ago. After living with it so long, he can't easily reverse himself.

"I've earned my keep, Harry."

"Sure you have. Tell me, who are you going with?" I ask.

"Myself."

"Yourself?"

I reel, off balance. I haven't anticipated he'd try doing it on his own. You need a pile more money to start a business now than when I began. Knowing how difficult it has been to raise money for Magic, a going enterprise, I'm astonished that he has found funds for a start-up venture.

"Myself, that's what I said."

"Alone, or with—?"

"With Gary."

"Not with that sonofabitch. I assume you'd know better."

Leering, he says, "Funny, he calls you the same thing."

But hasn't Fran often complained about Gary's arrogance? On occasion he has even admitted going out of his way to avoid him because he doesn't like him. I marvel that Fran's ambition could transform Gary into an ally, that it has the power to delude him into thinking their mutual incompatibility will disappear.

"Well, I wish you luck," I say, reaching out my hand. "You'll need it. I can't blame you for trying. I tried and, well—I have no regrets. You definitely know more than I did when I started. You should have no illusions. At Magic you've learned the right way to do it." Still gripping his hand, I try to catch his evading eyes. "Y'know, Fran, I wish you had leveled with me; I'm sure we could have worked things out."

"How? You denied me the same chance once," he says in a tight voice, releasing my hand.

"Huh? What are you talking about?"

"When you quit on me at MPI. Did you let me in on your plans then?"

"That was more than ten years ago. A lot's happened—"

"You didn't cut me in. Remember? Instead you chose Rob. And look at the trouble he's given you. You've got this coming, my friend. I've been waiting a long time." His voice is throaty as he revels in his vengeful words.

"How can you compare what happened then with now?" I ask. "My God, have you been carrying this—this resentment all these years?"

To think that he has been my secret enemy all the while I defended him against Rob, always trusted him and supported his interest. To think that in a few short minutes he could trash the years of my goodwill toward him.

Intensely wishing that he leave my office that instant, I rise from my chair. "You'd better leave, Fran, get out of my sight. I mean forever."

Janet had warned me to be wary of Fran from the beginning. And a few years ago my psychologist friend had cautioned me. But I want to trust; I want to believe that others are as well meaning toward me as I am toward them. I dismissed all warnings as ridiculous. Do I simply assume others are the way I wish them to be, still perceive them through the eyes of early innocence? Does a remnant of a fragile, trusting child still linger within me? Am I less sophisticated, less street-smart, than I think I am? Fran's betrayal shatters me far more than Rob's declaration of war. I could not predict or prevent the breakup of my alliance with Rob, but I blame Fran's actions on my naive blindness.

"The situation has changed," I tell Rob over the phone, the only way I can reach him, since he no longer comes to the office.

"How so?"

"I'd like to get together with you and discuss it."

"No. Talk now." His voice is terse, stiff.

"I've just learned that Fran and Gary are setting up their own business."

"Yeah, I'm not surprised."

"You knew about it?"

"They invited me in, but I've had enough of the color business."

It fits. Fran, Gary, and Rob, three of a kind. How long has Rob known?

"Well, it's a new ball game now."

"In what way?"

"I mean, they're bound to take a big chunk of business with them. It changes everything. Now my projections are out of whack. I'll have to revise the terms of my offer."

"Not on your life."

"Christ, Rob, you can't really expect me to make it under these new circumstances. I based my offer on—"

"Tough shit."

"Be reasonable. It's in your interest as well as mine."

"You're exaggerating the situation, as usual. They won't put a dent in you."

"Of course, they will."

"Then, tough shit is all I have to say."

I can hardly expect more. Rob is my declared adversary. Why should he be magnanimous? I pray that the bank hears nothing of Fran's defection, or it will be all over before it begins.

At Fran's departure the scenario drastically changed. Fran and Gary embarked on a deliberate campaign to damage Magic. Fran took many customers with him, some of our largest, making up 25 percent of our business. Having had access to our most important proprietary formulations, our prices, and our management style, which was the very source of our high efficiency, extraordinary product quality, and innovativeness, he knew the formula for our success.

But Rob was right. I needn't have been concerned. Magic's management style derived from the way I was, my personality. By my openness and trust of the employees, my decisiveness and honesty, my utter dependability, I had encouraged a cooperative spirit, a willingness to speak up and a sense of security and freedom among the employees. They were also driven to adopt my neurotic striving for perfection. I surrounded myself with clones who were capable of replicating those of my characteristics with which they were most comfortable. A business is the top man expressed in organizational form. For all that Fran had learned at Magic that worked, he would inevitably run his business his way, even if it didn't work.

While the bank is going through its rigmarole and the lawyers are fine-tuning the buy-sell agreement, Fran is broadcasting to the world that Magicolor is about to go under.

Sammy, now our top salesman, reports that Fran is telling customers of the squabble between Rob and me and claiming that since he and Gary were indispensable to Magic's success, Magic can't survive without them. Confident of the faith our customers have in Magic, I shrug off the resulting possibility of damage. But when Howard Carl, the president of Perfection Plastics, Sammy's largest account, calls, I acknowledge that Fran's actions are a serious threat.

"I hear you've got some big problems, Harry."

"We've had a few, Carl," I say lightly, "but they're behind us now."

"Are you sure? When I hear bankruptcy, I start to worry about my supplier."

"Bankruptcy!" I laugh, covering my distress. "Absolutely not, Carl. You have my word, absolutely not."

Fran has gone too far. He must be stopped.

Briefly I explain that I'm buying out Rob, that the bank is totally supportive, and that Magic will soon become employee owned, a fact that impresses Carl mightily. I assure him that the transformation is under control.

"Tell me, Carl, have you experienced any decline in our quality; have we faltered on service?"

"No, your performance has been, as usual, excellent."

"Right. And isn't that the real test?"

"Okay, Harry, I'm satisfied. I just had to hear it from the horse's mouth."

"I appreciate your telling me of your concern."

Carl's call and Sammy's reports are strong evidence that Fran is still on a revenge kick and that he isn't content to compete ethically. Before dealing with this outrageous calumny, for the next few weeks I personally visit every major account across the country and, as with Carl, I clarify Magic's status. And to all employees, customers and suppliers I send the following notice:

To: All Interested In Magicolor
From: Harry Simon

As a result of an irreconcilable disagreement on policy between Magicolor's two principals, Rob Starr and myself, the company is acquiring Rob Starr's total equity based on an amicable agreement. Over the years a substantial portion of the acquired shares will be transferred to the employees through an Employee Stock Ownership Plan. I will continue as president and controlling stockholder.

Magicolor is not only alive and well in Massachusetts and Illinois, but also never more motivated to serve you. With all our employees having an ownership stake in the company, please remember, when you talk to any one of us, you'll be dealing with an owner.

In October Rob and myself, my lawyer and his partner, Rob's lawyer and his partner, the bank's counsel and a loan officer, and a recording clerk meet in the boardroom of the bank in Providence, where we spend an entire morning signing the transaction papers. (See Appendix D for a list of the documents and the purpose of each.) Throughout the signing everyone is friendly and relaxed, even Rob and myself, as if there had never been a smidgen of rancor. The turbulence between Rob and me began a year ago this very month. Now that it's over I feel as I did on that first day in my own business—free, free to deal in my own way with whatever comes. Only now it's different: I'm familiar with the various negative forces out there. I feel I can defeat them all.

Of course I hadn't yet learned that the world offers far more than my experience, my imagination and my dreaming had prepared me for. I hadn't learned that I can't control things for long and to stop trying.

DRIVEN

In addition to the employees, the bank in a sense is also my partner. The bank requires maximum limits on Magic's debt, limits on my salary, on lease contracts, and capital expenditures, and compensating limits on checking account balances. Certain kinds of insurance are mandatory, including insurance on my life, the bank as beneficiary. The bank also insists on approving every major policy decision I make. But I'm not in the least troubled by such constraints, for I consider them judicious, in Magic's best interest. The bank offers me another sounding board. And I believe any veto the bank would make, unlike Rob's, would be constructive.

I appreciate the bank's need for oversight because its risk is enormous. The $550,000 owed to Rob plus the $400,000 long-term note owed the bank result in a negative net worth of almost a quarter million dollars on Magic's balance sheet. Yet because the bank's loan revolves and no repayment of debt is necessary during the current year, Magic's financial circumstances are quite manageable. Indeed Magic's key operating ratio, its current ratio, (current assets to current liabilities), is almost a healthy two to one.

As my lawyer, Dan, and I drive back to the plant to celebrate after the signing, he says: "You know, Harry, I have never known a bank to gamble like this. They sure as hell must believe in you." He places his hand on my arm approvingly. "I think you ought to feel proud."

I grin. "Yup," I say, "I remember a time when they wouldn't tell me what day it was. Now they believe in me."

"With cause, I'm sure," Dan says.

I sigh. "All I've got to do is deliver."

"If anyone can, it's you," says Dan.

I think fresh beginnings are so full of hope because they signify the conclusion of unhappy endings. Of course for every unhappy ending there has to have been a fresh beginning. I hadn't thought through that logic. Just as well. I hadn't a glimmer that the toughest part yet lay ahead.

CHAPTER XV
Year Ten
1976

Sales: $3,987,000 (+4.8%)
Profit: $16,000 (-76%)
Debt: $1,439,000 (+131%)
Net Worth: - $215,000 (-152%)

"It's a tough market here. New Yorkers have no loyalty, no humanity," says Sammy. I'm having lunch on Long Island with Sammy, who covers southern New England, and Bailey Cooperman, a shrewd and successful New York trader in plastic materials who once offered to buy out Rob and replace him as my partner. (I turned him down as substituting one evil for another.) I inform Bailey during lunch of the deal I made. Sammy feigns disinterest but listens closely.

"I'm glad for you, my friend," Bailey says. "To tell the truth, I never believed you'd find a bank to go along—not at your partner's price."

"Neither did I," I say reaching for the rolls. "Frankly, for a time I thought you were my only recourse."

"How'd you do it?" He winks.

"By sharing. I'm giving company stock to the employees." I outline how the ESOP works.

"Don't you think it's dangerous letting your employees know your business?" Bailey asks, taking a sip of his wine.

"It doesn't bother me in the least," I say self-righteously. "What have I got to hide?"

"Nothing and everything. As for me, I like the Caddy and the boat and the membership at the country club. And no one's going to tell me they're verboten."

"I don't need those things, Bailey. The trappings have never been important to me."

"I'll take them," Sammy cracks and laughs.

"I hear Francis left you," Bailey says. "Wasn't he your top salesman?"

"Yes, he was a good man."

"Starting his own shop, is that right?"

"He'll never make it," Sammy interjects.

"Sure he will, Sammy," I say. "There's plenty of room for us both—"

"Except he's playing dirty. He's a crook," Sammy states, slapping the table.

"News spreads fast," I say. "The bastard is bad-mouthing us."

"Better watch him," Bailey warns. "He's going after you. I hear he's got Edgar too."

Sammy and I stare in perplexity at each other.

"I'm afraid you've got it wrong. Edgar is still very much with us, very much in charge of the lab," I say, pushing away my full plate of food.

"A really good man, Edgar," Sammy says. "I don't know what we'd do without him. He'd never leave. Sure as hell not to Fran—a start-up operation."

"That's right," I affirm, addressing Bailey. "In the six years he's been with us he's never complained. I'm sure it's just idle rumor. Nothing to it."

"Maybe so, but I heard it from a customer who's doing business with Fran."

"Here on Long Island?"

"No, up your way, one of your former customers —Consolidated."

"Well, I don't believe it."

"I'd check into it, if I were you," suggests Bailey, stuffing his mouth with a forkful of steak. "Remember, an employee is only an employee. As I say, you're a fool making them your partners."

Sammy jostles awkwardly in his seat. I'm uncomfortable at Bailey's insensitivity to Sammy's presence. My stomach tightens and I'm unable to eat. Edgar may or may not be a problem, but Consolidated is a loyal account of long standing, I thought, one of my first.

After lunch we go our own ways, Sammy to his next call. I head for the phone booth located at the edge of the parking lot to call Edgar at the plant.

"Congratulations, Harry. You made it off the Island Expressway. Ha, ha," Edgar jokes.

"I'll put it to you straight, Edgar. Are you leaving me?"

There's a delay, which answers my question even before he responds.

"Gosh, you see—son of a—. I planned to tell you but you took off for the Island; it's damned embarrassing that you had to hear about it through the grapevine. I'm sorry."

"Wait a minute," I say impatiently, "you didn't do this all of a sudden."

"No, that's true, but I didn't want to leave you in the lurch. I know you've had your hands full with Rob and—"

"That's real decent of you, Edgar, real decent, but I don't need your favors."

"I'm sorry you're sore. I was thinking of what's best for you, y'know."

"You're going with Fran, is that right?"

"I'm not at liberty to say where I'm going, but wherever it is it won't hurt you."

"You're going with Fran."

"I can't say."

"What did he offer you? A piece of the action?"

"Harry, I'm willing to stay on as long as you need me, give you time to find someone else."

"What time is it now?" I ask.

"Two ten."

"Okay, whatever you're doing, turn it over to Earle, and in one hour, by three ten, I want you out of there. That will give you time to clean out your desk and say good-bye to everyone."

In seconds I formulate a reorganization of the lab. Earle, Edgar's assistant, will step into the top spot, something he's been after. It's marvelous how quickly I adjust to Edgar's departure. Now I'm eager to see what Earle might do in a job he so coveted.

"You don't have to do this, Harry. I'm willing to stay on until you're ready."

"I'm ready, so go, get out." My anger is building and I'm hurting.

"You don't seem to understand, Harry. I bear you no ill will. I want to leave on good terms."

"Aren't you listening?" I shout into the phone, "I don't want you around another minute—"

"Earle's coming with me," Edgar says quietly.

My legs go slightly soft and I lean back against the door of the phone booth as an instantaneous surge of defeat overwhelms me.

Finally, with dry lips, I whisper, "When I come in tomorrow morning, I just don't want to see you there. Understand?"

Fran is raiding Magic. He knows who the cream are, who to woo. Where will he stop? Earle says Fran offered him a 25 percent wage increase and promised him an annual paid vacation in the Caribbean (where he was reared and where his parents live) and in time Edgar's position as technical director when Edgar moves up to vice-president. I can't match the offer nor do I try; I doubt that Fran will live up to it. Though I think Earle will regret the move, I don't try to dissuade him. Whenever an employee decides to leave for whatever reason, it's best to let it happen. Every move is an experiment to find out whether the grass is actually greener on the other side of the fence or whether, as is usually the case, it's brown on both sides.

Losses are accumulating. During those rare months when Massachusetts makes money, Chicago loses more and voids any precious gains. Behind my every action lies a nagging awareness of our enormous debt, almost $1.5 million, and the cost of servicing it. It is like a contract of indenture. Add that burden to Francis's actions against me, his taking of my best people and his slander, and I am frustrated and enraged and fear sliding toward disaster. I must stop him if only to assuage my anger; I must strike out, do something, take control.

But I will not resort to his tactics. Not that I don't have a realistic basis for doing so. After all, considering Fran and Gary's natural dislike for each other, their partnership has little chance to endure. And from what I hear, their financial backing is extremely limited.

Several customers are splitting their business between Fran's company and Magic. They tell me that the quality and service are comparable. "Of course," I say, "that's what I would expect. Fran learned how to do it from us."

"Don't adopt their methods," I tell our salesmen. "Say nothing negative about Fran, avoid discussing him. If a customer won't drop the subject, tell him you have no information. Don't show bitterness no matter how angry you are."

The salesmen are happy to rise above the battle and be proud. But our mild approach belies the storm that rages within me. In a phone call I consult the attorney who handled the buy out.

"How do I stop them, Dan? They're stealing our people, slandering us. I think they've stolen formulations and prices because they consistently bid just below us. It's too much of a coincidence."

"Well, there's no law to prevent them from hiring your people. No one's forcing your employees to leave."

"What about all the lies they're spreading?"

"You need witnesses. Would your customers be willing to testify, confirm what they're saying."

"Sure, some would—I think."

But would they? For the sake of friendship? They aren't really friends. Not so much that they'd be willing to get involved.

"I'm not sure," I say. "I'll have to find out."

"Is there anything else?"

"Such as?"

"A contract or something."

My brain does a somersault.

"Yes, there's a contract. I forgot about it. Francis and Gary signed an employment agreement when they were hired, which stipulates that they can't go into the business for three years after leaving Magic. But I considered it little more than a deterrent. Anyway, in principle I have no objection to an employee becoming a competitor. I did it myself. Now it's a different story."

"That sort of contract may be hard to enforce, but it's worth a try."

"You mean the no-compete feature?"

"Yes, you can't stop someone from making a living."

"Well, the contract also requires that they devote their full working time and energy to Magic. I have proof that for at least six months before leaving they were using

Magic's time and facilities to organize their business. An equipment supplier has informed me that they purchased their machinery from our phones during the working day. Frankly that galls me more than anything else. They set themselves up right under my nose."

"Now why would he tell you that?"

"Who?"

"The supplier."

"He's courting my favor; he wants more of my business. But you're right. I'd never trust an equipment salesman—any salesman for that matter."

Dan roars. "As I recall, weren't you a salesman once?"

"Yup," I said. "That's how I know."

"Okay, okay, Harry, I'll file for an injunction."

"What'll that do?"

"Shut them down if we get our way."

"Oh, that would be fine," I say sadly.

Strange, the idea depresses me. I'm forced to act against the principle of live and let live and I resent them for that too.

Despite the rankling events with which I have to contend, I feel exuberant and optimistic and more relaxed and patient than I have been in years. Like having a painfully abscessed tooth pulled, Rob's departure is a marked relief.

"You're not the same man," Emma comments. "It's a real pleasure to work with you now."

"Huh? Was I that bad?" I inquire.

"I'd say you were—well, irritable—but with cause. We understood; no one blamed you."

I can always count on Emma's frankness and forgiveness. A destructive relationship is the worst tyranny of all. The enmity between Rob and me made us both miserable and as a consequence we made everyone around us miserable. Nevertheless the rupture is surprisingly painful, not unlike a divorce. For years Rob and I trusted and believed in each other, especially in the early years when I was autonomous and we consulted and cooperated and the future extended beyond the horizon. My disappointment is deep and I can tell that Rob, despite his easy manner, is no less disappointed.

"Magic is ours now, Emma. We're one family, free to make it into whatever we want. No one will put his own interest above the company's anymore. And whoever doesn't see it that way, well, he's out. That's the way it has to be."

She smiles in assent.

We share the excitement of a fresh beginning, its terrifying risk and its mystery. It is the underlying theme of our experience. I am a new and changed man and Magicolor is overnight a new and changed company.

Dan calls. "The judge has shut down your competitors for two weeks," he informs me.

"Good," I say, elated. "That ought to keep them quiet."

"When the injunction expires we can go to court, claim damages, and shut them down for good."

"I don't want to do that," I say, "so long as they agree to stop spreading false rumors and give up their claim to the profit sharing and retirement plans."

"Getting them to do that shouldn't be a problem," he says. "You're really letting them off the hook. But they're bound to ask for an indefinite release from any future complaints."

Hard though it is to give up the potential satisfaction of seeking retribution, I consent.

The rumors stop but not Fran's continuing attempts to steal more of our good people. Nor does his uncanny knack of consistently just underpricing us cease.

He pursues Perfection Toys with some success. How can I blame Howard Carl for taking advantage of Francis's lower prices? But now that we are no longer Howard's sole source, I sense a lessening of the long-standing good feeling that prevailed between Magic and Perfection. My relationship with Howard, having resembled that of a father and son, is no longer the same. I trust him less, and our dealings are more businesslike than before. I no longer exceed his requests as I used to to show my appreciation. Of course, our past quality and service and attentiveness to his needs remain. I can't let on that I'm hurt. In business I must hide my true feelings, else I know I'll literally pay for it.

Despite the new competition, the economy and the plastics business are booming, so that Magic's sales keep growing. Under such conditions there's room enough for everyone in the business to prosper. Having expected a harder time to recover, I'm now free to relax. Although the debt service this year is almost $73,000, Magic is generating enough cash flow to afford it. By contributing $19,000 to the employees through the ESOP, I reduce taxes by that amount. And I willingly cut my salary to $47,000 without causing my family hardship. Magic nevertheless shows only a marginal profit, but I'm satisfied since all obligations and then some are being met.

Julius Hillman also relaxes, too much I think. Each quarter he's slower in preparing our statements, slower than I wish to put up with in view of my need for up-to-the-minute results. I accuse him of taking me for granted.

"Your service isn't what it used to be," I tell him. "You've got to do better, Julie."

"We're doing the best we can," he says defensively, as if I had no choice but to accept it.

"If I don't have the figures by Thursday, I'll have to find someone else," I say, quickly regretting my bravado. Ultimatums are rarely constructive because they constitute a clash of egos.

Whether deliberately or not, Julius doesn't deliver on time, and to save face, if nothing else, I change accountants—no small deal. It's like leaving home. Our beginning together was planted in the fruitful soil of trust and generosity. He has to feel hurt from what I have done.

Perfection Toys' order volume continues to decline. I consult with Sammy, who has been servicing the account ever since I turned it over to him when he came aboard years ago.

"I can't imagine Francis taking the lion's share of Perfection's business away from us, can you?"

"Certainly not, Harry. We haven't lost our position by a single pound," Sammy says. "They're having a slump. That's all."

"That's baloney, Sammy. Business is good everywhere. The toy business has never been better."

Sammy shrugs. "I talked to Howard Carl. That's what he told me."

Over the following weeks Perfection's sales slide further. Sammy insists that nothing is wrong. I call Howard Carl.

"Is there a problem, Howard?"

"Problem? I don't think so, Harry."

"Can I see you? Lunch, perhaps."

"Fine. You say when."

DRIVEN

As Sammy and I drive the thirty miles to Howard's plant, we speculate on why we're losing the business. Sammy is mostly concerned because the account, making up more than half his total sales, produces a substantial portion of his income.

"Maybe we should drop our prices to Perfection," I suggest as a possible approach to energizing sales.

Howard is, as usual, cordial.

"Come in. Sit down, gentlemen. Good to see you again, Harry," he says, reaching for a handshake and directing us to two richly upholstered chairs facing his desk.

Though I have always found Howard considerate, I know he has a reputation for being tough. It is common knowledge that he fired his right-hand man on the spot—a man whom he was grooming to step into his position upon his retirement—when he overheard the man remark that Howard had divorced his fifty-five-year-old wife "for a young chick."

"What can I do for you?" Howard asks, leaning back in his desk chair. His youthful sixtyish figure is trim from jogging regularly. He speaks quietly, using words as if they're chessmen.

"In a word, Howard—no, in two words: more business." We laugh together. "Maybe I should ask, what aren't we doing for you, Howard?"

"I've got no complaint, Harry. Production and purchasing tell me you're doing your usual good job."

"Then why the big drop in your purchases?"

Clicking his fingernails on his desk, he stares off beyond Sammy and me before replying. Then lowering his eyes to mine, he says, "In about three months, when we're fully on stream, I'm afraid you'll be getting a helluva lot less." He pauses a moment to let his statement make its impact. "The fact is, Harry, we've started making the color ourselves."

Although neither my facial expression nor my posture reveal the extent to which Howard's news jolts me, I must fight to keep my spirit from collapsing. After all, Perfection, our largest account, has just announced that we will shortly lose 35 percent of our total sales by withdrawing their business. It is a killer blow, a brutal karate chop. As I glance at Sammy, I see he's near tears.

Regrouping my thoughts, I say, "Forgive me if I'm presumptuous, Howard, but are you producing a quality product—I mean material as good as ours?"

"Frankly, no. Naturally, we are more forgiving of ourselves. But we'll get there."

"We go back a long way, Howard."

"Yes, we do. I know this hurts."

"I only wish you had told me earlier of your intentions."

Howard shrugs.

"Well, if you ever get into trouble, call on us," I say, forcing a smile.

"Of course, Harry." He comes over to me as we rise. Placing one arm over my shoulder, he reaches to shake my hand while leading me to the door. "It's business, eh, Harry?"

How can I tell him that six months ago we purchased a production line costing a quarter of a million dollars in order to keep pace with his then increasing demand. But that would be laying it on him—the wrong thing to do. Yet I'm indignant that he intentionally misled Sammy by blaming his declining purchases on his own declining sales, a patent falsehood. And why didn't Sammy nose around more, see through the obviousness of Howard's phony excuse? Unable to vent my frustration at Howard Carl, I redirect it toward Sammy.

DRIVEN

"Damnit, you should have known, Sammy," I say on the drive back to the plant. "It's part of your job. When I kept telling you there was more than meets the eye—"

"Look, I'll make it up—somehow, I'll make it up," Sammy says, contrite and self-condemning. "Don't worry, I'll replace the business with another account. I know I can find one."

"You'd better," I say, "or else we both starve."

We drive the rest of the half hour in silence, brooding over the debacle, fully knowing that we'll never capture another Perfection Toys.

As if struck by an earthquake aftershock, a week after the meeting with Howard Carl, I learn that Perfection has hired away our best remaining lab technician and one of our top machine operators, offering them a wage in excess of what the jobs normally pay. To meet their offer would shatter our entire wage structure. Perfection's action is not unusual; it poses no moral question. The code of small business is to act in a business's best interest regardless of the damage it inflicts on another business. As for any actions that are considerate and decent, they are rare events, strictly voluntary.

The small business environment is clearly laissez-faire, the economic survival of the fittest. Although I acknowledge this fact of life, I can't deny that the human part of me feels outrage, all the worse since I can't attack without sacrificing what business remains to be had at Perfection. It is a rational jungle. I can and sadly do write off Howard Carl as a business friend and I mourn the loss of our mutual goodwill and trust.

The accountant I select to replace Julius is cooperative, prompt, stiff, cold, and uncommunicative. I miss the easy familiarity I had with Julius.

"I'll have the final figures for you by the end of next week, Mr. Simon," he says after he and an assistant spend a long day gathering the quarterly figures from our books.

"Just call me, Harry," I say.

"Sure thing, Mr. Simon."

I realize I've made a mistake. Efficiency is only one criterion for employing someone; the quality of a relationship is more important. Given my error, I'll allow the new man more time in the hope that as we get to know each other I can crack his shell.

My oldest child enters college this year. I'm pleased that I can send her even though it consumes a healthy portion of my after-tax income. My savings are negligible, since I've loaned most of my cash to the business. Being in control, I'm confident all will work out for the best. Furthermore I feel no need to personally make a lot of money. Magicolor's financial well-being and success are no less important than my own because both are intertwined, both are one. Magicolor is my cause, my raison d'etre, serving a purpose beyond my ego. Don't we all wish for an aim larger than ourselves to give meaning to our lives? I do, and I possess it through Magic.

My marriage is a model on the surface, a model to our children and our friends and perhaps to ourselves, for we have no confrontations. We simply accept the status quo as sufficient, like getting used to pain, eventually a sufferable condition. Janet and I perform adequately, if not for each other then for the sake of the family. The sex is lousy. We give to each other sparingly but, lacking for nothing material, our physical lives are comfortable.

Cathy and I sleep together occasionally. Having given up trying to persuade me to leave Janet, she is reconciled to being my mistress. Perhaps she prefers that role, which requires no commitment and possesses that certain forbidden quality that erases her sexual inhibitions and invigorates her.

Janet and I fly to San Francisco, where I am attending a five-day plastics engineers convention. We stay not in the big hotel recommended by the sponsors, but in a small, intimate place off Union Square. Each morning a cart of hot coffee, fresh fruit, and pastry is waiting outside our door. We ride the cable cars, visit the art museum and the chocolate factory, walk the waterfront, dine in Chinatown, take the ferry over to Sausalito, rent a car and follow a mapped tour of the city. They are successful days, happier than any we've had together in ages, until the night when Janet says she's too tired for sex and clings to her side of the bed and falls asleep.

I leave the bed, dress, and take the elevator to the lobby where I call Cathy early in the eastern morning.

"Where—where are you?" she asks, confused partly from having just awakened and partly from knowing that I should be on the West Coast.

"San Francisco," I say. "I had to call you."

"All the way from San Francisco. How nice, Harry. Oh, if only you could be here with me," she purrs. "I'd keep you warm. I miss you, Harry. God, I miss you."

"I had to hear your voice—to—to tell you I love you."

"Oh, Harry. Rush back. I can't wait."

"It can't be soon enough for me. Well, good night."

"Don't go, Harry, not yet."

"We'll be together in only a few days."

"How is it with you, being alone? In a strange place."

"Lonely, Cathy, damned lonely."

"So you called. Oh, Harry, you should have taken me."

"I couldn't. As I told you, it's all business. Only a few days left. Happy dreams."

"Happy dreams, my dearest."

Most of what I say to her is a lie. But it is true I could not feel lonelier.

As so rarely happened, I could take it easy. Nothing major was happening in my life. It was a time of waiting for events to make the next move. And move they did, but not as I expected.

CHAPTER XVI

Year Eleven

1977

Sales: $4,600,000 (+15.4%)
Profit: $49,885 (+212%)
Debt: $1,463,000 (+1.7%)
Net Worth: - $157,000 (+27%)

Looking at the figures above, you'd never know that 1977 was a year of crisis. Neither did I. Figures, which we tend to hold sacrosanct, don't lie, only people do. We often forget that figures, which are merely a numerical version of the past, do not speak for the present nor predict the future. In 1977, sales reached a peak that we were never to attain again. Profits were on the upswing and net worth was moving toward the plus side. Everything was going right. Only in hindsight did I recognize our eleventh year for what it was: a turning point toward disaster.

By September Perfection had stopped placing orders. Since our fiscal year ended in July, the final figures hadn't reflected the loss of that account. Nor had I an inkling of the steep climb in bank interest rates that was soon to begin. Indeed the continuing inflation was working to our advantage: I could pay Rob with ever cheapening dollars and charge customers who had become inured to higher prices accordingly. Furthermore, since we could count on the value of raw materials increasing, we maintained a healthy inventory.

"How would you like a new car—a Porsche hatchback?" I ask Janet over the phone. It is hardly five minutes after I get Magic's stupendous year-end results and decide to increase my salary to $150,000 to make up for my sacrifice of the past two years.

"I'd love it, Harry," she gushes. "A new car all my own, my size, I'd love it." Until now she has been driving hand-me-downs, currently my old company station wagon.

I also buy Janet a ring in which is embedded a string of small diamonds. I give Cathy a gold watch. She wants a ring, but I refuse. It's too symbolic, implying commitment and permanence. She forgets her acquiescence to the role of mistress and becomes extremely angry, saying that despite my declarations I don't really love her. My refusal is a constantly bitter subject, one she can't easily put aside. The more she nags me, the more determined I become not to budge. Often we part in acrimony.

Unlike Janet, who sets small store by material things but can afford them, Cathy yearns for but can't afford them. Except when she indulges herself in flamboyant, not necessarily expensive clothes. Cathy is a peacock and Janet is a pigeon.

Finally Cathy buys a ring for herself, paying more than a thousand dollars, a prohibitive sum for her. She gleefully displays the jewel one night when we're at a dine and dance place.

"Why in hell did you do that?" I explode, feeling cheap and well aware that Cathy is exacting a retribution of guilt from me.

"I just needed to give myself something," she counters. "If I'm not worth anything to anyone else—"

"Godamnit, Cathy, I gave you a beautiful watch."

She looks from beneath her lowered eyelids and smiles victoriously.

Janet is pleased with my gifts and I'm pleased to give them. They succeed in bringing us closer together—for a while. Eventually their effect wears off—they are only an aberration, she thinks—and we are soon back to our mutual separateness.

From August through October, our first fiscal quarter, losses begin to mount again due not only to the disappearance of Perfection's business but also to Fran's success in competing against us. By taking certain accounts entirely and sharing sales with us in others, Fran has succeeded in reducing our total sales by 20 percent, a hard fact to accept.

Finding it impossible to contemplate decline in these prosperous times, I hire Harrington Archer, a first rate sales manager, from a major plastics resin corporation for $35,000 per year, a most generous salary. His credentials are prestigious: Cushing Academy, Harvard B School, high-density polyethylene sales manager for ten years with his last corporate employer, a resident of the posh Boston suburb of Westwood, tennis partner and neighbor of the president of the Second National Bank of Boston. Archer is tall, trim, auburn haired, smooth, eloquent, always congenial, and "loaded with personality," as many who meet him say.

"So why do you want to leave a secure expanding corporate niche for our ten-cent operation, Arch?" I ask in the first interview.

"Simple, Harry, my friend," he replies with exuberance. "I'm really sick of corporate politics, of having to constantly go by the rules. Y'know how it is. There's no place for fresh ideas. I'll take a small pond any time. Any time, yessir. Y'know."

Saying exactly what I prize most in an employee, he charms me. I don't let him get away.

In several months I review Archer's contribution to Magic: no new accounts, no program for enhancing sales, no fresh ideas, no attempt to improve the status quo. He follows a staid routine, consisting of a half hour each morning in the john reading *The Wall Street Journal*, then calling his wife, who apparently sleeps late, then talking over the phone for an hour with his former colleagues at the old corporation, then taking a two-hour lunch, unless he takes it with me. In the afternoon he closes his office door and, I suspect, takes a nap. But he makes friends indiscriminately with our customers, the rest of our staff, the postman, even the waitresses in the local restaurant. His stock response when answering the phone: "Archer here, at your service."

If he would perform as well in substance as he does in making himself liked, he would have to be the sure winner I thought he was. When I fire him he is surprisingly nonchalant, as if he expected it all along.

"I have no hard feelings, Harry," he says. "And I hope we'll remain friends and you'll always think kindly of me."

"By all means," I say, "but I'd like to offer a suggestion: On your next job try being a tough guy once in awhile."

"Oh, I've been tough, Harry, oh, have I," he says with sting, "and it cost me my job. I had to leave."

"Your last one?" I say, having had the impression he quit to join me.

"Yeah. That one too. I crossed the wrong guy."

So he plays it safe at Magic to protect himself and avoid repeating his corporate mistake, only to get himself fired again. Poor Arch can't win.

DRIVEN

I am now my own sales manager. Seeing my major task as improving sales—the usual route to profits, which I must increase if I'm going to meet our future obligations, mostly to Rob—I hire more salesmen and start an advertising campaign in the trade magazines. Such measures obviously require cash outlays and increase our overhead.

It never occurred to me that another viable approach to enhancing profits would be to cut back. My ego wouldn't allow it. Having had sales growth each year from year one, retreat was forbidden, not even considered. It never occurred to me that by allowing sales to shrink and, as a result, expenses also, every dollar saved would go directly to the bottom line. In contrast, every sales dollar earned from increased sales is worth only a fraction; that is only the profit remaining. Furthermore it takes time, a year, possibly two, and cash, to increase sales before seeing results from your effort. In my stubborn commitment to forge ahead, I had acquired shades of Rob Starr.

The three new salesmen I hire are Jud, a former Patriots football player, or so he claims; Wally, a former professional golfer; and Abel, Janet's cousin, whose father, Janet's wealthy half uncle, is a high-ranking executive with a food conglomerate. All are young, sharp looking, energetic men, excited over the opportunity to go out and capture the world.

I have purposely chosen men who have no experience in our business, which makes them more amenable to our training, our ways, our thinking: that selling quality, service, and dedication to a customer's needs is superior to selling simply on price. Being inexperienced, the new men have nothing to unlearn. (I consider hiring saleswomen, but Emma points out that the turnover among women who call on her is excessive. Our society makes it uncomfortable for women on the road.)

Since sports is of major interest to most of our customers — the common ground on which macho men come together — I believe our new salesmen have a special qualification for success. (On the other hand, I have no interest whatsoever in sports of any kind.)

Jud, the former football player, is particularly winning with his rather "aw shucks," loose manner.

"Why did you give up the game? The big money and all that glory?" I ask.

"Gosh, it was tough, real tough. I was going places, right up there, y'know, and I got this here knee injury and that was it."

He shakes his head and clicks his tongue to emphasize his bad luck.

I have to sympathize. It sure was damned tough having his career aborted like that through no fault of his own.

"Do you know what it is you're selling?" I ask the new salesmen in a training session.

To a man they look puzzled, because the answer is so obvious. "Color. Color concentrate," they say.

"Bullshit," I answer. "Color is incidental. You're selling a relationship, two relationships really: between yourself and the customer and, if we give you the right support, between the company and the customer. Although the product is the reason you're there, it is not enough of a reason for the customer to buy from you. He is first a human being, which I assume you all are. (Everyone laughs politely.) Like all other human beings he thrives on relationships. So the real reason he buys from you is you. You are the star, not color concentrate, even though ours is the best in the world. (More laughter.) But the sad news is that you must suffer the pain and the joy common to all relationships. To make them last and maintain trust, you must always deal gently, respectfully, and honestly. But you cannot always count on reciprocity."

I instruct them to "avoid the little guys," specifically, avoid any account that can't potentially give us $25,000 worth of business annually. And call on no account less often than once every two weeks and, in some cases, at least once a week.

"Your secret weapon is simplicity itself: call frequency," I advise. "Inevitably, at some point, the competitor will become overconfident, take the customer for granted, and slack off. But no one wants to be neglected, least of all a customer who is beginning to feel that he's giving more than he's getting. By hanging in there, maybe for years, and showing him that he matters to you, that you are willing to meet his needs, you are giving him good reason to favor you with his kindness and his business."

"But no payola," I add, "nothing beyond a lunch or a dinner, maybe a token Christmas gift—a pen with our name on it or a desk calendar."

Although payola isn't prevalent, I do run into it. Some of our competitors pay for their customers' vacations and send expensive gifts—TVs, High Fidelity components—to their homes. One notorious competitor provides a car every year or two to his largest customer. It galls me not so much that we must forfeit such a buyer's business to remain honest, but that he is cheating his own company of opportunities and profits.

I walk away from any customer on the take. On one occasion, knowing firsthand that a buyer we are calling on is accepting payola, I chose to go over his head to complain to the vice president he reported to. The VP, conceding that his subordinate may be accepting favors, nevertheless defended him, even praised him for the excellent contribution he was making to the company.

"But how can he know that he's paying a fair price if he sticks to only one supplier?" I asked.

"Well, let's ask him," said the VP, picking up the phone to summon the buyer to his office. As the buyer entered I sensed collaboration from the way he and the VP made eye contact.

"Harry here says he offered you a better price than you're paying." The buyer didn't flick an eyelash. "And you won't give him the time of day," continued the VP.

"Oh, yeah? How's he know what I'm paying?" the buyer asked, ignoring my presence.

I knew that I gave the low bid because I had intentionally quoted below cost to get a foot in the door.

"What was your price, Harry?" asked the VP.

"Fifty-eight cents a pound in ten-thousand-pound quantities," I replied.

"That's more than I'm paying," the buyer responded.

He had to be lying. I wanted to demand proof but held back. I knew I had lost. The VP should have requested our competitor's invoice verifying the price paid and presented it to me. By his not doing so, he implied either that I was gullible or he didn't much care whether or not his buyer was telling the truth, or both.

"Are you satisfied?" asked the VP.

"Are you?" I countered.

Shrugging, the VP threw up his hands. What more did I want? he asked. Here was an account I'd better forget, at least until the day the buyer—and maybe his VP—retired or died.

Of the three new salesmen I hired, the former pro-football player soon turns sour. A beautiful hulk, blue eyed and strong jawed, he is a male sexpot. Although his personal habits no matter how extreme are perfectly acceptable to me as long as they don't interfere with his job, his sex life strangely does. Working the metropolitan New York area, he apportions his territory into rotating threes: one week calling on prospects in New Jersey, the next week covering Long Island, and the next covering Westchester County and southwestern Connecticut. For each week in each location he shacks up with a different girlfriend in her apartment, and submits an expense account listing dinner for two every night.

Of course, I question his extravagant dining expenses.

"What's wrong?" he says, quite innocently. "Hell, ain't I saving the company my motel expense?"

Makes sense, I admit.

"But what time do you get going in the morning?" I wonder.

"I'm making the calls, Harry," he says. "Don't worry."

There's no question that he's a big hit with prospects who follow pro football, his principal subject during every sales interview whether the customer is a fan or not. But after months of his football talk he doesn't generate enough sales to pay his way. He finally peaks out—his graph looks more like a low mound—his sales level flattening then dipping. After giving him several warnings, I decide to replace him. The exit interview is depressing.

"Jud, you told me you played with the Patriots when you know you damn well didn't," I confront him.

"I was on the second team," he says as he sits beside my desk fidgeting in his seat and staring at his shoes.

"That isn't the way I hear it. You only tried for the team, right? And—"

"Where'd you hear that shit?"

"I met your father. When he came by for your paycheck, we talked a little. You didn't play football with the team, did you?"

Avoiding my eyes he stares dreamily into midair.

"Is that right, Jud?"

"Right, that's right, I didn't make it..." he says, forming a cup with his enormous hands and covering his handsome, massive face and sobbing silently.

"I'm afraid I have to let you go, Jud. I'm sorry."

"Sure, sure, I know," he says as he quickly composes himself.

Jud is a living tragedy. All of us delude ourselves to some extent, but Jud has converted delusion into belief. He carries his fiction of having been a pro-football player into every moment of his waking life, into every relationship, whether with his closest friend or the most casual acquaintance. It is the sustenance he needs to keep going. Though it's hard to witness his pain at being revealed, I have no choice but to shatter his lie. Maybe it will be a small step in leading him to abandon it. Maybe not.

Wally, however, the pro golfer, turns out to be a winner. Making use of his expertise, he does a good share of business on the golf course. Possessing an easygoing, patient charm, he's modest about his golfing ability, which certainly wows the customers. After playing awhile they end up asking him for pointers on how he does it. Understandably Wally's sales show steady increases from month to month, and there's no telling where he'll peak out.

DRIVEN

"I wasn't good enough at the game," Wally says with refreshing honesty. "Not good enough to make a decent living on the circuit." But he's good enough to parlay golf into nice sales commissions at Magic.

"If you can't make it one way, try another, eh, Wally?" I say. "If you can't be a Michelangelo, then be a Milton Avery."

"Who's he?" says Wally.

Working out of the Chicago plant, Wally covers Indiana, Michigan, and Illinois, including Cook County. One afternoon while on a trip to a prospective customer in northern Michigan, he calls me nearly in tears.

"After months of trying I finally got an appointment with the purchasing agent, but now that I'm here he says he's too busy to see me. Harry, I just drove five hours. I'm so fucking angry, I don't know what to do. I just can't think."

"I know exactly how you feel, Wally. It's shitty. But there's nothing you can do, not yet," I say.

"Sonofabitch, I'd like to pick up the phone and tell him to go fuck himself."

"I don't blame you. First, you've got to decide whether you want to write him off or not. It's your decision."

"Christ, I feel like bawling."

"Good idea. Just go to your car and have a good cry."

Look who's talking. I haven't cried since I was a kid. I didn't cry when my father died.

"You're kidding me, Harry."

"I'm not. Look, drive to the middle of nowhere, then scream at the top of your lungs. It'll work wonders. After that, phone the bastard and tell him you've driven five hours to see him and you'd like to make another appointment."

"I don't know—I don't know whether I'm ready to do that."

"It's up to you," I say. "Being a salesman, having to swallow so much crap, is tough. You're pissed, right? Okay, let your anger work for you. Turn the situation around; put the bastard on the defensive. Make him feel guilty over what he's done. I'll bet he'll see you. You'll probably have him eating out of your hand."

"Do you think so?"

"I do. It's important to do something—even if it gets you nowhere. Don't accept his refusal. Just act. Take charge of yourself. Okay, Wally?"

"I get it."

"Let me know how you do."

"I sure will."

"I'd say your trip has already paid off."

"You're being a little premature, aren't you, Harry?"

"I'm not talking about the customer. He may still tell you to go fuck yourself. I'm talking about you."

Janet's cousin Abel, though a charismatic young man, has consistently failed at every task he has ever tried. Not that he isn't bright or personable or motivated. All his life he has lived in the shadow of a successful father, Gilbert Samson, a former marine colonel and presently a top executive with a construction conglomerate. He is Abel's infallible, macho god. Abel even tries to imitate his father's weight lifter's strut, except he doesn't have the broad chest for it. Taking a cue from his father, Abel becomes expert at smoothly manipulating others.

One Sunday afternoon in June, Abel, his parents, and his fiancée visit Janet and me on Cape Cod. Abel tells me that he recently dropped out of his last year of college and is recovering from a leg injury he suffered while waterskiing and is presently living off the monthly proceeds of a liability claim. He and is fiancée, a fragile feathery girl, the daughter of a well-known, shady union leader in Boston, plan to marry in August. It will be Abel's third marriage, her second.

"He only needs to find himself," his mother confides. "Why do kids nowadays have so many problems? Did you have to find yourself, Harry? I surely didn't. All I had to find was a husband."

"He needs something to sink his teeth into," his father says, taking me aside, "something challenging to show what he can do. He's very capable, Harry. I'm not saying that because he's my son. The trouble is the right thing has never come along."

Apparently everyone knows what Abel needs except Abel himself. Maybe Magic has what he needs. But does he have what Magic needs? I'm willing to gamble, as I did on Sammy.

In confidence his fiancée says to me, "Thank-you for giving Abel a chance. I'll see that he sticks with it and meets your expectations. I'm what he needs. He's never had someone like me to make him succeed."

To me Gil Samson, Abel's father, is a puzzle. I can't locate him in the scheme of personalities that I know. At one moment he is a sycophant, at another an inspirational leader, at another an entertainer, at yet another a demanding, irritable tyrant. A personality chameleon, he assumes whatever style gets him the most from the person he's with.

He invites Janet and me to Washington to spend a weekend with him and his whiny, barrel-shaped wife in their newly refurbished company-owned house off embassy row. He takes us to the city's poshest restaurant where the maitre d' parts the waves for us. Famous columnists and members of Congress nod to him and smile as we are led to our table.

"How are ya, Gil?"

"Great. How are you?"

As he mutters their names sotto voce for my sake, he's in rapture.

"In this town, Harry, all that counts is who you know. Influence is everything. It's how things get done. Take our overseas projects. Hell, I know prime ministers, foreign secretaries, kings, you name 'em. That's the way you do it." Blue veins bulge from his thick neck.

"Gil knows everybody anywhere who counts, Harry," his wife interjects.

"Y'know, Harry, less than one hundred people run this country. Did you know that? Less than a hundred people."

"Is that so?" I say.

"Old families, board chairmen, corporate titans, people you've probably never heard of are calling the shots. Deal with them and you can do anything."

"I never realized—"

"Anytime you need anything—some favor—just call me. I can get it done for you."

"Frankly, Gil, I haven't operated that way."

"Then it's about time you woke up, Harry. It's about time."

Later, while in the National Museum of Art, Gil shows no interest in the masterpieces before us. He talks on about his influence and the way his world works. Growing anxious for Sunday evening and the flight back home, I've had more of Gil than I can comfortably digest.

As a trainee Abel begins with a promising spurt, first in the lab, then the plant, and later the office. Not surprisingly he is bright, ambitious, personable, and resourceful. Conceivably in a few years, after developing his native abilities and management skills, he will be capable of running a new satellite facility. I might consider grooming him to be my replacement some day. There's no one else. My children have no interest in the business. It seems Abel has found his niche; as his mother would say, at last he has found himself.

His father, mother, wife, and father-in-law—the whole tribe—express their gratitude whenever I'm in sight. "It's miraculous. Abel's a changed man. How did you do it?" they say. Inviting Janet and me to their frequent parties, they fuss over us as if we were royalty. They introduce us to their friends: "Meet Harry Simon and his wife, Janet. Harry is Abel's boss—you know, the wonder man we told you about."

"See, you were wrong," I say to Janet for being against my hiring Abel.

"It's still too soon. What if he doesn't work out?" she says. "Do you really think the relatives will understand?"

"Nothing to worry about," I say. "He's born to the job, a natural. All the kid ever needed was the right opportunity."

It's been more than ten years since I gave Sammy his big break. His recent behavior isn't promising, however. Surely Sammy had a hand in losing Perfection. And new problems are surfacing. He insists on ignoring my counsel, calling on the smaller accounts rather than going after the dinosaurs, whose volume business we need desperately to fill our idle capacity. Now almost sixty, no longer ambitious, Sammy's coasting, satisfied with his coterie of small customers who are always glad to see him and gossip with him over a cup of coffee. I suspect he considers himself sort of semi-retired.

"Those are hungry machines out there in production, Sammy," I finally confront him. "We've got to increase sales. And you won't do it by calling on two-bit outfits. So forget 'em. Drop every account that can't give us at least $25,000 worth of business a year."

He appears troubled. "You mean my regular accounts?"

"You got it. Some of them."

"They're my friends, Harry. I can't do that."

"We're not in business for friendship, Sammy."

After pondering that wisdom, he defends himself. "Small accounts can become big accounts."

"Damn few. Name one that's amounted to anything."

"In time some will."

"When hell freezes over, Sammy."

It's no use. His sales figures remain on a plateau as he sticks to a losing routine. Under such circumstances any competent sales manager would replace him with fresh, young blood. Being a coward in such matters, I'd rather stew and evade the issue.

To boost sales I put on independent reps, straight-commission salesmen carrying allied lines. Though most turn out to be only mildly effective, two are outstanding: in Kansas City and Atlanta.

George, the Kansas City man, in his late fifties, enormous as an ocean liner, is a veritable walking "have a good day" poster. He's so likeable that the customers give him business to make their day. He drives a vast cream-colored, chrome-plated, Cadillac. People stare at it when it passes. I find riding in it almost an embarrassment. But since George brings out my better-natured side, as he does with everyone, I think it's fun.

In only a few months, the rapport that develops between George and me is exceptional. He's a giant of decency, patience, dependability and efficiency. He never exaggerates, as salesmen are prone to do. And he moves fast. For instance, he calls my home at 7:00 A.M. to tell me that he's got a hundred-thousand-pound order—no mean quantity—if we can match a customer's color target, make up a sample of concentrate, and get it back to him in Kansas City by the next day for the customer's trial and approval.

"No way, George," I say. "Figure a day to get the target here, a day to formulate the color in our lab, and a day to get it back to you. You couldn't have it before the day after tomorrow."

"I see. Trouble is, Harry, they're about to place the order with their present supplier tomorrow if we can't come through. I know it's asking a lot."

The sample request couldn't be processed any sooner by our Chicago plant. Anyway they don't have the capacity to produce such a large order.

"You're asking for the impossible, George."

"If I get the target to you today, can you make up the sample right away?"

"Are you serious? How are you going to do that?"

"Leave it to me, Harry. Just be ready, Okay?"

"You're on, George. We'll do our part here."

"You're a good man, my friend."

I shake my head. "And you're a dreamer."

His next call is at one o'clock in the afternoon. "How do I get to your place?" he asks.

"What?"

"I said—"

"I heard you, George. Where in hell are you?"

"At Logan Airport; I just rented a car."

"You flew in?"

"Yeah. Boy, are my arms tired from all that flapping."

"You're unbelievable."

"Is the lab ready for me? I've got a reservation on the nine o'clock back to Kansas City."

"You bet we're ready," I say in wonder and admiration.

When I offer to reimburse him for his trip expense, he refuses. It was his idea, his gamble, he says.

George secures not only the hundred-thousand-pound order but also all the rest of the account's business. After promising the customer that Magic, though fourteen hundred miles away, can duplicate the service of the local supplier only ten miles down the street, he proves it.

Every minute of George is pure excitement. Nothing is daunting. But that is his undoing. Besides being grossly overweight, he chain-smokes, often lapsing into an uncontrollable coughing fit. On my last trip with him, I say, "George, trim down and give up the filthy habit. Your life-style's killing you."

"To tell the truth, any other way would kill me sooner. Contrary to popular opinion, I'll go on forever."

"Well, if you don't care, I do."

"Why Harry, I didn't know you felt like that." He grins.

"I don't, you bastard. It's only because I need you."

He cackles. "Don't worry. Bastards like me don't die; we just get meaner and meaner."

"Whether you know it or not, George, you're already there."

Whether I knew it or not, I had come to love him like a brother.

A month later George calls, inquiring about the status of his accounts. In passing he says: "By the way, I'll be out of commission for just a little while."

"What do you mean? Are you sick, George?"

"Not really sick. My ticker's acting up a bit and they say I have a touch of emphysema, so I'm taking oxygen."

"So—"

"So they put me in the hospital—"

"You're in the hospital?"

"Right."

"You're calling from a hospital bed?"

"That's right, but I'll be up and around in a few days."

"Was it a heart attack, George?"

"Naw. Just a little ticker trouble, that's all, nothing to worry about."

In ten days George is back on the road, still refusing to quit smoking and to cut down on eating. I wonder whether he's suicidal or denying his mortality or rebelling against God or all or none of the above. A week passes and his wife calls to tell me, "My beautiful George passed away yesterday, Mr. Simon. He used to say you were like a brother to him."

"It was mutual," I say. I close the door to my office so no one would see me, and weep.

For the next six months, though our rep agreement terminated George's compensation in the event of his withdrawal without notice, I paid his wife the commissions that would normally go to him had he been alive. I thought he'd appreciate the gesture. In the territory he covered, he, not Magic's performance, was obviously the crucial ingredient in our sales success. No one else could have brought the subtle fervor and joy to a relationship that George could. I replaced him with a new rep, but we gradually lost most of the business George had generated.

Our Atlanta rep, Sal, in his late twenties, dark, confident, aggressive, and brooding, is a decided contrast to George. Formerly he sold for a competitor, becoming "his own master" as a rep when the outfit didn't meet the salary he "deserved" and demanded. Having an established following, he's a find and brings with him most of the competitor's business in the territory. However, after a few months I realize that in order to compete in the low-end market made up by most of his customers, we must sell at such marginal prices that, after paying him his commissions, there's no profit left for Magic.

While spending a few days making the customer rounds with him in Atlanta, I learn that he is separated from his wife and four children and lives in an apartment building occupied largely by female flight attendants.

"I sleep with a different bimbo every night," he crows.

"What's that do for you?" I ask.

"Hey, I'm a horny guy, so this place is paradise."

"Good for you."

"You don't approve?"

"It's none of my business," I say.

"Hey, I hear you do your fooling around."

His statement comes across as a stinging accusation, and I strike back.

"You've got a responsibility to your wife and kids. Why don't you grow up?"

"You're a sonofabitch," he says.

As of then our relationship stops dead, and over the next few months his sales dwindle to nothing. He found another company to represent.

My efforts to improve sales and thereby Magic's bottom line are slow to take effect. Meanwhile the cost of our debt burden continues to rise.

A salesman must show his face for months to establish a relationship and encourage confidence with customers. I figure it will take at least a year before results begin to appear and another year to take hold. But the question is, do I have that much time? That depends on the rise and fall of the interest rate, the keenness of our competition, the morale of employees during a slow period, and plain old luck. Having little or no control over these factors, I find next year frightening to contemplate.

CHAPTER XVII

Year Twelve

1978

Sales: $3,700,000 (-19.6%)
Profit: $14,000 (-71.9%)
Debt: $1,193,000 (-18.5%)
Net Worth: - $46,000 (+71%)

As sales are dropping, profits are plummeting three times as fast to a new low. My stomach is constantly roiling. Ever climbing interest rates are increasing our costs. The new salesmen, whose salaries and expenses are chewing into profits, are supposed to be the means by which our fortunes should improve. But that will take time, more than I have. I'm racing against a deadline — October — when I have to make the first $100,000 principal payment to Rob Starr. Until now I'm paying him only $25,000 per year plus interest. To default means I lose everything. Already leveraged to our eyeballs, we can't borrow money from the bank. Where will it come from? I feel helpless. I pray for a miracle.

Groping for a solution from my three directors, I ask the board to meet quarterly. Professor Hoyt Strong who had shown me the way to buy out Kob by means of the ESOP, says he fears the consequences of directors' liability for a man in his position. He resigns. Even when I offer to take out insurance to protect him, he refuses to reconsider.

DRIVEN

The local attorney—the secretary of the board—begs off attending meetings, saying he's too busy. Dan, the attorney who represented me and drew up the agreement between Rob and Magic, urges me to take a minority position and go public to raise money. This is abhorrent, out of the question. Doesn't he understand? Magic is my creation and must belong to nobody but me and my employees. To relinquish control is to negate the whole idea of entrepreneurship and my need to be as much master of my fate as possible.

I feel totally alone. No one—not Janet, Cathy, my employees, the bank—can help me. I'll just have to tough it out and put on the best front I can muster. Certainly I have more than enough everyday problems to distract me from what's happening in the big ring.

The new accountant isn't working out. He's still cold and uncommunicative, so that I feel we'll never relate—a serious constraint. I give him every chance to come around but then he fouls up our tax return, which leads to an IRS audit and a penalty—the last irritant I need now. Though I must contend with my pride, my desperation for wise counseling and some down-to-earth figure crunching and someone to talk to is overriding. I need Julius more than ever; I miss him as a valuable sounding board, I miss his calm insight.

"Will you take us back, Julius?" I plead over the phone.

"Of course, Harry, but to be honest I'm surprised. I never expected—"

"The other guy is impossible. He's screwed up the tax return and now I've got the IRS and the State on my back."

"I must admit this is a first for me. I've had clients write us off, but no one has ever come back. So, Harry, I'm yours." His voice seems to smile. "I know what it must have taken for you to call me."

We are like lovers making up after an argument.

"Frankly, I've missed following your progress," admits Julie. "And giving you my advice, which, of course, you never take anyway."

"Things aren't good, Julie. You may be sorry."

"Let me be the judge. You've been in hot water before. Remember the first years? You don't give in, Harry. You always land on your feet. I know you'll make it somehow."

"Well, this is a big one."

Julius's words are what I need to hear. I don't need a proposal or a promise or a solution to deal with the situation—just encouragement and someone to believe in me.

As if they secretly know I'm weak and vulnerable, the IRS, the Massachusetts State Sales Tax Bureau and OSHA choose this year to monitor Magic. In my state of mind, I half suspect they have somehow informed each other of our condition and have conspired among themselves to harass me.

OSHA penalizes us for, among other things, having toilet seats that are not open at the front. Most disturbing is a $10,000 fine for not having air-cleaning equipment to remove the dust generated in our process, although we have the proper equipment on order and due to be installed in a matter of weeks. The OSHA inspector, dutifully reminding me that I need not admit him to the plant, threatens to secure a court order if I resist, and with my involuntary permission spends several weeks examining every detail of the facility. I'm incensed when he prohibits me from being present during his interviews with our employees. I want to know my accusers if there are any, know if they are giving accurate answers. He says my presence would be intimidating. The employees inform me that he asks them questions on matters about which they have no knowledge.

I protest to the district director on a visit to his office in Providence. It's a small room, almost bare, without a window. With the inspector present sitting off to the side, I sit stiffly before his desk.

"Do you have any children?" I ask him.

"Two sons," he says, curious that I'm getting personal.

"And are you bringing them up correctly, to be honest and considerate of others? I mean, the best way you know how?"

He nods, more curious.

"Suppose one of your sons does something bad. Do you punish him?"

"Sometimes. Look, I don't know what you're getting at—"

"Please hear me out, sir," I say. "You will know in a minute."

"Well, suppose he says, 'Dad, I know what I did is wrong, but I promise I'll never do it again.' " I pause, letting the scenario sink in as he waits. "Then you strike him despite his words of contrition. You strike him hard." The director imperceptibly flinches. "He'd certainly resent you, wouldn't he?"

"Yes, I suppose so."

"And you'd probably lose his trust and confidence."

"Yes, I—"

"Well, just think, in essence that's exactly what your man here has done to us. He is punishing us for mending our mistake. We've shown him that as soon as we became aware of the unhealthy condition in our shop, we took action—immediate and unilateral action—to correct it. Here are the dated documents."

The director, his forehead furrowed, accepts the sheaf of papers I hand him across his desk.

"I see," he says. Turning to the inspector he adds, "Let's review this case. I think Mr. Simon has a point."

A week later the fine is dropped. It's a small victory, but a victory just the same and the sign I need that not everything is going against me. But my battle with the government isn't over.

The State Sales Tax Bureau fines us $15,000 for not paying sales tax on the dust-collecting equipment that OSHA mandated. Prior to submitting his report, the inspector had hinted to me that we had a "serious violation in the matter of a substantial sum that should have been paid but was not." He suggested that the matter need not go further if we would "have a mind to correct it" in advance. A payoff? I suggested he complete his goddamned business and get the hell off our premises.

Looking up the sales tax statute, I discover that our equipment is not taxable because it contributes to the employees' health and safety as well as the cleanliness of the air outside the plant. At the hearing I request (I don't hire an attorney) I refer to that specific portion of the statute.

The presiding officer castigates the inspector. "What are you trying to do wasting my time on this?" he says and dismisses the state's claim. Another victory. It's a fight to gain every inch.

Finally the IRS moves in with all their intimidating might. For more than two weeks an agent—a small, thin, seemingly mild, fastidious man—pores over every detail in our books, missing nothing. He also reviews my personal return and touches on returns for prior years. Although he appears easy and conciliatory, I'm wary not to be taken in by him. The first sign of disguised hostility surfaces one morning over coffee when he remarks, offhandedly, that here he is "working for peanuts" while I'm drawing an enormous salary.

"You want my headaches?" I ask. "My debt?"

"I was just remarking—"

"You don't have to stay with the IRS, y'know. You can go with one of the big accounting firms and earn more. Outsmart your IRS colleagues when they come around. And with little risk. You don't like risk, do you?"

"I didn't mean—"

"You know exactly why I make more than you, don't you? So keep your comments to yourself."

The battle is on. After that altercation, the IRS agent begins nitpicking at my expense account records, questioning one insignificant item after another. When he meanders into my office with one of my expense reports from the previous summer, the stage is set for another blowup.

"I see by this report you stayed at a motel in Gallilee, downstate," he says evenly as he sits beside my desk. "That's a resort area, isn't it?" I only stare at him. "I take it you wouldn't have business there, no customers."

"But, I do," I say, delighted with the surprise on his face. "My customer has a summer place and I took him out to dinner, where we discussed business, which is explained in my notes of that date if you'll turn the page."

Momentarily squirming in his chair, he quickly recoups.

"You were with your wife, weren't you, and you included her expense too? I'll have to disallow that."

"No, I was not with my wife."

"Where was she?"

"On the Cape where she stays all summer."

"Then who were you with?"

I explode. "None of your goddamned business. What are you, the Gestapo? I was alone."

"Well, it says here on the receipt, you had a room for two."

"It's wrong. I paid for a single."

"Well—maybe."

"Let's call the motel and get their rate for a single, okay?"

I pull out the phone directory to look up the number.

"That won't be necessary. Alright, I'll let this one go."

"Get off my back. I've got problems enough. Just get off me!"

But he is determined and finally, redeemed, finds a possible violation in a more substantial matter. Disallowing a deduction that Julius had taken on a three-year-old return, he levies a charge including a penalty of about $20,000 against Magic, a sum that I can't dismiss.

Julius had urged us to intentionally take small chances on our IRS returns, nothing illegal, just questionable. "In case of an audit give the agent a bone," he said. "Let him find something to justify his time and effort." But obviously he didn't intend to plant a bone worth $20,000.

Meeting with the agent, Julius argues until the agent eventually admits that the deduction might be allowed since it is based on a gray area of the law that hasn't yet been tested.

The next day the agent reneges: "I'm recommending that we proceed with the charge and penalty anyway." After discussing it with his boss, he lays down a challenge: "If you want to go to court, that's okay with us."

"Pay it," advises Julius. "It'll cost more to fight than the amount involved; we won't win even if we win."

I'm livid, especially since I'm battling so hard to conserve every dime and struggling to stay in the black. I feel a powerful bitterness toward all government. Don't they realize that business constitutes our nation's very lifeblood? Without business there'd be no revenue, no payroll to tax, no profits. In discouraging me they are deterring my entrepreneurial spirit and thereby Magic's future growth.

Under the circumstances is it really worth all the effort I've put into building Magic? Though I'm personally in the 50 percent tax bracket, that doesn't dampen my incentive because personal income is not my major goal. But who or what hurts Magic also hurts me. And most troubling to me is the hidden partnership arrangement, which the law imposed on business. Julius and I ruminate on it.

"The government is strictly a fair-weather partner," I say. "It takes its cut when you make it, but not your lumps when you lose."

"Not entirely true," says Julius. "Doesn't the government subsidize the farmers in bad times? You should be so lucky. And Harry, I wouldn't complain about taxes. Better to complain when you don't have to pay them—when you don't have profits. So pay and be grateful."

"Looks like my paranoia is showing, eh, Julie?" I respond. "Actually I wouldn't want to be subsidized. I don't want a handout. And I'm truly grateful to the government, the Small Business Administration, for helping me to get Magic going in the early years. Without the SBA I know there'd be no Magic as it is today, or any Magic at all, for that matter."

"And where would you be in Russia or China or socialist Sweden?" Julius asks.

"Probably in prison. I'd break every law they've got, maybe even murder."

"And compared to the frustrated entrepreneurs and iconoclasts in Russia, you're getting away with murder."

"Still, compared to most Americans, I'm making a tremendous contribution to the nation's welfare. So it's a fair exchange, isn't it, and I guess it's only right."

"I agree."

"Only they better lay off me."

That year inflation climbed to 13.5 percent; over the next two years the interest rate rose to 21 percent.

As was the case with most businesses then, except oil, Magic was a sapling struggling to stay rooted in an economic storm. To think I had believed that by having my own business I would have control over my destiny. What then is the main difference between owning a business and being an employee if in neither case are you in control? Simply, if you own a business, you can act, you can call on your inner resources, your ingenuity, and try to beat the forces arrayed against you. Even though you may lose, you will have had the opportunity to try to win.

Phil, our production manager, shows up one morning with a bandage on his temple. He explains in his clipped way that he had an accident the previous evening while driving the company van.

"The van's totalled," he says.

"How did it happen?" I ask.

"Fell asleep. The van went off the road." He offers no more details. Getting information from Phil is like prying a lid off a nailed crate.

The accident is suspicious, but accidents will happen. At least he's not seriously hurt. But I'm concerned. When Phil joined me ten years ago he was a dark haired, lean, enthusiastic young man in his early twenties fresh out of a technical college. Now he is bloated, his eyes are bloodshot, and his hair and skin are gray. He no longer shaves every day. No matter the time, Phil can be seen holding a bottle of Coke in his hand. He walks fast and paces nervously when idle. Is there something wrong? I care about him.

Two other auto accidents also occur within the month. Our upstate New York salesman rams a stopped car ahead of him on the Thruway. Helmut totals his car in Chicago while speeding into a fog bank on the Outer Drive. We're lucky that none of the men suffer serious injuries. But I castigate myself for having just cancelled our collision insurance policies; to save money I self-insured our vehicles after analyzing our excellent accident-free record over the last five years. I failed to realize that the longer our good luck holds, the greater the odds it will turn.

Is there conceivably a constructive point of view from which to deal with chaos — a philosophy, a theory perhaps, that provides an understanding of the senseless mix of events? I devise the AFU theory as follows: Since the normal state of affairs is to be, in three words, All Fucked Up, accept this as the way things are. Don't be surprised, don't panic. When things go smoothly, be grateful, but bear in mind that such conditions are abnormal.

It takes no great effort to brainwash everyone at Magic to believe that the AFU theory is valid. When things go wrong we now automatically remind ourselves and each other that, "It's only another AFU situation."

As troubles continue and losses mount with no end in sight, I need new ideas and an arena in which to debate and hone them into practical use. I change the composition and size of the board of directors, which has already been altered by defections. Abel's father, Gil, the corporate honcho, agrees to serve, as does an old friend from my MPI days, Jensen, a retired executive who had once managed MPI's color concentrate division in Chicago. I choose Gil, thinking he will bring a larger vision to our plight. Jensen will be valuable for his specialized wisdom derived from his prior experience in the business and, in the event of my death, for his ability to take over temporarily and see to Magic's continuity—both for the protection of the employees and for Janet, who would be left with the business.

To the board I also bring Meyer, another retired gentleman, a neighbor at the Cape who had sold his company, of which he was president, to a large conglomerate. In the deeper reaches of my mind the thought exists that I might sell Magic one day, especially if none of my three children are interested in taking over. If that should happen Meyer's experience would be most useful.

For Emma's insight into the employees' angle on things and also to add to Magic's continuity were I to die, I ask Emma to participate, which of course she is thrilled to do. Furthermore I think Janet would find it easier to deal with a woman, someone I know she can trust and who knows the ropes.

I don't evade the possibility of my death and since Magic is my legacy to the world and to all those who matter to me, I want to leave it in a safe and secure condition. Indeed, with a million dollars of insurance on my life, were I to die Magic's financial problems would be over.

At the first meeting of the new board I promise that I will abide by its recommendations even though I have veto power. As one member put it: "Good, Harry! What use are we if you do whatever you wish? Why should we spend our time giving you advice if it doesn't count?"

I ask Julius to attend all board meetings as an advisor. Being an ESOP company it's essential to have an appraisal of the company's stock each year. An economics professor from a local college serves in that capacity and attends only the annual meeting, but I keep him apprised of our financial results quarterly throughout the year. And I insist that Janet attend (though not as a board member for reasons of liability), since her fortunes are tied to Magic's whether she likes it or not. Reluctantly, to please me and seeing that it's prudent, she agrees. Now I have people whom I respect, who are objective and experienced, whom I can call upon for ideas and use as a sounding board, who will call it like it is and hold me accountable. I feel less alone.

I want the employees to participate more in the struggle, to gain insight into what it means to run a business and to have a say in the company's direction and therefore their own destinies. After all, they now own a piece of the action, albeit a small one. Already I'm disappointed that their ownership stake has not translated into the increased productivity I expected. The reason, I gather, is that the benefits of ownership are too remote. We are an impatient culture. When people must expend every dollar they earn to live, only the present matters, not the uncertain promise of the future. There has to be a way to motivate everyone for the now. To find the way, to experiment, I appoint a select group; their response is surprisingly enthusiastic.

For one hour five days a week at 8 A.M. we hold an uninterrupted meeting in my office behind closed doors. Precisely at nine the meeting is terminated no matter what is under discussion and left unfinished. If important enough, it can be taken up the following morning.

Those attending the meeting are Emma, the office manager and purchasing agent; Phil, the production manager; Wally, the new technical director in charge of the lab and quality control; a production worker chosen on a rotating basis for a term of one week; and any salesman who happens to be in the office and wishes to join in — and they do. Whenever Helmut, the Chicago manager, visits, he too is invited to attend.

No one presides; everyone is encouraged to speak his or her mind frankly and to bring up any subject pertaining to any area of the business. It's always okay to mind someone else's business and it's okay to be absurd. The essential requirement is to have an open mind; no defensiveness is allowed.

From these meetings, conducted religiously for the next two years, emerged a dazzling range of management ideas and experiments that shaped Magic's future beyond any of our imaginings. They included an innovative incentive plan involving teams, a method for eliminating layoffs, a flexible work program, the four day week, profit sharing, a unique reward system for the salesmen and more.

Although the Massachusetts operation is declining, the Chicago operation is making money. Helmut is doing nobly, even showing signs of brilliance, having created an entirely original kind of coloring product, which Magic has patented and is promoting. Since Helmut is his own man, aggressive and dedicated, I leave him alone, except to insist that he follow a standardized manufacturing procedure and use only materials that are common to both facilities. Such a policy is necessary to ensure product homogeneity and interchangeability between the plants. Were one plant out of commission for any reason, then the other could easily fill in and keep customers serviced without interruption.

Despite the logic of this stricture, Helmut ignores it, arguing that he can buy alternate raw materials cheaper than Emma can, or that certain materials he uses in Chicago work better than the materials Massachusetts uses, or that his procedures are more efficient than Massachusetts's. I reply that if all this is so, then he must share his knowledge and innovations with the other plant so that both plants can mutually decide whether or not to incorporate the changes. While agreeing, Helmut can't suppress his renegade spirit and continues to dart off in his own direction, cooperating less and less with the Massachusetts staff and causing frustration and confusion in both locations.

Finally, he calls me. "Everyone in the mother plant is deliberately trying to shaft me, Harry."

"I find that hard to believe," I say.

"Are you aware they're holding back my pay?"

"Holding back—"

"The staff up there doesn't really give a damn about us."

"That's absolutely crazy, Helmut. I'll look into this immediately."

My investigation reveals that the paychecks had arrived late on only one occasion when the payroll service we employ changed its procedure. Nevertheless, before the developing friction sparks a fire, I rush to Chicago. For two days Helmut repeats his claim that the Massachusetts staff treats him and his group like second-class citizens.

"They resent us, Harry. And do you know why? Because we're making the money and they're not. They're goddamned jealous, that all."

"You're wrong about the people in Massachusetts," I argue. "They have a high regard for you; everyone knows you're doing a super job. Look, if you have a problem with anyone specific, bring me into it."

"I don't want to bother you with that kind of stuff, Harry."

"It's okay, my friend. I don't want you to feel the way you do. I want us to be one harmonious family."

I try to remedy Helmut's paranoia by swapping personnel between the plants for two to four weeks at a time. I have Helmut visit headquarters more often and deal person to person with the staff. But these measures aren't sufficient to limit his compulsion to blaze his own path. Eventually he virtually isolates his operation, stops visiting headquarters, and pursues his independent goals. I can't allow his secession or support his need for autonomy. It's undermining the cooperative spirit on which I've gambled Magic's final success.

I fly to Chicago again to have it out with him.

"If you can't join the rest of the company, maybe you'd do better on your own," I suggest.

"I don't get you, Harry. My plant is making money and you're unhappy. I can't win with you." He throws his hands up in disgust.

"You don't seem to understand that the operation is not only yours, Helmut. It belongs to all of us."

"Before I took over, you were ready to shut it down. I made it what it is, no one else."

"I realize that," I say, "but that doesn't make you emperor."

"I think I'm more capable than anyone else in the company. Why don't you give me credit for my superior ability? What about all the new ideas and the new product I've given you? Why don't you appreciate what I've contributed?"

"I do appreciate what you've done, and I think I've shown it by steadily increasing your compensation."

"Well, I admit I have no complaint on that score, but—"

"Good. Then find a way to come back to the fold. I'll respect what you need if you'll do the same for me. Don't be so rigid."

I put my arm over his shoulder and pull him to me. I remember how he had flown to Boston on his own that night to plead with me to keep his job after I had let him go during Chicago's harder times.

"I've got to think about it. What you said, a little while ago—"

He paused in mid-sentence and stared into the distance.

"What did I say?"

"Maybe you're right, Harry. Maybe I should be on my own."

Sadly, I'm aware that I'm asking him to compromise his individuality, his very originality and natural aggressiveness, the entrepreneurial spirit, that I admire in him and value in myself. But I know also there is only room for one such person, one leader, at Magic. Being like me, I know he can't possibly contain his drive for the sake of the team. Like me, he must become his own master.

A week later Helmut gave notice. A month later he opened his own shop in Chicago and wooed away our top production operators; his brother, who ran the color lab; our best woman in the office; and our largest customer in the area. He sent out word to the trade that without him our operation was in trouble, which was true. From then on he was our arch rival and displayed a bitterness toward us that I never understood. But I suppose it's basic to kill the king in order to become one yourself.

CHAPTER XVIII

Year Thirteen

1979

Sales: $3,400,000 (-8%)
Profit: $40,000 (+186%)
Debt: $1,100,000 (-8%)
Net Worth: ($26,000) (+43%)

My oldest daughter is in her third year of college, my son is about to enter college, and my youngest daughter is a sophomore at a private academy. We have made two additions to our custom-built home, paying cash. I drive a big Buick station wagon (having long ago passed through the luxury foreign car kick) and Janet still has her Mercedes. We dine out at least once a week, then attend a concert or go to a movie, or do all three. Occasionally we entertain at home, hiring professional caterers to cook French cuisine in our kitchen and wait on us. For two weeks every February we fly to an island in the Caribbean to attend a management seminar, which is nothing more than a veiled tax write-off, a business perk. It's a comfortable life without financial strain, yet I feel insecure because I'm not sure it will last.

As I become increasingly preoccupied with the tenuousness of Magic's future, I withdraw into myself, fall back onto my own inner resources. I prefer to be alone. I see Cathy less and less. It seems I've gotten so used to loneliness that I need it to feel normal.

DRIVEN

Magic's performance lacks the strength we need to meet the enormous debt burden that stalks me like a hunter. Yet our net worth is slowly improving, thanks to the ESOP. And I'm given cause to hope from the new board and the involvement of the key employees in the larger and long-range problems of the business. To be able to act, to simply do something even if it doesn't always work, is itself therapeutic.

I wonder whether Chicago hadn't reached its zenith for all time under the able Helmut. Under his successor, Mickey, the operation is slowly sinking into a mire of monthly losses. Although I consider closing it down, as a matter of pride I remain determined to find one more solution before giving in.

"Don't worry about a thing, Harry," Mickey assures me. "I know I can do the job better than the other guy."

Mickey, a local fellow and a former policeman, who previously owned and operated a small custom plastics injection molding business is always silky and soft-spoken, demanding nothing, always cooperative, a happy contrast to Helmut. He also religiously believes that he can solve any problem. In his early forties, he keeps his waist trim and his shoulders thick; his black mustache is fierce and his features are lean and jet. His manner projects: I am a REAL MAN, cool, unemotional, in control.

"Your labor's too high and the inventory is getting away from you," I tell Mickey as we peruse the current quarterly P & L together. Though our sales have dropped, he hasn't adjusted his parameters to the change.

"Maybe so, maybe so. But I'll sure as hell take care of it."

That Friday he cuts the workers' wages; as a result no one shows up the following Monday except the office workers.

I fear that Mickey may be creating a hotbed of discontent, conditions that will attract a union—the last thing I need right now. I often state openly that if the employees were to bring in a union, I will have failed as a proper leader and would sell out. To fend off union attempts to organize our people, and there have been several, I'm alert to every complaint and never lightly dismiss any claims. I adjudicate them as fairly as possible in a give and take exchange; assuaging the unhappiness one on one so that it doesn't spread. Mickey may well be infecting Magic with a dread disease: managing by edict—shades of Gary. The sonofabitch.

The manager turnover in Chicago damages the morale of the workers. Should I fire Mickey or try to salvage him? I'll be damned no matter what I do.

The Massachusetts plant has become an experimental laboratory for testing fresh ideas. Some are original, some are copied from other companies whose innovations are described in the *Harvard Business Review,* mandatory reading for all Magic's key people.

At one of our early morning meetings Emma proposes eliminating the time cards for both factory and office workers.

"Let's treat the people with dignity; let's show them we trust them. They'll feel better about themselves and the company," she argues.

We discuss the implications of not having a written tally of hours worked. Won't we have to depend on everyone's honesty? Isn't it essential that every worker arrive on time to keep the machines operating during shift changes? How will we keep track of overtime?

"It's chancy," someone says. "Give people an inch, they'll take a yard."

DRIVEN

In spite of some reservations I'm for it. Won't trusting gain reciprocal trust? We adopt the suggestion by acclamation as a tentative experiment.

Upon announcing the elimination of the time cards on the bulletin board, the reaction is instantaneous: Everyone glows.

Doing away with time cards turns out to be one of our worst ideas. For the initial few months it goes smoothly, then gradually production drops off as machines start late or must be shut down while waiting idly for late arrivals of the subsequent shift. Seeing that only a few workers are habitual offenders and remain so despite warnings, I call a plantwide meeting.

"I think you know who the tardy ones are," I say. "Only a few are abusing the confidence the company has placed in you. If it continues, we have to go back to time cards." There's a grumbling murmur. "I used to punch a time card myself and hated it. If we have to do this, I'm sorry, but you know what it means when machines are down."

The tardiness improves for only a week or so before the same offenders begin arriving late. True to my threat, we reinstate the time cards. A small delegation of workers comes to my office and pleads that I trust them again. I say it isn't fair that most of them who deserve the company's trust have to be hurt because of the few, but I know of no other way. Neither do they, they admit.

I learn that rules are a painful fist to offender and innocent alike. If I thought that anarchy could work, I would be an anarchist.

Wally, our new technical director, proposes adopting a four-day week, which is the current innovation in factories across the country. The proposal: everyone works four ten-hour days, half the crew Monday through Thursday, the other half Tuesday through Friday thus ensuring five days a week coverage in both plant and office. (Management would still work five and a half days.) We elect to try the plan for three months after which we'll vote to retain or reject it.

Though we observe no significant increase in productivity due to the four-day week, most people seem happier. A surprise advantage is that the fifth day proves convenient for working overtime when offered and necessary. Of course everyone has a long weekend for personal chores. Nevertheless after three months the Massachusetts workers overwhelmingly reject the plan; the office staff and the Chicago employees vote to retain it. Each group is permitted to adopt the work-week schedule it wishes.

Another not so brilliant idea, it turns out, is mine. It created a problem for Janet. Wouldn't it be productive—a way to promote cohesiveness and more creative thinking—to combine pleasure and business at a weekend gathering of all the company's key people and their spouses at the Cape? The company would fly in the Chicago contingent—the two salesmen and their wives, and Mickey and his wife, and his office manager and her husband. The local staff, those in New York and New England, would drive. All would be put up in motels near our Cape house.

Admittedly it would be expensive, but, in my view, well worth it. I hoped to promote camaraderie and provide an opportunity to acquaint everyone firsthand with the troubled state of the company, explain what's being done about it, and seek proposals for a future strategy.

DRIVEN

Twenty of us would arrive on Friday, hold work sessions throughout Saturday into the late afternoon, have a cookout on our deck that evening, play on Sunday—sightsee, swim, golf, or sail—and return home on Monday morning.

Janet is dead against the idea.

"I don't want them in my house," she says. "I don't want them to see how we live. It will only make them resent us more."

"I don't see why they should resent us. I'm the boss and they expect the boss to live well. It helps them feel like they belong to a first-rate outfit."

"It makes them envious. They want the same thing for themselves and they can't have it."

I'm not for ostentation, but I refuse to live fettered by the fear of others' envy. This is not the first time Janet has expressed discomfit over our affluence. It's her goddamned guilt. It's a source of chronic disagreement between us.

"Who says they can't live the way they want? No one's stopping them," I shout. "Look, they know what I've done, how hard I've worked. They're free to do what Fran and Helmut did. I don't think a single person is discontented at Magic."

"Well, I think you're naive. Conduct your business someplace else."

I have cause to think as I do. Several of the employees have kidded me about the ordinariness of my car—not that a Buick is so modest. It reflects on them. They urged me to drive a Caddy or a Lincoln, something more prestigious and in keeping with my position as the head of a successful company. I find such cars much too flamboyant. However, my next car is an Audi Turbo which meets with their approval, if reservedly. It could have been more expensive.

"No, damnit. This is my house too. And the company can't afford more than we're already spending. Anyway, I'd like to share this place with them, show them our garden and take them out for a sail. Sunday we'll picnic on the beach, cook lobster and clams, have plenty of beer. I want everyone to have fun and be free together."

Janet lapses into silence, realizing she has no choice.

The gathering is not without problems or revelations. During the work sessions, Janet and the spouses, including Emma's husband, the only male, sit in the sun and the cool bay breeze on the deck. To Janet's surprise the women complain, occasionally bitterly, about their husbands.

"But I kept my mouth shut and just listened," she assures me. "You should be proud of me. I was shocked at what they said."

Why is she shocked? How often has Janet put me down behind my back and before others?

"So you're not alone in your misery, are you, Janet," I jab.

At the business meetings, though I gradually expose Magic's plight, the day ends on an optomistic note as I assure everyone that "I have a handle on things. Quite simply all our problems will be remedied by increased sales; I have faith that in time the curve will reverse."

Before dinner late that afternoon Wally and Mickey become intoxicated and loudly offer their opinion on how much it cost to build our beautiful home. "The house that Magic built," Mickey calls it. Nevertheless the cookout—grilled swordfish, Wellfleet oysters on the half shell, is a hit.

On Sunday morning I take Wally, Sammy, and Mickey and their wives sailing on the bay in my nineteen-foot open-cockpit sailboat. The day is diamond bright, the air is brisk, the water is flashing, and everyone is exhilarated. The women squeal in delight as the boat heels and slices through the whitecaps. For the first time we feel free together. I am no longer their boss; they aren't my employees. We are abandoned to the elements, having fun.

"I've got to get a sailboat," Wally shouts above the rush of the wind. "I've got to do this again." At this moment he speaks for the others as well.

In the afternoon we join the crowd of tourists ambling along Commercial Street in Provincetown, where Mickey criticizes the male couples who are holding hands.

"They shouldn't allow that," he objects. "They should all be put away."

"C'mon Mickey," Wally urges. "They've got as much right as you—"

"No, they don't. They aren't real Americans. I'd strip them of their citizenship."

Mickey's avowed macho fanaticism makes me uncomfortable.

Although no formal business agenda is scheduled on Sunday evening, business matters come up over dinner. Janet is chagrined. Cleaning up after everyone has gone, we find a silver decanter and several pewter wine cups missing.

"Never again will you do this," Janet announces. Angry over the missing pieces, contritely I agree. Maybe Janet is right. Maybe I tend to romanticize Magic and my employees.

On Monday morning I pick up the Chicago people at their motel in my station wagon and drive them to the Massachusetts plant, where they spend a few hours getting re-acquainted with the office staff before I take them to the Boston airport. We plan to have lunch on the way.

Driving down the interstate, a strange tightness grips my chest and I clutch it with one hand. My breathing quickens and I gasp for more air. A surge of nausea suddenly wracks me. I feel a pain in my left arm. I'm unable to decide whether these sensations are real or my imaginings.

"Anything wrong, Harry?" someone asks.

"I don't know," I say. "I'm sure it'll pass."

It always has. It's not the first time I've had this sensation, never as severe as now. I keep driving, assuring myself that it's nothing, probably indigestion. The discomfort subsides. When in a few miles it returns, I begin to worry.

"I don't think I can eat," I say. On arriving at the restaurant parking lot, I ask Mickey to drive me to the local hospital while the others have lunch. They can drive to the airport and leave the car there.

During the fifteen-minute drive to the hospital, Mickey attempts conversation but I withdraw into myself and don't reply. Why is this goddamned thing happening to me? I'm having a heart attack, at the worst possible time — when there are so many unsolved problems: the debt burden, the escalating interest rate, a second consecutive year of declining sales. Never has the business needed me more. Now Janet may be stuck with the mess. What a stinking legacy, hardly the way I'd choose to go out.

At the hospital emergency entrance I order Mickey to drop me off, rejoin his people, and leave for Chicago.

"No, I'll wait," he says.

"I don't want you to. Please."

"I can't—"

"Tell them I'm okay. Just a little indigestion — that's probably all it is. I'll be in touch. Say nothing about this to anyone. Everything's under control."

DRIVEN

As I struggle from the car, Mickey says, "I'll call you as soon as we land."

"Yes, do that."

Do that, if I'm still around. By my age my father had had his first heart attack. So had his four brothers. I announce to the nurse at the desk: "I think I'm having a heart attack."

As she comes around her desk and looks at me, I can tell that my eyes betray my terror. They are wide and intense, as if they glimpse death itself coming down the hospital corridor.

"Sit in the wheelchair," she says.

"I can walk."

"Follow me," she says, leading me briskly into a small empty four-bed ward. She pulls a curtain around one of the beds, tosses a johnny onto it, and instructs me to put it on. As soon as I lie down she slips a thermometer under my tongue, takes my pulse, and listens to my heart with a stethoscope. Making small talk she attaches a series of wires to various places on my chest. After leaving me for a moment, she returns with a form on a clipboard and asks for my personal statistics.

"Name?"

"Who me?" She smiles. "Just Harry Simon."

"Age?"

"Fifty-five and not counting."

"Weight?"

"One seventy-five, strictly around the middle."

"Blue Cross number?"

"Call my office. No, don't call my office. Call my wife. She has it. No, I'll get it for you."

"Married?"

"Unhappily."

"Children?"

"Seventy-five employees."

"Employer?"

"My wife."

"Occupation?"

"Failing businessman."

"Your doctor?"

"Me—myself."

A young, bearded, businesslike doctor in a lab coat sweeps into the room as the nurse opens the curtain. Standing beside my bed he reads the questionnaire, takes my pulse, and says, "Describe your symptoms."

I tell him my story as he stares at the TV monitor on a shelf across the white room.

"Have you been under any stress, lately, Mr Simon? Anything bothering you?"

"Nothing at all, Doc. I've got the routine problems everyone has in business. But things couldn't be better."

He feels my pulse again, now quieter than before but still running a fast pizzicato.

"What did you do yesterday?"

"Had a great relaxing get-together with some of my employees. It was at the Cape. We sailed and—"

"How do you feel now?"

"Pretty good. The pain is gone."

"Take a look at the monitor over there. That's a good strong beat, no sign of a problem. You haven't had a heart attack, Mr. Simon."

I study the jagged line as it forms a regular pattern across the screen. Deep relief, a surge of joy, passes through me. So I have time after all, thank God, thank God. I can straighten things out, then I can die.

"What in hell was it, Doc?"

"I'd say you've had an anxiety attack."

"An anxiety attack! Never heard of it."

"The nurse will give you a tranquilizer. I'd suggest you have a checkup with your personal physician."

"I will, I sure will."

"Take it easy, Mr. Simon," he says as he departs.

"How, Doc?"

"Rest awhile before you leave," the nurse says as she reduces the angle of the bed. "You're just like my husband—works his head off, never lets up. He drives me crazy." She laughs. "Men. You're all alike."

"You're happy with him?"

"I wouldn't swap him for anyone."

I can see she's a solicitous, giving woman, a fine nurse.

"Then don't worry. You'll never see him in here."

When she leaves I lie alone within the curtained enclosure, an unaccustomed luxury. I ruminate over what happened in the last hour, over my terror and how damned lucky I now feel, as if I've just had a last minute reprieve. Now I have an opportunity to save everything from collapsing. Everything? What do I mean by everything?

I get dressed, call Emma, explain briefly what happened, and ask that she keep it to herself. After she takes me to my car at the airport, I return to the office. It is late afternoon when I call our family physician, who, after hearing of my episode, insists on seeing me at eight o'clock the next morning.

"Stress agrees with you," he says after the examination. "Blood pressure, electrocardiogram, lungs—everything's in fine shape, better than with most men your age. Put on your clothes and let's have a talk in my office."

"I don't need your kind of doctor," I say. "There's a psychiatrist I used to see—"

"Certainly, he's the proper man. I'm one who believes there's no separation between the psyche and soma. You know, if it weren't for the psyche, I'd be out of the soma business."

Calling the psychiatrist, I say, "It's nothing urgent. In fact I don't think it's anything I can't handle, but the thing happened so — well, I don't really get what's going on."

He gives me an appointment for a week hence. I tell Janet nothing. I can't admit weakness. If she knew what had happened she would offer immediate support. Show a glint of vulnerability, just get sick, and she becomes solicitous. But long ago, I resolved to need no one and trust no one with the secrets of my soul. I must be — I am — the BOSS.

And I haven't told Cathy. After all, I'm her king of the mountain, top man of the snow pile, second son of God.

Wally, our new technical director, is smart and imaginative, often charming, and unpredictably moody. He persists in wanting more and more responsibility in addition to his lab duties. Divesting myself of some load, I put him in charge of sales, since the lab and sales functions are compatible. In fact, all Magic's products, being custom designed, originate in the field. So as director of sales, Wally is made familiar with a customer's requirements, and as technical director he has a hand in tailoring the product accordingly. As director of sales he is also in charge of the salesmen.

"Sammy is a bone in my throat," he says after a few weeks in his new capacity.

Though I know what he means, I ask, "How so?"

"He doesn't call on the big fish or any new prospects. Says he's happy with the way things are. But I'm not."

"You've talked to him?"

"More than once."

"I see. A satisfied salesman is no longer a salesman, eh, Wally?"

"Worse, Harry. The man's dead weight, a negative force. His territory is suffering. I don't know where to go from here."

"He was good in the early days, y'know. He's grown tired. After losing Perfection Toys he never really recovered."

"I know he's been with you at least ten years and he's a relative. It's a delicate situation. What do you want me to do?"

"You're his boss. I can only say, do what you have to do."

"Can I—sack him?"

"If that's what you decide."

"He won't change. What choice do I have?"

"No choice, I suppose," I say dejectedly.

Immediately I understand why I appointed Wally sales manager, the reason behind all other reasons. I'm ducking the issue of Sammy's decline and whether to let him go.

"You won't have to do the dirty deed," I say. "I'll do it."

"You know I'm willing, Harry."

"Yes, I know. But I'll do it."

Firing Sammy is only half my problem. Telling Janet is just as difficult, for Sammy's wife is her very close and favorite cousin. And Sammy enchants Janet with his laid back ways—so different from mine. Worse yet, Sammy's daughter is getting married in a few weeks and we're invited.

As expected, Janet erupts angrily when she hears the news.

"Didn't I tell you not to hire him in the first place?" she reminds me needlessly.

"He used to be a good man," I say. "For a while he was our best. I don't regret hiring him."

"Well, you're stuck with him. How can you fire him, a man his age—almost 60? What's he going to do?"

"He's hurting the company, Janet."

"The company. It's always the company."

"I can't afford a drag on us—not now when sales are falling. Anyway, it's Wally's decision. I'm committed to back him up."

"Don't give me that. It's your decision."

"You're damn right, it's mine," I explode. "I should have done it years ago."

Of my many defects as a boss, procrastinating at firing people has been the most costly.

"My name will be shit on my side of the family," she says.

"I'm sorry about that. The decision is already made. Anyway, Abel's working out. You can bet that part of your family won't turn against us."

Thank heaven her cousin Abel's performance continues to surpass my expectations.

"Who knows when you'll tire of him too," she says.

"You needn't worry. He's being groomed for better things," I say, holding in my anger at her unfair dig.

"Don't let Sammy go until after the wedding. Don't spoil it for them."

"Sure, I can hold off for a few weeks. But no longer."

CHAPTER XIX

Year Fourteen

1980

Sales: $2,850,000 (-16.2%)
Profit: $28,000 (-30%)
Debt: $960,000 (+12.7%)
Net Worth: $6,400 (+124.6%)

In my first visit to the psychiatrist, the story I tell is as happy as a Frank Capra movie; all the characters are honorable if not exactly ideal.

"In other words, you don't have a care in the world, is that right?" the doctor says. "And everybody is your friend."

"Well, sure I have cares," I admit. "Problems come with the territory. That's the way things are in business, by definition. But nothing I can't handle."

"And at home?"

"Status quo. We get along."

"I see. Can you tell me what those territorial problems are that you're handling?"

I mention my concern over Mickey's destructive behavior in Chicago, firing Sammy and its effect on Janet, and Gilbert Samson's zany suggestions on the board.

Nothing enlightening comes of that session—to me at least, except that it gave me time to examine my feelings. I now realize how seriously Gil Samson is annoying me.

At every meeting Gil harps on our lack of an active research and development program. "You've got to have new products coming on stream," he insists. "It's the best way to increase sales, gain market share. How do you think we became a multi-billion dollar corporation at Energy Construction? Research and development did it."

"Magic isn't a multi-billion dollar corporation, Gil."

"Of course not, Harry. Neither was Energy once upon a time. But there's a lesson to be learned here."

The other board members are content to listen, but I have the impression they are on my side of the argument.

"What I mean is you can't compare the two businesses," I say. "A rich man and a poor man don't live the same way. You've been pushing this R&D thing for months. We just don't have the dough right now. R&D is an investment in the future, but the problem is NOW—it's our fucking bottom line—and money is getting scarce. Meanwhile Rob's got to be paid. So, Gil, goddamnit, let up on your R&D. We aren't a research company; we're a production company."

While listening he darkens the doodles he's been making on his scratch pad and breaks through the paper, tearing it.

"Without research you'll die, Harry."

"Yeah, and if we do it your way we'll die sooner."

Obsessed with R&D, Gil is simply blind to our immediate situation. Yet the confrontation has a benefit: I see in an instant my own blindness and the error in my strategy. How fortuitous that obstacles can force us to find new ways and renew our faith.

In my argument with Gil, I spilled out my deepest worry: the threatening deadline of that first $100,000 payment of principal due Rob next month. I know there's no way I can meet it in time. I must finally acknowledge the futility of trying to improve the bottom line by boosting sales. In fact the attempt is having the opposite effect. I'm no less ridiculous than Gilbert when he touts investment in R&D—a long-term process that drains our meager resources—to solve an immediate predicament. By investing in salesmen, I'm only pursuing another long-term process, which has in the past two years still produced few results.

And why? Ego! Just ego. I'm obsessed with repeating or surpassing Magic's peak at $4.6 million three years ago. I have not even entertained the idea of contraction, retreat. Magic must regain it's former irrepressible youth. Am I equating Magic's decline with my own—so visible suddenly in my sagging flesh and retreating hairline and the deepening furrows in my face?

By my fifth therapy session, the truth is totally revealed.

"No wonder you had an anxiety attack," the psychiatrist says. "Only one?"

"Oh, I've had more than one."

"When?"

"Mostly in the last few months. I'd ignore them and they'd go away."

"But your fear is not in the least neurotic, you realize. The problem is real. What's neurotic is your denial that there is a problem. But can't you find a solution to the real problem?"

"That's the problem. I don't have a solution."

We both laugh.

"Forgive me," he says. "Your logic is overwhelming."

"I'm that way."

"You can no longer sweep it under the rug, can you?"

"I'm not trying to."

"Good. I'm certainly no businessman, but isn't there help to be found somewhere? Have you gone to the bank?"

"The bank's the last place I'd go. If they were to find out—"

"But they are going to find out, aren't they?"

"Sure, but—"

"Delaying doesn't change a thing, does it?"

"No, I suppose it doesn't."

"You say there's not enough time anyway."

"Yeah, I've run out of time. Nothing can be done. It's too late."

"You mean you FEEL nothing can be done."

"That's right."

"Then if everything is lost what do you have to lose by going to the bank and seeing if they will help?"

"I—I—it would be an admission of failure."

"You FEEL you're going to fail."

"No, I'm really going to fail."

"Not necessarily."

"Well, it hasn't happened yet but—"

"Then you won't know until it has actually happened, or not happened. What do you think of taking control of your failure?"

"Taking control of—"

"Yes, letting it happen on your terms, so to speak."

"I see. That's an interesting idea. A very interesting idea. I see."

"Sort of a wonderful swan song should you fail."

"I see, I see. Like making a success of failure."

"Yes, you can put it that way. But you're calling the shots."

"I like that."

DRIVEN

In cutting the federal deficit, the alternatives are to increase taxes or reduce outlays, the latter being more dependable and direct. I realized after my argument with Gil that trying to increase profits by increasing sales is an erroneous strategy under Magic's prevailing time constraint. Cutting expenses is the obverse solution. This approach appeared so obvious and simplistic that at first I failed to appreciate its power, and I introduced it as if it were a child better seen than heard. Only after it was in force for a full quarter did I see that only a fraction of a sales dollar adds to profits whereas one hundred cents of every expense dollar saved goes directly to the bottom line. Blinded with pride, I wouldn't have considered such an alternative two years before. All I knew was to attack.

Sacking Sammy fits the new policy perfectly. By assigning his territory to two salesmen who cover the adjacent territories, we would eliminate his hefty salary, benefits, car and expenses. But I hesitate to eliminate him outright. Janet is right to point out the difficulties he will have being unemployed at his age. And I personally like him. (Attending his daughter's wedding is extremely awkward. I'm not good at hypocrisy.) I devise an alternative that I believe is fair and generous, perhaps ideal from his point of view.

In dread, when he calls in from the road I ask him to see me in the morning.

"Let's have a talk," I say.

"What about?" he inquires.

"Your job."

"Again?"

"That's right, Sammy. We've got more to talk about."

Asking him to close the door as he enters my office, clues him that our talk may be momentous.

"What's up, Harry," he says, sitting warily beside my desk.

"I understand Wally's unhappy with you."

He grins arrogantly as if to say, so what else is new? Sammy feels immune to disapproval because of our special relationship.

"What about you? Do you have any complaint?" he asks, his grin still fixed.

"You know what I think."

"I'm an old dog, Harry. I can't change."

"Sure, Sammy, that's too much to ask, right?"

"You can ask, but I don't hear well."

"So I've got a proposition for you."

"I don't want to hear any propositions. I go to work every day. I make the calls. I'm doing okay."

"How would you like to go on straight commission, keep all the small accounts, the ones you prefer, actually be your own boss?" I ask in my most convincing voice.

"Are you saying—d'you mean I wouldn't be on the payroll? Is that what you mean?"

"Well, that's right. But you'd be making 5 percent like all the reps. With the accounts we'd give you, your income would be cut about in half, but, of course, you're free to take on allied lines. Reps can do better than any salesman. By the same token, if you'd rather ease off, being a rep would make it feasible."

"So you'd cut my income in half and expect me to get by. After being with you for over ten years, giving up a good job and bringing in Perfection Toys, our biggest account, this is what I get?"

"Just a minute, Sammy. You were unemployed before I hired you."

"You're wrong."

"You didn't bring in the Perfection account. I turned it over to you when you came aboard."

"That isn't the way I remember it."

I marvel at how Sammy rewrites history to suit his purpose.

"No, I suppose not. It's the world according to Sammy." He studies the floor, refusing to meet my eyes. After a minute I go on. "Based on your present sales, Magic is subsidizing half your income. My proposition brings you in line with reality. And I think that's perfectly reasonable."

"I'm not interested," he says, rising from the chair.

"Think it over, Sammy, don't be hasty," I say. "It's in your interest, too, a genuine opportunity."

"I don't need you. You're a sonofabitch. You'll regret this." He walks out.

For the next hour, holing up in my office and accepting no incoming calls, I try to reckon with my guilt and deep sadness over having made an enemy of a man I'm fond of, whom I had once helped and considered a friend and tried up to the last minute to do right by.

When I call Greg, the bank vice-president, to ask for a slot of his time, he says, "Funny thing, I was going to call you today. It's time we reviewed things."

We meet in his well-appointed, mahogany paneled office on the main floor of the bank. A mild, demure man in his early forties, Greg speaks with some hesitancy, which is deceiving for he is quite sure of everything he says. Not once has he misled me. It was he who engineered the loan that enabled the company to buy out Rob Starr three years ago. We never became friends—he keeps a professional distance—yet I know he believes in me.

Greg says he isn't concerned, but he wonders what our sales might be for the year. "Could you give me a projection, Harry? Just an estimate, nothing that I'll hold you to."

Of course, having seen the quarterly statements I routinely send him, he is also aware of the dire trend that has developed.

"In other words, you're wondering whether our sales will keep dropping as they have been these past two years," I inquire, addressing the issue directly.

"As I say, I'm not concerned. You consistently manage to stay in the black, which is all that matters to us."

"Greg, I'm afraid it's not going to be a good year—maybe our worst in a long while. The industry is down and you know what's happening to interest rates. To tell the truth I don't see how we're going to make the $100,000 payment to Rob."

"Hmmm. That may be a problem. Of course, you are aware that your line of credit is fully extended. We can't do better without more collateral."

"I know that only too well."

"And if you default to Rob—"

"I'm out. He'll take over and you'll have to deal with him. Then you'll own me—house, car, wife, kids, every goddamned thing."

"We don't want that. It's a last-ditch alternative. There's no need to talk about it, Harry."

"To be blunt, were Rob to move back in, I think you can kiss Magicolor good-bye."

Having placed his faith in me, Greg's own position is on the line; he is committed to justify that confidence to both himself and his employer.

"What are your assets, Harry?"

"You're kidding. They're all collateralized to the bank. Remember? I signed the notes personally."

"You never know. Think about it. How about your home?"

"Fully mortgaged. I took out a home improvement loan for an addition last year. Nothing there."

"Anything else?"

"The house at the Cape is also mortgaged. Greg, I'm up to my neck. Most of our savings are gone since I cut my salary way back. I just don't have it."

"Are you sure? Think, hard."

"Well, there's the factory building, which I own personally after buying out Rob's share. But that's mortgaged too."

"For how much? How old is the mortgage? The building's near the interstate, right?"

He is suddenly alert, firing questions as if he's onto something. I think he's poking air.

"The mortgage? Christ, I don't remember the amount. Couple hundred thousand, I guess."

I'm embarrassed at my ignorance, but I've never given the building much thought. It's there, serves us well, and the mortgage is paid automatically every month by the bookkeeper.

"Is the mortgage assigned to us?"

"No, because the building was already heavily mortgaged to another bank when you made the loan. You never asked for it."

"What do you think the building's worth?"

"No idea."

"Well, Harry, let's find out. I'll have our appraiser up there either this afternoon or tomorrow at the latest."

I shrug, convinced that Greg is wasting his time. As I drive back to the office, I feel discouraged; default seems inevitable.

That evening about eight when I walk into the kitchen I tell Janet I'm tired and going to bed. Having no idea why I'm depressed — I won't admit that I am — she is concerned.

"You're working too hard these days," she says. "You said after you got rid of Rob, things would get easier."

"I've still got to pay him off, y'know."

"The company will do that, won't it?"

"I don't think you understand. I am the company."

"Oh, I know that. El Presidente, the big wheel."

"I'm going to bed."

Not having seen Cathy in months, I call her at home in the early morning before she leaves for work. Suddenly, mysteriously, I yearn for her.

"It must be telepathy. I was just thinking of you, Harry," she says. "I'm always thinking of you. Is it the same with you?"

It isn't but I say it is.

"Can you stay with me tonight? We'll have dinner," I ask.

"I was going shopping with my girlfriend, but—"

"No, no, that's okay. If you have something planned—"

"I'd rather be with you, Harry. You know I'd rather be with you. I miss you so very very much. Do you miss me? I want you. You don't know."

Suddenly I'm restored; my heart lightens and I'm eager for the night.

Late that afternoon right on schedule Greg is on the phone. "I've got a figure on the building, Harry. Our appraiser came up with a million dollars."

"A million— That's incredible."

"Well, it's the location. The interstate. Also every parcel in your industrial park is taken. The value of the land alone has skyrocketed."

"But we paid less than a quarter million."

"Yes, but when?"

"Ten—twelve years ago."

"You made a good investment, Harry. Tell me, how much money did you say you needed?"

"I never got that far. I didn't expect—I'm—I'm overwhelmed. Bless you."

"It's all in a day's work. Just get back to me with the amount."

Greg's voice as he gives me the news seems to sing with joy. True, our two interests coincide. But the fact remains that in this harsh world of business someone is helping. I have no doubt Greg wants me to succeed, for my sake too. And I feel both of us are enriched for it.

The irony of it. Had Rob taken up my offer to remain my partner in the building, I would have closed off the opportunity to refinance it. Certainly I can claim no credit for my good fortune. It's entirely fortuitous—as so much in business is. Nor could Rob have ever guessed what his decision not to take up my offer would cost him.

"Rob," I say over the phone, "how would you like to be paid off?"

There is a provision in our agreement, added by my lawyer, permitting prepayment, but neither Rob nor I ever took it seriously.

"It all depends. Did you find an angel someplace?"

"One just landed on our roof from money heaven." He laughs. "Let's get together, Rob. My office."

In the three years since Rob's departure, our once bitter feelings have decidedly mellowed; in fact, when we run into each other accidentally in restaurants we dine together and catch up on how the other is doing. Rob is kept abreast of Magic's status anyway from the quarterly reports I am obliged to send him. During an impromptu lunch I learn that he attempted business twice and failed. The day I call him he is home, taking time in between projects, he says, to do some sailing and golfing and traveling with his wife. I can tell from his voice that he's somewhat down.

"What's the chance of my coming back in?" he asks after he settles onto the couch in my office, his arms stretched along the back. "Then you wouldn't have to pay any principal. We could work out something."

"Forget it, Rob. It was over long ago."

He flinches. "From your financials I see things could be better."

"That's right. We've got problems. The tunnel's dark at both ends. So I'm proposing some kind of settlement."

"What's that mean?"

"Something less than the 750 G's we still owe you."

"What are you talking about? Do you expect me—? No, this is ridiculous." He starts to rise.

"Hear me out, Rob."

"How much less?"

"Like half."

"You're out of your mind." He stands, ready to leave.

"Less is better than nothing, Rob. I can tell you now we aren't going to make the principal payment due you next month." He sits again, as if struck.

"How do you figure that? One minute you've got enough to pay off half and the next—"

"Our angel's offer is conditional upon Magic buying ALL your stock."

It's a lie, of course. Were he to know that our source of funds is the bank, I would lose my bargaining advantage. He must believe that I'm under an investor's stringent constraints. Moreover, where I secure the funds is none of his business.

"That's too bad. You and I have an agreement. I'll just stick with it."

"You want me to default?"

"I sure as hell do."

"You'd like to take over? Is that it?"

"Exactly right. In a minute."

"Let me warn you, I'll see to it that you inherit a fucking shell. I'll strip Magic of every fixed asset, every goddamned gear, every paper clip, every plastic pellet, before you can set foot in the foyer."

"In a couple of weeks? You don't have the time."

"Apparently you've forgotten. The agreement provides for a three-month grace period, which permits me to cure a default before you can move in."

"You wouldn't—"

"Try me, Rob. You're not going to reap the benefit of my years of struggle on the cheap. Just try me. I'll bring the roof down on our heads."

My fury is bursting. He is in visible turmoil.

"I can tell you I won't go for half," he says.

Pouncing, I say, "It's obvious Magic is not generating the earnings to pay you off. To make matters worse, a recession's starting. I'm offering cold cash. These days you can earn fifteen, sixteen percent just in CD's. What am I paying you, a lousy eight percent? I don't think my offer is such a bad—"

"Okay, Harry. Let's split the difference."

"Huh?"

"We're $375,000 apart. Let's split the difference; I'll settle for $562,500."

"Five hundred thou."

"No, $562,500."

I sigh, feigning resignation. "Alright, Rob. It's a deal, it's done."

As I extend my hand to shake on it, he stands abruptly, turns to the door, and walks out saying, "I hope you sink."

Oh, what heavenly retribution this is. It is of the first rank. Never have I forgotten Rob's refusal to provide me some relief after I informed him that Francis, taking the most talented of my staff and workers with him, was starting his own business. Never have I forgotten his words: "Tough shit." Now in so many words I have retaliated and I feel I have just lit up the night.

By uncanny coincidence, 1980, the very year Magic reached bottom, in which, discouraged, I had thrown away all hope and left our fate to entropy, that very year we went from negative to positive net worth. How often it is that when life seems at its worst, the forces of recovery are already working.

Hadn't a similar result occurred many years ago when I had negotiated to buy out Cal with my last dollar despite Magic's grim promise? That year too, Magic surprised me and turned the corner. All current events, seemingly so spontaneous, are invisibly cast by events that have occurred long before. Freed of the merciless debt to Rob, I steered Magicolor into a new era during which things happened that I couldn't have imagined.

CHAPTER XX

Year Fifteen

1981

Sales: $3,100,000 (+8.8%)
Profit: $44,000 (+5.7%)
Debt: $1,000,000 (+4.2%)
Net Worth $50,000 (+681%)

The $750,000 debt that formerly had to be paid off in three years is now reduced to $562,500, payable over twenty years—an easy commitment for Magic to meet. With a broad margin for error in place, I grow more daring and innovative.

During our morning meetings I ask everyone to indulge in "blue sky" thinking. "No matter how ridiculous an idea might seem, let's bounce it around. Let's be free, like shameless kids again. Since we'll all be equally as crazy, no one should hold back."

We are all disgusted with the way Mickey is running Chicago. "Get rid of him," most say, "and replace him with one of our own."

Of course, why hadn't that dawned on me long ago? Such a simple concept: to use management people who are already steeped in the company's style and philosophy, who are already part of our family, rather than bring in outsiders. Phil proposes giving Dave, his best foreman, a chance at running Chicago, starting him off with not only a good salary but also 10 percent of the annual pre-tax profits of the operation. No one has to twist Dave's arm to make him accept.

The very first month Dave takes over, conditions dramatically improve. He discovers that Mickey had been on the take, paid off by several vendors and truckers. And he had threatened his workers jestingly with a handgun which he kept in his desk, causing them to fear him. He had thought himself still the cop.

After fifteen years of being in business, I am still slow to recognize evil. Perhaps it's a refusal to acknowledge such a human capability. Or perhaps I suspect and must deny a destructive and hateful bent in myself.

From our meetings, we develop what proves to be the granddaddy idea of all: an incentive system. Not that the principle is new. But the way we implement it is original and makes the difference between mediocre success and triumph.

"What do people really want from a job?" someone rhetorically asks.

The answers:

"Money."

"A sense of participation. A say in what we do."

"Instant gratification."

"A challenge."

"Recognition."

"Security."

"Right," I say. "All these. Now why can't we come up with a system that satisfies everyone?"

"That's a lot to ask, isn't it, Harry?"

"Yup. A lot to ask."

Phil, the production manager, goes right to work and devises a highly effective system.

Magic's manufacturing process is currently made up of sequential steps performed by individual workers. Essentially they are blending various materials together—both solid and liquid, under heat and pressure—which when fully mixed form a specific finished coloring product. Phil proposes that those workers who depend on each other in performing their respective tasks compose a team, even across shifts.

The team's productivity standard will be based on the historic norm. At the end of each month, a bonus, derived from a formula in which a quantity produced in excess of the standard is the governing factor, will be distributed equally among the interdependent members of a team. Only in the event of a technological change—say, the installation of new equipment—can that standard be altered.

Before being installed, the incentive system is explained in detail during a series of companywide meetings in which objections and suggestions are sought. I tell everyone that if the incentive system does not work to the satisfaction of most after three months, it will be either revised or dropped. "If it works and you are pleased with it, and I'd like to predict you will be, I ask that we keep it to ourselves. Don't broadcast what we're doing."

I suspect we will be surprised at its success. It will be our secret weapon. We have invented an incentive system that can restore our profitability to its former 5 percent level of six years ago when we peaked. I have no wish to share it with our competitors. It is ours, born of our tiny culture.

The good results I anticipated were tame compared with those that actually occurred. All the motivating factors we had established as goals at our meeting were achieved. And the beneficial fallout spread in startling directions. Again, my imagination fell short of reality. Life is so marvelously, tantalizingly humbling.

Life tastes sour sometimes, too. Sammy gets his vengeance. He goes on the road for Francis's company, which is rather ironical because he hated Francis, hated him for his superior airs and his heedless ambition. But I have to smile, for Francis has taken on a loser, a man who has given up the challenge and is content to coast into retirement. It seems Francis will automatically hire anyone who has quit or been fired from Magic, as if having a common enemy is qualification enough.

Emma is as saddened by Sammy's bitterness as I am, since she and Sammy and their spouses were old friends. In fact I had met Emma through Sammy and hired her in the early days as receptionist and typist on his recommendation. Now Sammy and his wife expect Emma, our well-paid office manager and now member of the board, to quit Magic as an act of loyalty to them. To her chagrin, when she doesn't they stop speaking to her and refuse to return the phone messages she leaves at their home.

Having so many former hostile employees out in the world, I am dubbed the king of bastards, and all in my kingdom are surely citizen bastards.

From out of nowhere an opportunity for revenge drops by in the person of Earle, the color-matching genius, our former Indian lab technician, whom I have not seen since he joined Francis three years ago.

"I've quit them," he says, "and I'm suing Francis and Gary and their company for a million bucks."

Though happy to hear such elevating news, I'm skeptical. Earle, I recall, frequently felt indignant and sued organizations and employers, often to no effect.

"On what grounds, Earle?"

"Discrimination. Not honoring an agreement. They reneged on their promise to pay for my vacation in the islands. And by now I was supposed to be in charge of the lab but Edgar still is. And they refused my demand for a 25 percent salary increase, which I deserve because it's obvious I was holding their lab together. They won't get away with it, Mr. Simon. I'll win."

"As I recall, you sued the outfit you worked for before you joined us—and you won that one. But didn't you lose against the country club, and wasn't there another—the private school?"

He grimaces and waves my question away.

"Mr. Simon, you have good reason to help me in my complaint."

"How so?"

"Francis and Gary, they really shafted you."

"That's not new, Earle. I got what I wanted from the injunction."

"Shutting us down. That hurt," he says. Then with a leer he adds, "I'm not talking about the shit they spread around about Magic. I'm talking about what Francis and Gary did to you."

"Oh, that's ancient history."

"But you don't know the things they did."

"Like what?"

"Francis copied all your formulas and prices before he quit. He stole your customer list and went into your payroll register and found out everyone's pay."

"Really? I figured as much."

"I'm willing to testify. I was there. I saw him do it."

Feeling fresh outrage, I'm tempted to join his cause. But it is old stuff, sins forgotten and best left that way. Involving myself with Earle will only distract me from enjoying Magic's entrance into a new era. Francis and Gary are no threat to me now; in fact I expect the situation is quite the reverse.

"I'm not interested, Earle. I'd rather spend my time concentrating on Magic."

"Uh huh. Well, if you don't care about justice, if you change your mind—"

"Sure thing, Earle."

"They got their problems, y'know."

"Who doesn't?"

"Did you hear that all the formulations disappeared from their lab?"

"What? My God."

An uncontrolled giggle slips out of me. To reconstruct lost formulations would take months. Meanwhile, because they could not deliver on time, they could lose, at least for a while, a substantial portion of their sales.

"Just disappeared? How in the world did that happen?"

"I wouldn't know," he says, assuming a beatific expression.

Earle is the perfect surrogate for expressing my unvented vengeance. But his methods are far more daring and vindictive than any I could conceive.

Though I rise from my chair, signaling him to leave, he remains planted in his.

"I'm a damn good color technician, don't you think, Mr. Simon?"

"I'd say one of the best, Earle."

"Well, do you—maybe—I mean, would you have a place for me?"

"I'm afraid not. We're pretty well staffed." And to drive home a point, I add, "We don't have much turnover. Our people stick with us."

DRIVEN

No doubt he has an extraordinary eye for color, possibly better than anyone presently employed at Magic. Yet I feel lucky that he left us before he had a chance to find some fault and sue us. Francis and Gary deserve him. Let their mistake be my lesson.

"Yeah, I hear no one wants to leave Magic. Gary approached a few of your boys; they wouldn't even talk to him."

"I'm not surprised," I say smugly.

His head bowed, he finally stands.

"Look, Earle, I know someone in the vinyl compounding business who's looking for a colorist. I'll call him for you."

A few months after Earle and I talked, Edgar, our former technical director and Earle's former boss at Fran's place, shows up at my office. He too is looking for his old job back. He has been fired for reasons he "prefers not to discuss at this time." Like Earle, he too is bitter. Qualified though he is, when politely I refuse to reemploy him, he suggests an alliance.

"Fran and Gary are bastards," he says. "You were well rid of them when they left Magic."

"It seems so long ago," I say. "I don't worry about them. I don't think about them. I don't care about them."

"Right. You don't have to, Harry. If I can be of any help—if you need any of their formulations, prices, that sort of thing—"

"We're doing okay."

"Right, Harry. But if you're ever in a tight competitive situation, let me know. I might be able to give you an advantage."

"Thanks," I say, rising abruptly. I lead him out and pray that I've seen the last of him.

Is it possible when Fran and Gary raided Magic a few years ago, they also inadvertently purged us of our secret undesirables? There exists an underlying unspoken morality within every company. Do only those employees who are comfortable stay, while others, whose personal principles or lack of them silently clash with the company's, finally leave or are fired?

Is there not also a certain justice that has nothing to do with morality but rather with the price we must pay for every advantage? Earle and Edgar expected a free ride from Fran and Gary, who they thought would give them more than their talents justified. They were programmed to delude themselves into believing that Fran's outlandish generosity was realistic and genuine.

Steve Bluestone further strengthens these speculations when he visits my office asking for a job. He had been my boss in a family-owned company during the early years of my marriage. I was to have been his production control manager, except that he never got around to delegating the responsibility to me. Now in his mid-fifties, tall and distinguished looking, his hair graying attractively, he sports a custom-made suit. From his demeanor one would never suspect that he isn't still head of the company he inherited from his father, a company he ruined by expanding over-ambitiously in a market that was under attack from foreign firms who could produce more cheaply.

"I hear you're doing well, Harry," he says.

"We're surviving," I say.

"But you can always do better, eh? There's always room for improvement."

"If that's what you're looking for," I say, suspecting he's leading up to something.

"And the best way to do better is to bring in a fresh slant from the outside. With my extensive management experience and expertise, I can offer you that. Of course, you know more than most what I can do."

It comes back to me—his vast ego, his arrogance, his insolence toward vendors, toward his workers. I remember his father, Steve's model, a demanding prototype of arrogance: The day his net worth reached a million dollars, when making a million was a rare achievement, he cruised through his plant bragging of his success to his workers. He handed his spoiled and wild son power and authority without making him earn it.

One incident I'll never forget: A room in the plant was engulfed in flames and a worker lay writhing on the floor. Steve gave me hell for calling the fire department because his insurance rate would rise.

"We're pretty well set, Steve," I say with finality. "A recession's on, interest rates are going crazy. The fact is we're cutting back."

"Those are tough problems. No doubt about it. But, Harry, they can be beat. And I can show you how." He takes a hard swallow. "I don't have to tell you, do I? We were a team. You know my experience. You know what I can do."

Steve, like Sammy, rewrites history.

"Tell me, Steve, how did it feel—the business falling into your lap when your Dad died, then in less than five years the whole thing going down the drain?"

This is hardly the response he intended from me.

"Some things are beyond a man's control," he says categorically.

"You mean like a recession and rising interest rates?"

"It's okay, Harry. I get you. I understand your situation. Here's my card. When the going gets real rough, call me. I'm an expert on bad luck. I've learned a lot. And you know, based on our old friendship, I'd give you my very best."

His card reads:

> Steven Bluestone Associates
> Business Consultants
> Mergers, Acquisitions, Systems Analysis
> Bankruptcy Specialists

"You canned me. Don't you remember, Steve?"

"Oh, no, Harry. Not me. It was my father. He figured you were too smart for us. You'd learn the business and—well, you'd go out on your own."

"That may be, but you weren't worried, were you?"

"Actually, I wasn't. You were a dreamer. You said you wanted to write."

"The truth is I was a zero because I was an outsider. You had cousins, a brother-in-law aboard, a son ready to come in. Anyone not a member of the family didn't stand a chance to get ahead. Isn't that right?"

"I suppose—well, can you blame us? Blood's thicker than water. It was nothing personal."

"This is nothing personal either," I say as I reach out my hand to dismiss him. "We don't need your help."

Beginning at the top, Steve was deprived of the opportunity to struggle, to court disaster, to know humility so that when he experienced his first serious reversal he was too smug to acknowledge its consequences. Now he is battle trained, but too late. He has a reputation for failure. There's no guarantee he's learned his lesson; I'm not about to take a chance to find out. Anyway, what service could he render me?

Abel, our newest star quality salesman, assumes the territory that Sammy had covered: Massachusetts, Connecticut, and Long Island. The customers easily take to his informal and charming blend of studied innocence.

DRIVEN

He is everyone's precocious son. With many he forms a weekend relationship, inviting them to spend a Saturday or Sunday to play golf at his father's exclusive country club. Gil, Abel's father and one of our dedicated directors, enjoys contact with our accounts, which allows him to feel closer to the action than the other directors. I sense a deeper interest in Magic than is appropriate. I'm not sure whether to be pleased or to worry.

After being on the road for a year, Abel reveals that he's dissatisfied. We are having one of our many soul-piercing talks in the dark corner of a quiet local bar. Thinking he should be making more money, he resents Wally, his direct boss, who has given him no satisfaction.

"You're compensated just like all the other salesmen," I point out. "Everyone is treated alike. Wally's going by the rules."

"I've seen their paychecks, Harry. They make double what I make."

"Sure. But they've built up a following. It's taken them years. When they started out they were worse off than you—they were on straight commission. At least you have a base salary in addition to a commission. Be patient, Abel. The way you're going, you'll get there. Remember, I told you at the beginning it will take five years to make it big and after that there's no limit."

"Actually it's not me. I'm under certain pressure. They think I'm worth more than I'm getting."

"You say 'they'. Who do you mean?"

Taking a gulp of beer, he hesitates momentarily.

"I'd rather not—the family."

"I'd be very happy to explain the situation—"

"To tell the truth, my father."

"Gil says that?"

"Please, Harry, don't say anything."

"No, no. Of course not."

But I'm steaming that Gil is interfering in what is none of his business.

"When I worked for my father's corporation I was earning $78,000 a year, so you see I've had quite a comedown."

"What did you do for all that money?"

"Nothing. Absolutely nothing. I was bored sick."

He seemed almost ashamed, remorseful.

"And you quit?"

His employment application had been vague about his separation from the corporation, and because he was related to my wife no attempt was made to check him out.

Abel takes another gulp of beer and wipes his lips with the back of his hand.

"They let me go during a companywide austerity program."

Is that a polite way of saying he was discovered as deadwood?

"Look, son, give yourself time. You've got the stuff, and so far you're doing fine. Eventually you'll reach $78,000, and more. I've got ideas, plans— You never know how far you'll go with me."

He doesn't react. I seem to be flying past him. Having said too much too soon, I go back on tack.

"Keep in mind how good it feels to know that you've earned every buck you've made. To know no one handed it to you. You can always hold your head high, be your own man."

"I guess you're right."

"Don't let anyone tell you it's easy. Work for it. Earn it. Do it yourself. It'll give you a sense of self-worth."

We embrace and I pat his shoulder.

"Anytime you want to talk, kid, let me know. I'm for you one hundred percent."

"Thanks, Harry, thanks for talking to me."

DRIVEN

Privately I review the counts against him. Gil paid for renovating the house that Abel and his wife have just bought; Abel inherited his father's year-old Lincoln; Gil gifted Abel a membership in his exclusive country club. The young man hardly stands a chance.

Wally soon comes to me complaining that Abel has persistently refused to visit the Long Island territory for the past three months on the excuse that he must stay close to home due to his wife's pregnancy. Abel is adamant that any overnight stays are out of the question. Of course, Wally must enforce our policy mandating a three-week call frequency for all accounts.

"If he weren't your wife's cousin, I'd tell him either do what I say or get out. Harry, your relatives keep making things damned awkward for me. It makes it tough."

I concur, beginning to see that I've blundered. The whole matter is a distasteful and unnecessary complication.

"Let me talk to him," I say.

I discuss the issue with Abel over the phone. Perhaps "discuss" is too mild a term.

"How far along is she?" I ask.

"Four months," he replies.

"Hell, Abel, what are you worried about? You can make at least four visits to the Island before she's a month from term."

"Well, she'd feel better if I stayed near home, just in case something happened."

"Why? Is she having a special problem?"

"No."

"Then I don't get it. Can't you keep in touch with her by phone from the Island and if she needs you, drive home—it's only five hours—or hop a plane if you have to?"

"I'd rather stick around. That's the way it is. The Island will have to wait until after our child is born."

"You mean the company, which is hemorrhaging and in weak condition and needs sales, doesn't matter to you?"

"Take it easy, Harry. Sure it does. But my wife and newborn kid come first. What do you expect?"

Though my question and his reply are rhetorically sound, both exaggerate our real situations. The company will not suffer greatly if he delays visiting the Island. His wife will not be in jeopardy if he does. Nevertheless, I conclude that he is willing to sacrifice his career to his wife's unreasonable demands.

"Listen, Abel. Either you go to the Island by next week or I'll instruct Wally to turn over that part of your territory to someone else. We can't afford to neglect those customers any longer."

The receiver, as I await his reply, reverts to a dial tone.

Gil calls me at home that evening.

"Abel tells me you're threatening to cut his territory," he says in a tight voice, omitting his usual introductory small talk.

I feel a pang of disappointment that Abel, like a hurt child, seems to have appealed to his father to pressure me rather than deal with the conflict directly.

"Gil, I'd rather not discuss it. I'm sorry. This matter is between Abel and Magic and doesn't concern you."

"Hell, it doesn't. He's my son. And I think you're being completely heartless. Where's your humanity, man? You've had kids. Have you forgotten what it was like the day they were born? Where were you then? Off calling on customers? Hell you were."

I'm startled at his intensity.

"As I say, Gil, this is an employee matter. We're not a kindergarten. We aren't in the habit of settling an employee's complaints with the parents. So I have nothing to say to you."

"Then you won't budge?"

"It's a closed subject between us. If your son wants to talk to me, he knows my office door is open."

"Goddamn you," Gil says as he hangs up.

Gil fails to appear at the next directors' meeting. In a way I'm relieved, now that I no longer have to listen to his constant harping on the R&D issue. I try to reach him by phone but he doesn't return my calls. Finally I write him, requesting that he resign his directorship. He responds, from an obvious need to express himself, with a phone call.

"I used to think you were something terrific, Harry. Now I know what you really are. You couldn't tell me man to man that you wanted me out, so you had to take the cowardly way and write. I'm very disappointed, very disappointed."

"I'm sorry that's how you feel," I say. "I'm sorry this has happened. I guess there's nothing more to be said."

Janet is disturbed by all this, of course. Now that the last vestige of goodwill is eradicated, she knows her name is bound to be shit throughout her side of the family. To her credit she withholds judgment and hesitates to condemn either Gil or me though I would welcome her automatic support. I do regret that, as she feared, my actions in defending the business have complicated her personal life.

Abel's weekly reports show that he has resumed his visits to Long Island, as Wally demanded. However, by accident, I discover that every word of Abel's reports are phony. I sit behind my desk trying to sort out my disillusionment and decide how best to deal with Abel when the phone rings.

"Why are you avoiding me?" Cathy demands.

"Cathy, I can't talk now."

"Is there someone else? Tell me the truth."

"Don't be foolish. You're enough for me. Look, I'm busy, I can't—"

"Harry, I can't go on. It's not worth it."

"I'll call you back."

"I want to end it all. My life's worthless."

"Don't be ridiculous."

"No one loves me. You don't love me. What's the use?"

"I do love you. Your kids love you. You have every reason to want to live, every reason."

"I feel so—so unwanted."

"Look, Cathy, I'll see you tonight. How would you like that?"

"Oh, would you, Harry? Would you stay with me?"

"Sure, sure, but I've got to hang up now."

"I love you, Harry. You can't imagine how much I love you. I couldn't go on if you didn't love me."

CHAPTER XXI

Year Sixteen

1982

Sales: $3,300,000 (+6.5%)
Profit: $114,000 (+159%)
Debt: $791,000 (-21%)
Net Worth: $50,000 (+228%)

I discover that Abel's weekly reports are phony as I spot-check bills from vendors as part of my self-assigned oversight function. Normally Emma approves them and one other office person checks her before they are paid. Having just changed over our telephone service to a new provider, I'm curious and review the first month's bill. There I discover a baffling series of anomalous charges against Abel's company credit card. Some calls originate from his home during midmorning and midafternoon, when he would have been on the road; others are from Newport, where we have no customers; and several are made to Florida, Arizona, and Hawaii, far from his territory.

In comparing Abel's itinerary listed in his weekly call reports with locations listed on the phone bill, it is obvious that the reports are calculated deceptions. I'm demoralized at having been so taken in. I cling to a faint hope that I'm mistaken. I must give him a chance to explain.

When Abel calls in from the road, I ask to see him the next morning. Saying that he is far from home and intends to stay overnight, he wishes to delay. No, I say, it's urgent that I see him. He becomes flustered. Apparently my sense of urgency tips him off that something is up and he wants to know more. I tell him that I'd rather not discuss it over the phone. I enjoy the thought that I may be causing him to stew over any number of imagined possibilities.

"When did your disillusionment start?" I ask early the next morning when he breezes into my office and slouches on the chair beside my desk.

Abel understands my question precisely, the implication being that his claim of devotion to the values we had discussed, his concern for the company's welfare, and his taking me into his confidence on personal matters were all pretense, designed to sucker me in. With sneaky casualness he glances at the phone bill and the small stack of call reports lying on my desk. Evading my eyes, he looks off into space as he speaks.

"A long time ago," he says, curling his lip insolently.

Again he glances at the papers on my desk. I toss them toward him; he tosses them back instantly, ignoring their content.

"Can you explain them?" I demand.

"You can't fire me. I quit."

"Too late," I say as I reach into my desk drawer and retrieve his paycheck. "You're already fired."

He stands up to leave.

"Wait a minute," I say. "Sit down. I'd like to know why you've done this?"

He remains standing. "At the beginning I was the best, most enthusiastic man you ever had."

"Yes, I know that. At least I thought so. What happened?"

"I realized there was no future with you."

I gasp. "You couldn't have been more wrong. Why, I had plans—"

"Nothing like my plans—our plans—you can bet."

"What?"

"Gil says the way you're going you'll never turn this company around. If you'd listen to him, you could do it just like that." He snaps his fingers. "But you know it all. And you think small, which is all you'll ever be." Astonished, I stay silent. He goes on. "In fact, we considered making an offer for Magic; we'd show you how it should be run."

"You mean Gil and you?"

"Right."

"How far back have you had these ideas?"

"A long time."

"A month, six months, a year?"

"Soon after joining the board, Gil saw that everything you were doing was wrong."

"Such as?"

"You were killing Magic's unrealized potential."

As if observing a photo slowly developing before me, I begin to see more and more clearly that Gil's role as a director was entirely self-serving and that he envisioned eventually taking over Magic for himself and his son. Now I understand the motive behind his involvement with our customers. Now I understand why he entertained Janet and me at his ski lodge, his Washington town house, and his seaside cottage. But when he saw I would brook no interference from him in dealing with his son, he knew I was beyond manipulation.

After I dismissed his father as director, Abel knew that their grandiose plans would never be realized. The scheme was the reason behind his staying so long—more than two years—suffering through our intense training program, which included hard physical work in the plant and the lab. Quite plainly, Abel no longer cared.

Before he departs, Abel makes a tour of the plant, lab, and office, shaking hands and saying good-bye. Meanwhile I advise Wally of Abel's dismissal and ask Emma to immediately terminate all his benefits, secure the keys to the company car, and arrange for someone to drive him home thirty miles away. Upon hearing this, Abel storms into my office. He needs the car, he says, and refuses to part with the keys.

"And you're not getting them until I'm good and ready."

"The car is not yours to use," I say. "You are no longer an employee here."

He gives me the finger.

My anger rising, I shout, "You goddamned thief, you dishonorable bastard, give me those keys."

He turns and rushes from my office, through the outer office and into the foyer, where, in pursuit, I catch up with him. Grabbing his arm I swing him around. At that moment my rage reaches an intensity I have never experienced before; with a fist so tight it is white, I strike a blow to his breastbone, stunning us both momentarily.

"Okay, Okay. You've done it. Good. I'll sue you for assault, I'll sue you," he screams and dashes out the door.

I shout after him, "If you take that car, I'll call the state police and report it as stolen—I'm warning you."

As I pass back through the main office to mine, I find most of the staff distraught and confused from the drama. I assure one crying woman who is seated at her desk that it's over. Sitting in my office, I am trembling and my heart pounds and I try to fathom my violence.

Abel's disloyalty has shocked me to the core. Beyond growing fond of him and believing in him, I had in a way adopted him as my own and felt protective and parental. I saw him as the means of extending into the future what I had built after my own powers would wane. His seeming development and growth had given me satisfaction and joy. Now I feel betrayed, manipulated, and used. Abel has trampled my loyalty and my best intentions into dust. In their place I now have only hurt and a desire for revenge. I have caught the disease of his evil; hate begets hate.

Heeding my threat, Abel allows himself to be driven home. A few days later he calls Emma to plead with her to keep his health insurance in effect in view of his wife's pregnancy. After Emma appeals to me on his behalf, I reluctantly agree to maintain the medical coverage until after the birth of his child.

Janet's reaction to firing Abel surprises me. She is one hundred percent supportive. Weeks later she has lunch with Abel's mother, who admits that Abel, her eldest son, is spoiled and unmanageable.

"He is his father's son, not mine," she says. "Still, as his mother I feel bound to take his side. Your husband swore at him and struck him."

Janet denies that is what happened. Harry is a mild person, she says, and hints that Abel lacks principles.

But the two women rise above the event and arrive at an unspoken compact to remain friends. Both have men who leave much to be desired.

"Did you strike him?" Janet asks as soon as I walk into the kitchen that evening.

"Yes, I'm afraid I did," I say. "But not hard. I lost control; I don't know what in hell happened to me."

"He had it coming," she says. "I told her the truth about her son. But I wish you had never hired him. Let this be a lesson. No relatives ever again."

"Right," I say and leave the room.

Even though last year showed an 8.8 percent increase in sales over the previous year, and this year 6.5 percent over last year, in dollar terms we are actually losing ground due to inflation. In other words we are selling fewer units. A column headline in the *Journal of Commerce* reads "Plastics Hit By Slump." We are following the industry pattern.

To make matters worse, interest rates have also been escalating to unprecedented heights, ultimately reaching 21.5 percent. The cost of servicing our enormous debt is seriously draining off profits. The year before Rob departed, our interest expense amounted to $34,000—barely 0.9% of sales. The following year our interest expense climbed to $73,000, a still manageable 1.8 percent of sales. But three years later our interest expense had risen to $95,000, 2.8 percent of sales, more than twice our profit for that year. The year before last our interest expense reached 3.3 percent of sales while our bottom line figure fell virtually to break even. The interest expense is like a leech sucking away our lifeblood and dashing my hope for the future.

Finally after years of accepting conditions beyond my control, I appeal to Greg at the bank for relief.

"There's nothing I can do," he says apologetically. His large brown eyes widen, signifying futility. "Our rate is firm; it's bank policy. Anyway, it's not us, it's the Fed."

"You're forcing me to shop around, Greg. I don't want to do that."

"Go ahead. I think you'll find we're competitive," he says confidently.

"I don't mean just locally," I say. "There's out of state—Boston, New York."

He shrugs. "I know. Try. Best of luck."

In a few weeks, after interviewing a half dozen banks, I strike gold. An aggressive small bank in Hartford, whose loan officer and president meet with me, offers to fund our debt at a rate several percentage points below prime and with conditions more favorable than our current ones. Under their note, no longer would insurance on my life or a compensating checking account balance be required. Nor would we have to put up our receivables as collateral. But I delay committing myself, frankly explaining that I feel obligated to offer our present bank one last chance. They say, all smiles, they understand.

Without revealing all the specifics, I visit Greg at his office, inform him that I've found a better deal, and offer him a last opportunity to revise his terms.

"You said you were competitive," I say. "But you aren't. Now, I ask, are you willing to be?"

"Below prime, you say. We can't possibly match it," he replies coldly and shifts in his chair.

"Then I have no choice but to walk away, Greg. Do you understand?"

"Yes, I know your position; I'm sorry we have to lose you, really sorry, but my hands are tied."

"I appreciate all you've done, Greg, especially the confidence you placed in me at the buyout—sticking your neck out the way you did—and later helping me find a way to pay off Rob. I'll never forget it."

His eyes grow moist and with his voice thickening he says, "You've given me one of the few joys I've had in this job." He places his delicate hand on my shoulder. "I feel I've helped contribute some small part to your success. You and your people have worked hard and you're all decent. Harry, you've proven me right."

For more than ten years, until he made that small speech, he had always kept his distance, always been businesslike and stiff and proper. We embrace freely, an uncommon sight in the bank, and say good-bye.

Magic's profit this year is the second highest in its history to date. Contributing to it is a $26,000 reduction in interest expense as a result of the improved terms given by our new bank.

Our good-byes the day Greg and I parted are not the final ones. He calls a few weeks later.

"I've been asked to offer you a better situation, Harry, if you're interested."

"Why in hell didn't you come through when I asked for it?" I say. "Damnit, Greg."

"I argued for you, but it was no use. Now the committee is rethinking its strategy. Seems like you're not the only customer we've lost."

"It's too late, Greg. You know I can't flip from one bank to the other. I'm sorry."

"It's okay, Harry. I just thought I'd sound you out. See whether you got what you wanted. I understand. So good-bye, good-bye again."

Despite only small increases in sales, profits are booming. Last year was a turning point in Magic's history. Last year the bottom line had not increased significantly in real terms. This year it surges 159 percent. Is it only an aberration?

I don't think so. Owing to the stupendous impact of Phil's ingenius incentive system, I believe our gain is solid and lasting. The bonus given to every employee every month, amounting to several hundred dollars per person—about a month's rent—is having an electric effect on morale and productivity. In the first quarter of the plan, production has increased 15 percent, double what Phil had forecast.

"What it means is, our workers have been screwing off for years," Phil says at our daily meeting.

"And why not?" I say. "Why should they have done better? What incentive did they have? Everyone got the same pay whether they were good or mediocre."

The incentive is so designed that the monetary gain resulting from increased productivity is split 50-50 between the employees and the company. Not only does Magic receive its equivalent share, we are finding that the improvement in productivity is being accomplished with fewer workers. To the amazement of our "brain trust," the superior workers are pressuring the poorer workers on their team to produce more. In effect the workers are now supervising themselves so that our foremen have become redundant. Even more surprising, they have no objection to "going on the bench" since under the incentive system they can now earn more there than as salaried supervisors.

Due to the social pressure, the slackers, formerly carried by their brethren, are quitting. Those staying with us ask that we not hire replacements and assure management that they can get along just as well with fewer numbers. Since the bonus is split among the members of a team, the fewer the members, the more money each one receives.

In the frenzy to improve productivity, we recognize the danger that quality might be sacrificed. To make sure that this does not happen, Phil proposes a negative incentive which stipulates that the cost of replacing or repairing any defective product shipped from our plant and later returned by the customer be deducted from the incentive bonus earned by the team responsible. The result: our quality level, already high compared to that of our competitors, now borders on perfection. We simply have no more complaints.

Magic is experiencing a phenomenal revolution. Phil is our company hero. We have employed a simple but powerful idea: offer the opportunity for increased reward and recognition for work done well. Like a mantra, I repeat, "For every sales dollar made, only a percentage goes to the bottom line. For every operating dollar saved, one hundred cents goes to the bottom line." At our meeting at the end of each month we indulge in mutual praise as we observe the production rates increase 18 percent then 20 percent and finally 22 percent where they hold steady.

How can we not be satisfied? Twenty-two percent. It's beyond anything anticipated. Then at one of our daily meetings, the production worker chosen to represent the workers astonishes us by saying: "Actually we can still do a lot better."

"Better than 22%? I find that hard to believe," Phil says, and we all nod our heads in agreement.

"It's up to you," says the production worker.

"I don't get it," I say. "If you can do better and make more money, why don't you?"

"Because, Mr. Simon," the worker explains, "we're afraid you'll change the standard rates—the figures you base the incentive on."

Of course, their suspicion is perfectly realistic. As most piecework laborers know, were they to produce at a faster rate, they can be sure that management will reduce the piece rate in order to limit the worker's income. After all, the principle underlying most American business is greed, not sharing. My ex-partner Rob was definitely in the mainstream.

I write the following memo:

To: All Personnel
From: Harry Simon
Subject: Incentive System Standards

I, Harry Simon, guarantee that while I am president of Magicolor, the standards presently established to compute your incentive will remain in effect indefinitely. However they may be changed when a machine or a process is modified. In that event a new standard will be negotiated between the team concerned and management to their mutual satisfaction.

Immediately I call a brief company meeting at the end of the day. I read my memo and assure everyone of management's sincere intention to share the spoils. The memo is posted on the bulletin board. Now it's a matter of time to see what happens.

The results that follow surpass by an incredible margin those of the past. In the quarter after the announcement, productivity increases to 50 percent above our historic standards. Over the next six months the number of employees drops from seventy-five to fifty-two, this while production is improving. The superior workers, pressuring the slackers to perform, force those that don't shape up to leave. They ask that replacements not be hired so that each team member can receive a larger share of the incentive bonus. By year's end, eight months after the announcement, we are down to thirty-five, with unit volume exceeding that produced by the seventy-five. Magic and its employees are on the road to unimagined riches.

At my urging, Phil devises a method for awarding a bonus to management that is not, as would be typical, based on bottom line results, because the bottom line can be subject to arbitrary distortions, such as one-time charge-offs. Rather I ask that he tie the bonus to specific performance with respect to those factors over which the management employee has control and which ultimately affect the bottom line; for instance, maintaining a tight inventory, seeking the lowest price for raw materials, reducing the length of time customers take to pay us, or minimizing overtime. By determining a historic standard for all cost factors, just as he did in production, Phil develops a formula to compute a bonus for each member of management—except the president.

Now all of Magic, including the lab, operates under a system of reward for superior performance. Every person remaining among us is motivated. Our revolution is over. A marvelous renaissance is in progress and it is sheer joy to be in business.

But Phil, sadly, seems unable to bear the success he has so brilliantly earned and brought to us.

CHAPTER XXII

Year Seventeen

1983

Sales: $3,400,000 (+3%)
Profit: $159,000 (+39.5%)
Debt: $626,000 (-21%)
Net Worth: $315,000 (+92%)

Julius, our trusted accountant, is impressed with the progress exhibited by our financial statements. They, of course, only symbolically represent Magic's performance; they don't tell much about the how or why. Julius is fascinated to learn what real life activities have made such dramatic results possible.

"How do you account for such enormous increases in profit and net worth after only small sales gains?" he asks. "You're doing something right. What is it?"

"An orange can't give more juice than it contains," I tell Julius. "In the compressed market of a recession every competitor is hard put and fighting with equal determination for fewer sales opportunities. So I reduced our sales staff."

"I don't see the logic. It sounds risky—just what you shouldn't do, if you don't mind my saying so."

"Typically entrepreneurs try harder for sales as the going gets tougher, when more selling obstacles arise. My approach is don't fight the situation, work with it. When the economy improves we'll get aggressive again."

"That still doesn't explain why your labor costs have dropped from 15 percent of sales to 8 percent," he says, slapping the sheath of statements with his hand.

"And still dropping, I hope," I say proudly. "We're aiming for 5 percent."

"Just a minute, Harry. Labor and administrative costs are down. Are you telling me your people are working for the love of it?"

"In a way, my friend. They're working for the love of money—and a sense of participation. We've got a smaller organization now, fewer than half as many as two years ago, and we're producing more goods than ever. By passing back part of the increased profits, we enable our people to earn more money than before. More than a year ago Phil came up with an incentive system that really works. The rewards are quick, fair, and generous. Everybody in the company—except me—is included. I honestly believe Magic can now withstand anything short of an earthquake."

Julius shakes his head. "You're a radical SOB, Harry. I don't have another client who would take the kind of chance you've taken."

"You mean your other clients don't believe in giving to get?"

"I think they'd give if they had a guarantee they'd get more back."

"Or is it just plain greed?"

He ponders my statement for a moment.

"Possibly that's what it boils down to."

In fact, Julie's figures mask an even better performance than is obvious, for hidden among them are voluntary contributions to the ESOP, and extra bonuses to key employees, write-offs of recoverable inventory, and the expensing of some capital items, all done for the purpose of reducing income taxes. The year before last, those contributions totaled $65,000, last year $170,000, this year $210,000, and next year they should be about $231,000. We are afloat on a money boat.

That year, Magic's third consecutive year of gain, was a turning point for the economy and the beginning of the longest sustained upswing the United States has had since the sixties, or perhaps has ever known. Magic's continued prosperity into the foreseeable future was assured.

For the first time in years I feel fearless and secure in business. Partly from a strong sense of achievement and partly from the approval of those around me, my self-confidence is enormous. The approval of all except Janet, that is, who takes what I have done for granted and gives no sign that she respects me any more for my success than for my anxiety-driven failures. Cathy, of course, who always thought I was a virtual superman, sees nothing unusual in my accomplishments.

As the business problems gradually retreat into sweet, safe nostalgia, I find myself growing bored and unfulfilled. Perhaps I need the mortal danger, the almost lost battles, the adversity of entropy to feel alive. I'm puzzled, confused, by this new set of feelings, this inexplicable ennui. Somehow I have a sense of completion, of having reached the hard-won goal, and that the time has come to find a new goal and begin again. But this is a vague sort of feeling, as if shrouded in mist and mystery too elusive to grasp.

Apparently Phil, our production genius, is having an even harder time reckoning with himself. Daily now he arrives at work in the morning unshaven, his graying hair tussled, his clothes unkempt, and his dark eyes bloodshot. He heads for the soda machine first thing and keeps a Coke warming in his hand all day long. Many more production mistakes than usual are occurring. In tracking them, quality control finds they are mostly Phil's judgment errors. Wandering the floor recently, I noticed a new procedure that appeared questionable.

"Why are we doing it this way?" I asked the worker.

"Don't ask me, ask Phil," came the angry reply.

Though I am witnessing the slow deterioration of the man, I don't feel that alarm is yet warranted, perhaps because some weeks Phil appears to be his old self. And despite his mistakes, he is just as cooperative, insightful, and attentive to his work as he has always been.

Until the morning he enters my office, closes the door behind him, and paces the floor like a caged tiger. In a frenzy of distress, between swigs from his first Coke of the day, he demands a 50 percent increase in salary.

"You're taking advantage of me, Harry. I should be earning double what you're paying me."

"By what standard, Phil? I mean, how do you come up with that figure?"

"My wife says I'm not earning enough. She says I've never earned enough, nowhere near what our friends are earning. You've got to do something about it."

This Phil is not the calm, decisive, independent-thinking man I knew.

"Your wife! How about you? You've got a mind of your own. What do you think? You know how your wage stacks up in the industry. Why, I can hire the best around for what you're getting, for less than you're getting. Our entire wage and salary structure is better than any competitor's."

"She'll leave me, Harry, if you don't do something."

DRIVEN

A wife in a long marriage is complaining. I know about this. A relationship is in trouble: it always goes two ways.

I leap up, place both my hands on his shoulders, and fasten my eyes to his. "Phil, do you really think my giving you what you ask will solve the problem? Is it really the money or is it only an excuse? Aren't you what she's really unhappy with?"

Slumping onto the chair beside my desk, he bows his head, buries his face in his soiled hands, and begins to sob. "She's seeing some guy, Harry."

I soothe his bent neck with my hand. "That's a tough one, Phil, a real tough one. I'm sorry."

"She waitresses nights after I get home. We hardly get a chance to see each other or talk. She's sick and tired of working so she's going to quit. I don't know how we'll make ends meet if she does. Two of the kids are planning to go to college soon. If I can't support them decently, she has someone who can. Christ, Harry."

Phil has the largest family of anyone in the company: six children ranging in age from less than a year to seventeen. What madness leads a man to take that on? But that's not my affair.

"We've had a record month," I say. "You'll be getting a good bonus. And at the end of the year, actually in just a few months, you're slated for a 10 percent pay increase. I'm willing to move it up beginning next week."

"I'm afraid that won't help. It's not enough; I know her."

"That's the best I can do, Phil."

Though still early in the day, unable to pull himself together, he leaves in a state of depression—I suspect to go to a bar. The following morning, appearing less disheveled, more organized than the day before, he enters my office again.

"She's asked me to leave," he announces in surprisingly high spirits, as if having the threat over with is a relief, as if the contemplated breakup of his family left only one place to go—up. "I'll level with you." He lifts the bottle of Coke to his lips, throws back his head and takes a gulp before continuing. "I'm drinking too much."

"That stuff?" I say in nervous jest, pointing to the Coke bottle.

"I wish this was all. I'm an alcoholic, Harry." He watches my face for a reaction. Seeing none, he continues. "But I joined AA last night and I think I can kick it." Handing me a brochure, he says, "Would you be willing to read this? It's all about AA? How we work?"

"Of course. By the way, Phil, when you had that accident a few years ago, ran off the road, smashed the company van. How did that happen? Did you really fall asleep?"

"No."

"So it's been going on for some time."

"Yes."

"I had no idea."

"Neither did I, Harry."

I marvel at how well he's covered himself for so long. Or was I simply unperceptive, too busy with myself?

Keeping Phil in a critical role of major decision making might have dangerous consequences for Magic. Under the circumstances it might also be an excessive burden on him. Yet I don't want to demote him, make him feel that he's less than he is.

"How would you like to take a breather, make it easier on yourself, temporarily turn over your production responsibilities to Pete?" (He's our best foreman.)

"Maybe I could use a break," he says, "but you know how I am, I can't be idle. I have to do something."

DRIVEN

"You can become my administrative assistant. Sounds fancy, eh? First off, work up a customer analysis, find out which ones are giving us enough business to justify the lab work they're demanding. You could research the territories covered by the commission reps, determine whether we should drop them and put our own men out there. I've got projects galore for you, Phil."

During the following weeks, he confines himself to his office and works on the projects I assign him in his usual diligent fashion. He seems no less tense and driven, but the Coke bottle has disappeared.

Grateful for the hiatus, opening up to me more, he talks mostly about his failing marriage. He says his marriage has been everything and he is dying inside. Soon, he announces that he has to leave the area. To not see his children or visit his home while living so close by is intolerable. Could I find a slot for him as a salesman, out in the territory, the farther away the better? He reminds me we still haven't found a satisfactory replacement for George out in Kansas City and St. Louis.

"But you're a production man," I say. "You're not a salesman. You don't even think like a salesman. Anyway you wouldn't be using what you know. You'd be wasting your talent."

"I don't agree, Harry. You always said the more you know about a product—how it's made, the problems involved, everything there is to know—the better you can sell it. Who's more qualified on that score than I am? I can't stay here anymore, Harry, I'm sorry."

Seeing his determination and understanding the unhappiness of his predicament, I need no time to think it over. Surely he knows his stuff, he's always worked hard, and he'll make a good impression on customers.

"Under one condition, Phil—that you stick with AA on your travels wherever you go."

"It's a promise. I'll find out what night they meet in every town I'm in and schedule my itinerary around it."

"Good. And I'd like you to call in every day."

Phil rents a room in a private home in Kansas City. At the end of each day, true to our agreement, he phones in and we discuss his sales calls while I keep him informed about the plant.

"How do you feel?" I inquire.

"Great. I'm jogging every morning before I start on the road."

"And the AA meetings?"

"I don't miss a one. They're in every town, Harry. You can't imagine the kind of people that attend these meetings: surgeons, judges, politicians, college professors, and ordinary bums like me. I'm in good company."

"You're no bum, Phil. You're up there with the rest of them. When are you going to realize that?"

"I don't know, Harry. I've got a long ways to go."

Despite his finest achievement—our imaginative, brilliant incentive plan, which has proven to be the very core of Magic's salvation, despite the recognition he has received for that important contribution and for solving many other difficult practical production problems—he gives himself no credit.

But working relentlessly, jogging every morning, attending AA meetings every evening, in six months he has restored the Kansas City territory to the level that George achieved. Phil's call reports astound Wally and me by the resourcefulness and good judgment they show. In a year Phil becomes our number two salesman. In his opinion, however, what he has done still isn't good enough. My heart aches for him.

At the end of the year, Phil comes home to join his family for Christmas. It's a happy reunion. Phil is a man remade—on the wagon, clear eyed, looking lean and healthy.

"My wife wants me back," Phil says as he enters my office beaming. "I'd like to pick up where I left off, take over production again."

"Damnit, Phil, I can't do that. What do I do with Pete?"

"I always thought the job was mine."

"It was. You were slated to go back, but Phil—remember, you were going to assist me for a while—but instead you wanted to leave the area, start over someplace else, so I gave you that opportunity. Once you were gone—well, what was Pete to think?"

"I just thought, if I ever wanted to come back—"

"I'm afraid you thought wrong, Phil."

With my blessing, Phil found a job elsewhere, managing a plant in another industry. A good manager is a good manager in any kind of business. Phil had been with me fifteen years. I missed him for a year afterward, missed our brainstorming together, missed watching him pull himself together and then soar. Some things happen in business that make past struggles worthwhile. For all its agony, being the boss has its rewards, least of them the money.

Something is happening inside me I don't understand, a crazy sentimentality, a softness I never knew and I don't know what to do with it.

Wally walks into my office to tell me that Abel is now a representative of Fran's company and has been bad-mouthing us to our customers.

"Can you beat that?" he says. "Right away he runs over to Fran's and, of course, Fran'll take anyone who's been here."

"Fran's only getting our throwaways now," I say. "It's okay."

It occurs to me that Gil and Abel might have designs on Fran's company as they did on Magic.

Sure enough, word seeps out that Abel and Gary, Fran's partner and our ex-vice president of production, are plotting together to buy out Fran. No doubt Gil is the money behind the move. However, Fran, having no wish to sell, asks a ridiculous price. A stalemate prevails that leads to a cold war.

Sometimes business is a challenge, sometimes sheer misery, and, if it weren't for people, sometimes a joy. But business IS people.

After three years committed to Magic as technical director, Wally is still chronically dissatisfied. To make him happy, I've given him all the authority and responsibility he sought, which includes overseeing the lab, sales, and quality control, and dreaming up an advertising program in collaboration with a local agency. I've tried to make him happy since I value his keen intelligence, although not his unpredictability and moodiness.

Wally nevertheless drops his bomb: "I'm sorry, Harry, I'm giving you notice."

"Why?" I inquire dumbfounded. "Why aren't you happy here? When you asked for more responsibility, I gave it to you. Your salary is right up there."

"I suppose I'm as happy as I'll ever be. I've got no complaint."

"Then what's this all about?"

"I've been offered a special deal by Colorcon, too good to turn down: a piece of the company, a percentage of the profits, and the entire plant will be my show."

The president of Colorcon has a reputation as a tightwad and an unreliable flake. After five years his company is still going nowhere.

"You got all this in writing?"

"Certainly. Hey, Harry, I've learned a few things from you."

"Then you know owning a minority piece of a closely held company isn't worth very much," I say while he stares at me coldly. "You won't have any real say and I doubt if he'll declare dividends and subject himself to double taxation."

Wally wriggles uncomfortably in his chair. "Still, a minority stockholder has some rights, such as seeing the financials."

"But you see them at Magic too. I presume you're referring to the profit figure."

"That's right. I get 25 percent. That's nothing to sneeze at."

"Twenty-five percent of what?"

"Of the profits."

"What profits?"

"What do you mean?"

"How do you know there'll be profits, Wally? What's the guarantee?"

"Hell, of course there'll be profits. I'll be able to see to it. I know I can do a job."

"I don't doubt your ability, Wally. For your information, your so-called partner can make the bottom line pretty much what he wants. All he has to do is raise his salary or have his real estate company charge more rent, or write off inventory. It's easy to manipulate profits. Everyone does it to beat taxes.

"Do you know why so many of my business friends call me a fool for going ESOP? There's too much visibility. Under the law, I must abide by a disclosure rule. I can't hide anything from my employees. But your partner, as majority stockholder, is still going to call the shots. And don't kid yourself, he will. You'll see the figures but you won't even know what's going on right under your nose."

Wally's eyes glaze over and he isn't listening.

"I've made up my mind, Harry. If it doesn't work out, I'll be on your doorstep." He reaches for my hand and shakes it vigorously. "Thanks for everything. I've enjoyed working with you. I'll miss this goddamn place, I can tell you."

"Y'know, Wally, I don't think you're happy with yourself. You have everything going for you here at Magic, but you're not miserable enough. You're climbing out of a nice, clean pool and purposely diving into a swamp. Maybe that's what you've got to do. Well, good luck anyway. If I can help, call me anytime."

"I might just take you up on that," he says as if acknowledging the truth in my words.

For weeks after Wally's departure, we feel an inexplicable relief, like a communal sigh. The entire staff laughs more, kids more, relaxes more. And we talk about the change, how remarkable it is that Wally's grumpy disposition, his litany of dissatisfaction, had infected us all without our knowing it. We had grown used to him, like a shrill chain saw screeching in the background.

Wally called me two years later to see if I'd take him back. Exactly what I had warned him against happened.

I turned Wally down, remembering well the salubrious effect of his departure on all of us. He then found a job with a supplier as a salesman and began calling on Emma and me. After awhile he confided that he was unhappy in that job too.

"The only time I was ever really happy was with you, Harry," he said. "Only I didn't know it then."

"And if you came back, Wally, you still wouldn't know it. Stay where you are. You're working for a good company. There's plenty of opportunity."

"Yeah? Where?"

Poking my index finger to his head, I said, "Right there."

What is this spent feeling I have? It's not burnout. I'm no longer working hard, at most eight hours a day, and the pace is easy. I even have time to peruse *The Wall Street Journal*, see how some of my investments are doing. The staff people are handling the day-to-day functioning of the business like pros. I ask myself what's left to be done. Build more plants—in the Southeast, the midsouth, the Far West, Canada. Why? For the money? I don't need more money. For the challenge. I've had enough challenge. To prove I can do it? I'm satisfied with what I've achieved, proof enough of my competence and my worth. Then is my job done?

What irony! I always thought having my own business was the be-all and end-all of my life's work. Now, it's not enough. Why? What in hell's gone wrong? In fact, I'm even questioning whether Magic contributes anything to the world. We pollute the environment, our factory building adds nothing aesthetically pleasing to the landscape, our products enhance life only negligibly.

I'm fifty-eight years old. Should I be like a smart poker player—cash in while the pot is full and I've got a good hand? Why not move on to something else? What, I don't know. I don't know yet. Use my business experience, take what I've learned these past seventeen years. Maybe at last I can give myself to Janet, not to a business or another woman. Sounds good, sounds possible. What can I get for Magic? I'll find out.

While helping Janet clear the kitchen table after dinner, I tell her that I'm considering selling out.

"I don't think it's a good idea," she says cautiously. "What will you do to keep busy?"

"Do? Why, I'll have plenty to do. Manage our investments, for one thing. Remember, we'll have a few bucks after I sell out. I'll write; I've wanted to write ever since high school. In the summer I'll garden and sail. We'll travel."

"And you think that will be enough?"

"Certainly."

"You don't think you'll miss being chief honcho, having all those people report to you, giving orders, all the excitement, you know, your respected position—el presidente?"

I stiffen. "Sure, maybe I'll miss it at first. But are you saying I can only be happy when I'm the boss?"

"I'm saying you're a very controlling person."

"You have a will of your own, Janet. I can't push you around."

"Not that you don't try. I won't let you. If you're going to be around the house, in my hair, all day, I'll scream."

"It'll work out. You'll see."

She doesn't see, but seeing that I've made up my mind, she has no choice in the matter.

When I tell Cathy of my decision, she reacts in panic.

"I'll lose you," she wails. "I'm afraid. You'll be on the Cape and I won't see you anymore."

"Of course, you will. Why do you say that?"

"What reason will you have to come here?"

"You're the reason."

"I mean what excuse? How will you get away? Your wife must never know."

"Leave that to me."

"I never thought it would end like this."

"Godamnit, nothing's ending. We won't see each other as often, but—"

"I can tell, it's over."

"Listen—"

"Why don't you leave her? She's not good for you. It's so obvious. I said I'd never marry again, but, Harry, I love you. Being with you would be different; I know it would work with us. You know how great I am in bed. You've told me. We're wonderful lovers. Don't cast me off like this. I don't want to be alone."

"I can't leave Janet. We've gone over this before."

"Why? I don't understand. You're miserable."

"For crissakes, I don't know why," I bellow. "I just know I can't. I love her too. She's the mother of my children. I have to give it another chance."

"I'm sorry for you, my sweet love."

The stronger my insistence that Cathy's fears are unjustified, the less convinced she becomes. I despise myself for not having the courage to level with her, to confess that I want life to be cleaner, less complicated. I'm counting on that trite truth: "Out of sight, out of mind." Still, there's time, for I haven't sold the business yet. Having sent out only a few feelers, nothing more, I'm not psychologically ready to give up Magic.

But now Cathy's a problem. Long ago, I told her not to push, that we must have no strings tying us to each other, that our freedom, hers and mine, contained the essential beauty of our relationship. She had agreed. It was what she wanted too. Now she seeks to change that premise. I can't allow it.

CHAPTER XXIII

Year Seventeen
(Continued)

1983

Business is like a sine wave and we are riding its up phase, the very best time to cash in. Last year I took a salary of $175,000, more than my standard of living required. This year I raise it to $235,000. Next year it should exceed a quarter million.

Magic can now afford to add more salesmen and more administrative staff. A new receptionist in the office, nicknamed Flea (for Felicia), is notable. The day she is interviewed for the second time, Emma phones and asks that I also check her out, which is certainly not necessary since Emma has authority to hire the people who work for her.

"Why bring me into it?" I ask.

"Well, I'd like to hire her but I'm just not sure. She's bright and I checked her references. They're beyond reproach; the way she looks isn't really her fault—"

Thinking that Emma is describing a sinfully unattractive woman, I'm certainly willing to offer my opinion. After all, a receptionist is our face and voice to the world.

"Okay, send her in," I say.

In a couple of minutes, led by Emma, an arousingly beautiful woman in her mid-twenties, dressed in a conservative skirt and blouse, glides into my office and sits down next to the desk. Emma introduces us and withdraws. Immediately I understand Emma's problem, of which I am indubitably a part. Without saying so, she remembers my "secret" affair with Cathy, which led to a scene and eventually her quitting.

The interview is routine. I learn Felicia is separated from her husband and contemplating divorce. She has no children, lives in a small apartment barely two miles away. Her answers to all my questions are smooth, credible, and businesslike. She can type at a fast speed, has had experience answering the phone, does bookkeeping, composes letters, even performs inside sales. In short the woman is Emma's dream of a qualified person, except that she looks as though she should be modeling bathing suits.

When I ask Felicia why she wants to work at Magic—an interviewer's stock question, she replies, "Your company has a good reputation, Mr. Simon. I think it's the kind of place I'd like to work—and I live nearby." This is a direct and sensible answer and has the added effect of making me feel good. I like her—perhaps in a troubling way I can't acknowledge.

She waits in the foyer for the verdict while Emma and I talk.

"What's a girl like her doing here?" I ask. "She should be a model."

"I doubt whether she realizes how attractive she is."

"She must know the effect she has on men. This girl lights up the sky."

"So, should I hire her or not?"

I'm aware that Emma knows I'm also wondering about myself. But after the episode with Cathy, I had long ago realized that you don't mix personal business with business business. I'm not susceptible, at least that's what I convince myself.

"As you say, her qualifications are perfect," I muse. "The question is, will she cause a problem among the men, or even among the other women?"

"I think I can deal with *those* problems," Emma says, implicitly excluding me.

"I don't think she's leveling when she says she was laid off her last job," I comment, not wanting to appear too eager. "That company is running straight out these days. They would need to keep her."

"She confided in me that her boss was getting personal. He was very persistent."

"I'm not surprised," I say. "Well, it's your decision."

She smiles. "I'd rather you make it, if you don't mind."

Damn her. She's asking for an implied promise that I stay clear.

I say, "Go ahead. Hire her. We'll keep our fingers crossed."

Once on the job Felicia proves to be more than anyone expected. She is consistently in fine humor; by her manner and tone of voice she makes everyone feel important and warm. But there is no getting used to her beauty. In fact it grows on you.

Lithe and tall, taller than I, she has a shapely figure, firm breasts, a compact derriere, slender thighs and a flat tummy. She exceeds ordinary reality. Only in calendar art, an exaggeration of provocative femaleness from an artist's imagination, have I seen the likes of her. The smooth planes of her face, her delicate chin, her perfectly geometric nose, and her inviting lips, her eyes like warm chocolate, brown hair that streams in a long sweeping curve to her shoulders — these form a remarkable composite of feminine lushness.

As anticipated, the male traffic to the office from the plant and the lab booms. The men seek the slightest excuse to gaze upon and, if possible, chat with her. Eventually Emma issues an order that all employees direct their inquiries to the office through their shift supervisors, not that they too aren't immune.

Felicia's phone manner and her voice are so captivating that customers call in, not to do business but just to talk. "Does she look as good as she sounds?" they ask our salesmen who, of course, extoll her beauty. "Better," they say.

Although customers visit our office only on rare occasions, one of our customers finds small excuses to return again and again. After dating Flea a few times, he proposes that they both quit their jobs and go South together. This despite the fact that he is already married and has a family. She turns him down cold, much to Emma's relief. She has in less than three months become Emma's most versatile and valued employee. Her work is flawless, her intelligence remarkable.

After awhile I too can no longer resist her. My married life, of course, is no joyride, and now Cathy, pressuring me for commitment, is driving me away. I yearn for a change, a fresh relationship. Though Flea treats me no more warmly than anyone else, I find cause to imagine that I stand a special chance with her. After all, the boss can't be easily dismissed.

She is now always in my consciousness; she even invades my dreams. I want to know how she lives each moment in every detail. Purposely going home late, although out of my way, I drive by her apartment hoping to see her. I'm a slave to an infatuation more gripping than anything I've ever experienced, even as a young man. I'm puzzled that at age fifty-eight, having a certain mature vision of life, I can be so consumed without any care for safety or sanity. I'm like a lovesick adolescent. Recklessly, I throw myself into the abyss of love.

Often delivering rush correspondence to my office, Flea sits beside my desk waiting for me to sign them so she can prepare them for the next mail. At such times we engage in small talk, rarely anything personal.

"I see you're pretty popular around here," I say on one such occasion, curious whether she is as innocent of the power of her beauty as she seems.

"I try to be nice to everyone, Mr. Simon."

"But certain ones don't know where to stop, I take it."

"Yes, sometimes."

"I suppose your attractiveness is a problem. You can't really know whether someone loves you for yourself or simply wants to go to bed with you. And that can be hard, right?"

"I guess so. But I manage."

"All the time?"

Laughing she says, "Not always, Mr. Simon. I've been disappointed."

"If I were to ask you to have dinner with me, do you think I'd disappoint you?"

She considers my words seriously for a moment, then says, "No, I don't think so, Mr. Simon."

"Please, make it 'Harry' when we're alone."

She giggles. "Okay, Harry."

"How's tomorrow night?"

"But you're married. I don't go out with—"

"My marriage is a wreck. All I'm asking is that we have dinner together. How about it?"

"I guess—well, all right Mr.—Harry."

On our first date—it's at a Chinese restaurant—she talks about her separation from her husband. I gather it's on her mind most of the time.

"Why did you leave him?" I ask, assuming that's the case, since no sensible man would abandon such a beauty.

"Oh no, he left me," she says, becoming teary. "Still don't understand. I was good to him; I love him."

"Yes, it's hard to figure," I say. "I'm generous to my wife. I loved her once, still do, I suppose, but nothing about me makes her happy anymore."

"He used to demean me so, say I was stupid—I'd feel worthless. He'd strip me naked, make fun of my body, and tell me I was ugly. Somehow it gave him pleasure."

"That's incredible. God, you're so lovely—so competent. Did you actually believe that shit?"

"He'd strike me."

"Strike you? Goddamn, Flea, how could he do that to you?"

"Somehow I felt I deserved it."

I lend her my handkerchief to dry the tears coursing down her cheeks and dampening her hair. Tempted to leap across the table and comfort her with an embrace, instead I place my hand over hers, a gesture she welcomes. How entirely different she is from the confident, cheerful, popular person I'm used to seeing at the office.

"You took it and still he left you," I say, shaking my head.

"I don't think I could have ever left him. No matter what he did to me. He needed me—I thought so, anyway."

I stare at her in futile silence. Couldn't she see that she had been his victim, collaborated with him in her victimization?

"Could you leave your wife?"

"No. Never."

"So, you must know how it is."

My God! A flash of insight pierces my dumb brain. When Janet wanted to leave me long ago, I pleaded with her to stay. Why, we were both wretched victims of each other. Flea and I are in the same boat.

In front of her apartment she lets me kiss her gently on the lips once, only once, before dashing from my car. I drive away elated, making plans to see her on a steady basis. But our thirty-three-year age difference nags at me, and her unsettled emotional state is an obstacle, albeit temporary. I am ready to accept that gentleness and patience will be needed. But there's a doubt that she could possibly get serious with a much older man—maybe a dirty older man.

For the next month we see each other after work twice a week, either by going to dinner at a restaurant, or to a movie, or watching TV in her apartment. During my embraces, when my hand falls to her breast or cups her buttocks, she pulls it away.

"I'm not ready to make love," she says. "I'm sorry, Harry. You'd better go."

As my frustration grows, so does my anger. Soon I find more cause. Several young men call on her during lunch hour and chat with her in the foyer. One in particular, wearing a soiled black leather jacket and sporting a ragged beard, comes several times a week on his motorbike to take her out to lunch. Shortly after he appears on the scene, she makes transparent excuses not to see me as often. I confront her in my office.

"We get along together. You seem to like my company. Why do you prefer someone else to me?"

"I do like you, Harry. But I like others too."

"Bums, you mean. He's a loser, Flea, just like your husband." She shrugs. "I don't understand. You're falling into the same trap again. I treat you like a—a movie star and you—"

"It's my life, Harry. I'm sorry. Anyway, I can't see you because I'm thinking of taking a night job. I need the money."

"Doing what?"

"Well, as a bar lady at the Hello Club. I tried it one night and liked it. It was real fun. The boss is teaching me how to mix highballs and stuff like that. He says I catch on faster than anyone he's ever trained."

"Christ, you have too much ability to waste your time doing that kind of thing, Flea."

"I don't see it that way. I like the work; that's all I care."

"You like all the attention, showing yourself—"

At this moment I suddenly realize that she is very much aware of her attractiveness and uses it with purpose. No wonder her husband had been jealous. I put the thought aside.

"Never mind," I continue. "Does this mean we don't see each other any—"

"Of course, we'll see each other. When I get a night off, I'll let you know."

It isn't a whole loaf for sure, but I'm content with any slice or two she offers. From the time of our talk, or perhaps coincident with her work at the club, the lunch visitor on the bike no longer appears. She turns away the other admirers and in fact all male overtures that continually come her way. I'm, of course, pleased; my competition has disappeared; the road is open.

Over the next several weeks I imagine an idyllic scenario that I think will appeal to her. By interoffice mail I send her the following handwritten note:

"How about spending next weekend with me at the Cape? We'll have the ocean. Good restaurants. Hiking on nature trails. Biking. Anything else your heart desires."

Since Janet has spent the entire summer at the Cape and would rather stay at our winter home, I often go to the Cape house alone on autumn weekends. It is beautiful there then. The air is still balmy, warmed by the sea, the summer people have returned to the cities, and a soft peace descends on the peninsula. Alone I work in the garden, cleaning up the brittle remnants of summer. I sail in the bay, brisker now than in August, and read on the quiet deck.

Until I began my weekend sojourns, I hadn't known the pleasure of solitude since being married. But since meeting Flea I long to share my treasured haven by the ocean with her.

Returning my note, she scribbles on it: "I'm sorry. I'm busy."

Phoning her desk, I demand she come to my office.

Before she has a chance to sit down, I say, "So pick another time when you're not busy."

"I can't," she says, "I'm working at the club every weekend."

"To hell with the club."

"I can't. I'm sorry, Harry. But I can't."

"What are you afraid of? I won't touch you. The bedrooms have locks. You'll have your own room. I'll give you a key. You'll have a tremendous time, Flea, guaranteed."

"I'm sorry."

"I don't understand you. When you're there you can do whatever you want."

She shifts from one foot to the other like a child anxious to go out to play.

"Can I go now?"

My plan disintegrates and in a sense so do I. My disappointment is overwhelming.

"Sure, go. Go to your boozers and bums," I say.

On Friday after work I drive to the Cape distraught, confused, in an unfamiliar territory of myself. As soon as I enter the house, I sit at the kitchen table, raise my hands to my face, and sob like a child. My life seems over—over the hill. I feel I'm unattractive, ugly with age. Not a vestige of my youth remains. I'm old and lost forever and desperately lonely. Neither my money nor my position nor my power can compensate for my physical decline. Nothing I have or am or can be will assuage my ache—the ache to be loved.

I haven't written from my heart since college, thirty-three years ago. Now I'm possessed by an urge to write of my feelings. By putting them on paper, I'll be able to wrench the pain from my inner depths and get rid of it. Haltingly I write and rewrite, occasionally bursting into sobs, until I've put down as best I can what I feel. I wonder whether I'm not repeating that earlier period of my life, a period in which almost every young man has his heart broken.

Writing, spending time in the garden, and sailing in the bay are antidotes to my depression and I begin to heal. Gradually I come to accept myself as I am and see that the good life need not be over. I may be aging but I'm not unwanted. How could I have been so absurdly obsessed over a woman and so crazy at her rejection? Did I feel so omnipotent that I couldn't entertain her refusal? By Monday morning as I drive the two hours from the Cape to work, I am a normal human being again; the infatuation is over.

Flea senses the change in me and is not pleased. She looks for excuses to visit my office and tries to gauge my mood.

"Would you like to take me out to dinner tonight?" she asks playfully.

"No, Flea. I can't tonight," I say without bitterness, no longer vulnerable.

A few weeks later she comes to work in a new red Porsche convertible and parks it in front of my office window. As she enters my office to drop off some papers for me to sign, I ask, "Whose car?"

"Mine," she says jauntily.

"C'mon, Flea."

"Really. It's a gift."

"From—"

"I don't think it's any of your business."

"Okay. But I hope it's—well, legitimate. Have you found a sugar daddy?"

"A sugar daddy?"

"Yeah, that's a—"

"It's from my boss at the club."

"So that's it," I say.

"What's that mean?"

"You and the boss."

"He's just a friend."

"Some friend."

"Think what you want. You really don't care, do you?" she says huffily and leaves.

But the evidence confirms my suspicion. Looking up her personnel records I see she has given up her apartment and has changed her address to Providence.

Though I no longer swoon over her, I have trouble with her blatancy. She seems to be flaunting her new lover before my eyes as if she deliberately wants me to be jealous. I read her to be saying, if you had bid higher, you could have had me. She's intolerable.

On a Monday I send her a note: "Tell Emma you're quitting. I'll make it worth your while."

She comes to my office visibly distressed.

"What have I done?" she says on the verge of tears.

"I can't bear having you here," I say. "You know how I feel about you. I want to forget you, and I can't—seeing you here day in and day out. I'll make it easy, Flea. I'll give you three months' severance from my own pocket. That'll give you time to find something else."

"It's rotten, your doing this."

"It's not fair, I know," I say, my arms extended like oars, hands palms up. "But that's the way it is. You have until the end of the week."

She leaves my office disconsolate and resigned and gives Emma notice. I am ashamed of the dirty work I have done but I resume my business seemingly unperturbed. The next morning as I pass by her desk, I notice that her face is swollen, and on a closer look I see discoloration, bruises.

"What happened to Flea?" I ask Emma. "Did she have an accident?"

"The poor girl is afraid for her life, Harry. That man she's living with beat her last night; he's even threatened to kill her."

"Who is he?"

"The man at the nightclub. She's left him but she's afraid he'll hunt her down. It's even dangerous for her to come to work."

"Where is she staying?"

"At my place until this thing blows over. She has nowhere else to go."

"The poor kid, Emma, the poor kid."

"Terrible, isn't it? And such a beautiful child."

What have I done? What have I done to this girl whose only crime is that she's incredibly enticing? Has she ever deceived me, or pretended to be other than herself? I call her to my office.

"I've changed my mind," I say. "Asking you to leave isn't right. I can't live with myself." She is unresponsive, as if dazed. The bruises on her left cheek are ugly and look painful. "I would like you to stay, Flea, that is, if you want to after the way I've behaved. Stay as long as you wish."

"Oh, Harry!" she says, suddenly alive, embracing me and kissing me fervently on the lips. "Thank-you, thank-you."

Having relinquished any desire to be her lover, I now feel protective and fatherly toward her.

"Take some time off for a while," I say. "Take a vacation with pay. I'll speak to Emma."

While still in her embrace, I detach her arms from around my body as she has often done with me.

"Let's just be good friends, okay?" I say.

"That would be nice, very nice," she says.

As she leaves her eyes are brimming with tears.

I'm relieved that I'm over her for good, cleared to tend to selling the business without distractions.

Flea never came back to work, instead, moving to California to start over.

CHAPTER XXIV

Year Eighteen

1984

Sales: $4,200,000 (+23.5%)
Profit: $266,000 (+67.3%)
Debt: $540,000 (-13.7%)
Net Worth: $583,000 (+85%)

Once the word gets around that Magicolor is for sale, the wooing begins. Among our pursuers are sleek New York investment bankers and presidents of large and small corporations, some with entourages of executive sycophants, some alone who wish to keep their pursuit a secret from their staffs or partners. Others act as scouts — just looking — vice presidents or hired merger specialists who "do deals" for a fee paid by the seeker. Some are banks or corporate consultants, who offer to represent Magic either on a contingency basis or for an up-front sum. A covey of Japanese businessmen, only one of whom speaks English, come bearing gifts of gold cuff links and tie clasps with their company logo.

They arrive in private planes, in limousines, or in rented compact cars. Sitting for hours in my office, they pore over the figures as I extoll our projected future, the competence of our people, and how superfluous I am to the operation. I invite them to interview some of our key people so that they can ascertain their superior caliber.

Forewarned, my people present themselves astonishingly well.

Few potential buyers believe my claim that I have become virtually unessential to the business. To a person, our executives reply in substance: "We're a team. Once upon a time we needed Mr. Simon. He provided the drive and set the tone and the style of the company. Now he needs us. He stays out of our hair, lets us do our job. We, not Mr. Simon, are running the company." I feel proud.

The visitors' reactions vary wildly. Some are skeptical even of my audited financial statements; others are more than accepting. A few, trying to get us for a steal, outrage me.

Most who are willing to offer a figure near my asking price want me to take mostly "paper"—a payout over a period of years from Magic's future profits with dollars that would be sure to depreciate, and expose me to the risk of uncertain future performance.

I know precisely the deal I want: a cash-only sale, a stock sale (not an asset sale, which would require that I pay taxes on recaptured depreciation and equipment leasing costs), and a price that approximates eight times the average of our last three years' earnings. Most buyers, of course, prefer to purchase assets strictly because they would thereby avoid paying for goodwill—the difference between the book value of our assets and the selling price. Under the current tax law it takes thirty years to write off the cost of goodwill, too long a period to effectively reduce a buyer's taxes, whereas assets could be written off in one third the time or sooner. Thus an asset sale is to my disadvantage and the buyer's advantage.

Though I seriously consider every offer, some admittedly for only a few minutes, I obstinately stick to my terms. What's the hurry? Likening it to finding the right woman to marry, I feel the right buyer is bound to come along, given time.

For two years I spurned one suitor after another until I met the scintillating Timothy Van der Steele III, vice president of a large chemical company headquartered in New York City. On his initial contact by phone he introduced himself by saying, "I represent one of the richest closely held companies in America." He requests figures and Magicolor's history.

I send him a letter covering Magic's past eight and a half years. (See Appendix E.)

After reading my letter, Tim Van der Steele III calls, telling me to prepare for his early arrival the next day. He joins me at 7:00 A.M. in my office.

"A pleasure to meet you, Harry," he gushes in a deep, . booming, clear voice, his hand outstretched as he sweeps across the room to my desk. "You have a wonderful, wonderful company; it's impressive, very impressive."

He wears an immaculate navy blue suit. A broad smile stretches across his skeletal face, which is absolutely hairless, as smooth as a piglet's bottom, as is his glistening scalp. Yet in less than fifteen minutes I find his barren pink skull pleasing, yes, handsome, even though without eyebrows.

Unlike so many others who flail the hay interminably, after only a few minutes of small talk he gets right down to business.

"My company is looking for growth, Harry, not income, and we're willing to pour in money if we see that Magicolor's got potential," he says breathlessly. "I've read up on your segment of the industry, seen your projections."

"What projections? I didn't send you any projections," I say puzzled.

"Now do you believe for one minute that other people who have seen them—to whom apparently you've presented them—would keep them confidential?"

"Would you mind telling me who—?"

He beams some more. "Ah, I believe one must always keep things in confidence, Harry. Don't you? With me, you're safe—even under torture. And so I hold my source sacred."

Waiting to satisfy himself that I'm not terribly put out, which I am but I suppress it, he resumes.

"I think you've got what we're looking for, Harry. Most definitely, I'd say. Now I'd like to talk with your management team, the key people, if that meets with your approval."

"Be my guest," I say, finding his directness refreshing.

My people have long become used to the onslaught of curious visitors, some of whom have even quizzed them without my approval and angered me by so doing.

In a spare private office he first interviews Emma, our fifteen-year employee, whom I identify as our office manager and purchasing agent; then Tom, a five-year man, Wally's former assistant, now our new lab head; then Pete, production manager, Phil's former top foreman, who came up from ten years in the ranks.

Back in my office he concludes: "What impresses me about your company, Harry, is that you promote from within. That's holding out a promise. People don't feel stuck that way. Yes, sir, Harry, I'm impressed."

A week later he flys to Chicago "to look the place over and get acquainted with your manager out there."

To a person, they're charmed; to a person, Tim Van der Steele III thinks they are "the best damn most competent middle management staff I've ever come across—that is, in a company your size."

DRIVEN

Before I begin my campaign to sell Magic, I must contend with my conscience. If I am not an easy boss, often showing little tolerance for error and targeting perpetrators with blame, sometimes harshly, at least I listen to argument and try to be generous, fair, and truthful. Perhaps the positive factors are sufficient to offset the displeasure I cause. The fact remains, employee turnover is minimal—no one aboard is with us less than five years—and company loyalty, which I interpret as satisfaction with and loyalty to me, is considerable. I feel it my duty to reciprocate.

When I announce to everyone my intention to sell, they are confused. Some feel betrayed; in their opinion, I'm benefiting number one, myself, and forgetting about them and their past loyalty.

"What if I were to die in an accident tomorrow?" I ask in rebuttal. "What do you think would happen? My wife would inherit the business. She's certainly not competent to run it; for that matter she's not in the least interested in doing so. She would most likely sell it to the highest bidder for a price far less than I can get while I'm alive and in charge. So it's in your interest that I sell to a buyer who is able and willing to invest in Magic's future, which, I assure you, I consider essential.

"You will not only receive more money for your stock if I sell now, while we're riding high, but you may well have more opportunity under new ownership than I've been able to provide. I feel my job is done; I'm satisfied with what Magic has become and I don't want more. But many of you do. So I know I'm holding you down. You have my word, my solemn promise, that I'll not sell to anyone whose management is not farseeing, will not invest in Magic, and is not considerate of its employees."

With some the reaction is disappointment that they would no longer be owner-workers. Chances are, they say, the company would no longer be managed in the participatory mode that has stimulated and motivated them. I agree. It's a price they will probably have to pay, but in return they would receive more cash for their stock than otherwise.

Although I offer one rational argument after another, they seem inadequate. Despite my stated reasons for selling, despite that I'm satisfied, that my job is done, the explanation sounds too shallow, too pat. Although Magicolor has provided us all with a comfortable standard of living, I can't help doubting its intrinsic worth. I've been living a secret lie. Were I ever to confide this to anyone, they'd think I was absurd. Our system, our culture not only approves of what I've done, it downright admires it. So I merely go along.

As I probe deeper, the real reasons for selling emerge. I worry that I can't sustain our good fortune, that life's cyclical nature will eventually bring it all to an end and do me in. I've never believed in happy endings, rather that life always ends in pain, loss, decline, and nothingness. I didn't plan my success. It's only accidental, so its demise may well be just as accidental.

I know who I am now, thanks to Magicolor. I know what I've done. But I know I'm not enough. There's more to be, it doesn't concern business or making money. I think it's possible in a way that I haven't yet found.

I hope for a deal with Tim, if possible. His maneuverings seem the most sincere, honorable, and realistic of three prospects under consideration. I'm convinced that he is the right buyer because of his interest in my people, his assurance that my asking price based on a multiple of earnings is reasonable, and his faith in

Magicolor's future growth. I am further convinced after he informs me that he is so taken with Magicolor that he has applied to his company to be assigned as Magic's chief operating officer.

The next step is, as he says, "a meeting with the brass," which, it turns out, we never get to. He calls about noontime.

"Can you and I get together tonight over dinner?" he asks in an urgent tone.

"Tonight? Well, I do have plans. Where are you?"

"In the Big Apple. Can you change your plans, Harry? I intend to leave for your place in an hour."

"Something gone wrong, Tim?"

"Not at all. I'd say things are very right."

"Then, why the rush?"

It seems to me more like panic.

"You'll understand after we talk. I'll be there by 5:00."

His Jaguar enters our parking lot at 5:10. The front office is empty, only the plant is humming, and we are in quiet seclusion with no possible interruptions. Agitated, far from his usual beaming self, seated on the couch across from my desk, he says bluntly, "I want to offer you a deal that you can't turn down."

"I'm listening, Tim, listening hard."

"I'm prepared to meet your asking price, all your terms, one hundred percent."

I gasp inwardly. Such an offer is beyond my most extreme expectations. I wait for a "but."

"That's marvelous, Tim," I say, rising to shake his hand. "Your management people won't be sorry. When can I meet them?"

"This is my deal, Harry, not theirs."

"I'm afraid I'm not with you. Say that again."

Taking my hand, he holds it momentarily in both of his.

"I want your company for myself," he says, studying my expression.

"Wait a minute—"

"Please sit down and hear me out. I've been looking for a jewel like Magicolor for years. I may make a hell of a lot more money than you, Harry, but I envy you. What you've got here is special—something clean, free of politics. You don't have to kowtow to anyone. You're your own man; you can make decisions without compromise and reap the rewards. Sure, sometimes you pay a price for your screwups, but you're free to make them. I've had it with fitting in to get ahead. Most guys would give it all up, chuck the whole goddamned corporate culture in the trash, if the right thing came along. But it rarely does. I've been searching for a long time. Now I've found it, you betcha. Magicolor's too good an opportunity to pass up. Do you understand?"

"I understand," I say, with sympathy. He's obviously a frustrated entrepreneur. "Still, Tim, you can always start a business from scratch."

Does he think my enviable "freedom" came free? I'm not about to enumerate my past agonies. But I agree with him. I wouldn't have his world, couldn't survive it. Even when things were going badly and I questioned my wisdom, I knew I'd do it again. I'd like my epitaph to read: "He took a chance and lived free."

"I'm not gutsy enough to start at the beginning. Gosh no. Not at my stage of the game, anyway. I'll pay someone else for taking the chance and go from there. Yes siree, I think I've earned a break for kissing ass, and this is it."

"What are you going to tell your company? Aren't they interested?"

His betrayal of the corporation concerns me. How can I trust him? Certainly the corporation shouldn't have.

"Of course they're interested, and they'll come up with an offer, but it won't be as good as mine. Here's the deal I'm proposing: your terms entirely, as I said. Of course I'll need time to raise the money. About a month, I'd say. Rest assured it will be a cinch. I've got the bank connections, and for seed money I'll line up a few private investors—very big bucks, nationally known people, names that would surprise you; can't mention them yet. They're sold on Magic too; I've shown them the figures."

"Damnit, Tim, I've learned nothing's for sure until you've got it in your hand. Don't you think you've put the cart before the horse?"

From the inside pocket of his suit jacket, he retrieves a wallet and with a flourish withdraws a check and hands it to me.

"This is my good faith payment," he says.

The check, made out to Magicolor, Inc., is for $25,000. Taking it I stare at it, astonished.

"I'll move with due diligence. My letter of intent will be in the mail tomorrow. If I don't do the deal in a month, you keep the money. I only ask that you cease all negotiations with anyone else. Okay?"

He stands up from the couch.

"Is it done?"

"It's done," I say, ready to take his extended hand, which instead joins his other and encircles me in an embrace.

"Thanks, Harry. You're a swell guy. Now let's have dinner."

Tim is irresistible. This is the first time a negotiation has gone beyond just words.

Over the next two weeks he calls several times to assure me that his private parties are secure, his bank in

New York is "working on it," and there is no question they'll go for the deal. In the meantime my lawyer has drawn up all the necessary documents and forwarded them to his lawyer.

The third week Tim shows up in my office without an appointment in a harried state. The New York bank has rejected his application, saying that Magicolor's projections could not "throw off enough cash flow" to service the interest and payback of principal.

"They're ridiculous," he says. "I have some connections with a bank up here—one of my roommates from Yale is a loan officer. They have more of a stake in the local scene. He feels sure they'll approve it."

"Show me your figures, Tim," I say, curious to see how realistic they are.

A lender or investor is concerned with the past cash-generating capability of Magicolor derived from profits plus expenses and certain dollar contributions that could have been eliminated or would be under new ownership. For example, since the ESOP would be discontinued, past contributions to it may be added to profits to arrive at a truer picture of cash flow. Such a reconstruction is not a nebulous projection but rather a scenario of a possible option.

I had submitted figures to Tim showing Magicolor's potential cash generation for the previous four years after adding back nonrepeatable and unnecessary expenses. From these, Tim constructed his own interpretation and submitted it to the bank. For comparison the two are as follows:

DRIVEN

Reconstruction of Past Operating Income

($ in thousands) Years	1	2	3	4
Harry	$697	498	410	210
Tim	$710	677	645	371

Astounded at his exaggeration, I say, "How in God's name did you come up with these?"

"Your figures aren't valid, Harry. You didn't add back rent and depreciation. After all, since the company will own the factory building, it needn't pay itself rent, and depreciation isn't a real expense."

"It sure is," I say. "Someday you're going to have to modernize and replace the equipment. It's decreasing value and future replacement cost is accounted for through depreciation. As for the building rent, it's not free. It's at least equal to what the cost of the building would earn if that money were invested."

"Only paper figures, Harry, paper figures. Depreciation is really capital. Rent is income. All the bank cares about is the hard cash, and I've given them the true story."

"Well, if you can sell your figures, who am I to argue? More power to you."

"Of course they'll sell, my friend. As I said, my bank connection is rock solid."

A week later on the deadline date, Tim calls. The rock hasn't yet solidified.

"Another week, Harry. Just another week and it'll be clinched. Trouble is, July is the worst time of the year to be doing this. Either one member of the loan committee or another is on vacation. Will you go along this once?"

Technically once he failed to meet the deadline, I could have called off the deal and kept his $25,000, but wanting the deal to materialize I granted him an extension.

"Another week, Tim, no more. There are people waiting in the wings. I don't want to lose them. They won't wait forever."

"Of course not. I understand completely. Consider it done. It's strictly a formality now. Why, I've even got it in writing."

"You mean the bank has actually given you a binding commitment in advance?"

"That's right. All that remains is the committee's rubber stamp approval of the loan agreement—the exact terms and so on. By the way, a couple of their veeps would like to chat with you, get your input on Magicolor's potential, that sort of thing. Okay with you?"

A clutch of four young veeps, including one woman, come, as they put it, "to learn the secret of Magic's success." After they tour the facility and talk to a random sample of people, I tell them, "Now you know the secret." Although they say nothing of their intentions, they indicate that the deal is not yet sewn up.

On the scheduled deadline day Tim calls again. "Three more days, Harry. That's all I ask. The goddamn committee decided not to meet last week. I hope you can see it's out of my hands—a fluke of circumstances, that's all. But you can count on it—just three more days."

"This is it, Tim. Either we sign by Wednesday, or it's all off."

"I don't blame you. I appreciate your patience. I'll be in your office Wednesday morning. Have the papers ready for signing."

"They've been ready for weeks. Tim, I'm expecting you to deliver."

"Wednesday, you can be sure. See you then. Good-bye, my friend."

Midmorning on Wednesday Tim sweeps into my office like a raging river and launches into a diatribe against the bank. I certainly don't have to guess that he was turned down.

"I'm going to sue the sons of bitches, Harry."

"For what?"

"Read this," he says as he plucks a letter from his briefcase and rams it into my hands. "It's a firm commitment. Don't you agree? Never, no never, have I heard of a bank that broke its word. We don't do things that way in the City. But, Christ, out here in the boondocks, they'll do anything. I'm sorry, Harry, goddamn sorry. I want you to know I haven't been stringing you along."

While I half listen to his torrent of outrage, I scan the letter for its essentials. A telltale phrase, "contingent upon the approval of the loan committee" blares at me like a trumpet call.

"I never doubted your sincerity, Tim. But this letter is no commitment."

"It most certainly is," he says, stiffening. "It spells out the amount and terms of the loan unequivocally—"

"Right, but there's no guarantee they would approve—"

"No, no. I was given to understand that the committee had to essentially okay only the terms. My so-called friend assured me it was in the bag, merely a formality."

"That's not what it says here," I point out as I place the letter in his trembling hand.

"Listen, Harry, I have no right to hold you up any more. The 25 G's is yours." His eyes moisten. Choking back a welling sense of defeat, he puts on a resolute smile.

"I know you've got to talk to others now. But I'd like to come back again—only next time I'll have the financing all set before we talk. I want your company and I intend to get it. This boy doesn't give up easily. Okay?"

Though I admire his pluck, it contains a quality of unreality. Hasn't he learned when to give up? I am familiar with his kind of blind determination in myself and it makes me uneasy.

"I see you and your partners are putting up only a half million."

"That's right. And we were going to borrow $2.5 million from the bank."

"At twelve percent for ten years; that's an interest expense of $300,000 the first year. Add to that the $250,000 of principal due, you'd have to generate $550,000 cash just to service the debt."

"But my reconstructed figures show I'd have the money and then some, Harry."

"Provided things go along as they have been."

"That's right. And they're bound to be better."

What a daredevil! How can he speak with such confidence, as if the future were the past? I could never afford such arrogance.

"Remember," I caution, "times have been improving the last three years, but how long will it last? To the bank you're an unknown quantity. The margin's too close, Tim. I don't think you'll find a bank that will go along. As I see it, you'll have to raise more seed money."

"That'll be tough. I had to twist a lot of arms—"

"Look, Tim, if you can get your horse in front of the cart next time, I'll consider an offer, of course. But I'm aggressively going to try to make a deal elsewhere."

I swing between restraining myself not to blow up at him and berating myself for allowing him to take me in.

"Of course, of course, Harry."

"I've wasted a lot of time already, too much time. The other parties may have lost interest by now."

We shake hands. His shoulders droop as I walk him through the office and the foyer and out to his car, where he sinks behind the wheel and sighs.

"Maybe you're right, Harry, but I'll be back. I'm not quitting. You'll hear from me."

And I did, at least once a week for the next two months, even as I began negotiations with someone else. When finally Tim called and said, "I've got it all together this time, Harry. Let's talk," I replied. "I'm afraid it's too late, Tim. I just received a letter of intent. I'm sorry."

CHAPTER XXV

Year Eighteen
(Continued)

1984

Of the three prospects that were supposedly waiting to present their offers in the event negotiations with Tim fell through, two are no longer interested and the third returns twice for more discussion but can't make up his mind sufficiently to propose a specific deal. Meanwhile others are dropping in, some never to be heard from again after their first visit and some returning casually for a second or third look. Though I always remain polite and open concerning Magic's figures, I take very few inquiries seriously.

One of the casual lookers is Vic, a so-called group vice-president with a substantial family-owned chemical company (sales of $200 million). It's a related color business based hardly five miles down the road and coincidentally a company for whom I had worked as a production supervisor thirty years before from which I was fired. Vic drops by from time to time seeking information, then leaves. Nothing happens. On his most recent visit he wonders aloud what my lowest figure might be.

"No need to beat about the bush," he says. "Let's save everybody time."

Vic is a giant, relaxed, about fifty who usually sits slouched with one leg bent across the other at the knee, his hands in tent formation. He is given to long thoughtful silences before he speaks. Because his calm manner is so soothing, especially after my exposure to Tim's sustained activity, I often underestimate the import of his words.

"Let me put it this way, Vic, what's the highest figure you're willing to pay? As you say, let's not beat around the bush."

Snorting, he says, "I guess I'm going to have to make an offer."

Retrieving a small notepad from his pocket, he opens a page, slowly marks down a figure, and displays it to me.

"That's an insult," I say. "Where do you get the nerve—my God, how in hell did you even come up with that?"

"Hold on, Harry, hold on. It's equal to the value of your assets."

"What about our goodwill, our expertise, our organization? Aren't they worth something, for God's sake? I don't appreciate the way you do business, Vic."

After studying his tented fingers for a while, he says, "Well, the truth is, all we're buying is the building and the equipment."

"And our customers. What about them?"

He tents and untents his fingers some more. "Well, maybe you've got a point. Maybe if I know who they are—do you think I could have a list one of these days?"

"I don't think so. You are, after all, a competitor of sorts, Vic," I say, fearing that he might be on a hunting expedition. I also refuse to let him tour the plant.

Vic uncoils his legs and gradually rises from his chair. "Well, I guess we can't do business, eh, Harry?"

"I guess not, Vic. Give Gordon my regards."

"Oh, sure will."

Gordon, the chairman of the board, a low key deliberate man in his mid-seventies, is, I suspect, behind the scene dictating Vic's strategy. Thirty years ago when I was his employee, he was president, having, as a young man, already built his father's industrial solvents business into a strong, diversified plastics and chemicals company.

It was he that sacked me in a battle of personalities in which the company's then highly regarded director of research and I clashed. To Gordon's credit, I have never been sacked more politely. He was honest and apologetic, saying that he was "between a rock and a hard place," and sincerely wished me luck. I didn't blame him for his decision, even though I felt it unfair.

It was an early lesson in business: justice is second to expedience. It was also a lesson about power: the boss is not always the boss. As I came to understand later at Magic, the true boss is so only by consent of the bossed.

I grow weary of telling the same story, taking lookers on the tour and answering the same questions week after week. Selling Magic has become a circus and its promotion a line of hype.

"Come on in everybody, come one, come all, see the show, the machines, the wonderful operation in progress, nothing like it in the world, meet the performers, look at the figures, come on in—and make a bid."

Magic has been my purpose, my inspiration, and my life; its people are my family. I find the process of selling what we've built together humiliating and cheapening. Now I realize that I must pay a deeper price for cashing in. It's that enormous part of myself that I've invested in Magic.

"Let's sell our winter home and move to the Cape," I propose to Janet.

"What about the two hour commute?" she says.

"No trouble. My people are doing a first rate job running the company; I don't have to go to work every day."

"That's a new one," she says. "You used to say they couldn't get along without you."

"Well, now they get along better without me. This will give me a preview of what it'll be like after I retire."

"That's true," she says. "You might find you won't want to sell the company after all."

Frequently Janet makes it clear she thinks selling Magic will be a mistake. She believes rightly that the company has given meaning to my life and without its sustaining force I might emotionally collapse. I haven't divulged to her my deepest feelings, my disenchantment with the pursuit of money, of being constantly rational and calculating, and my weariness from battling entropy.

It would be even harder to explain my nebulous sense of something missing, of wanting to find the essence of life before I die, that I have more to give and receive but in an entirely different mode. Now that Magic is doing well and my presence is less critical, could she understand that I find it too demanding, and that I have to be rid of it before I can move on.

After so many years there is still no genuine communication between us; we are a devoted couple outwardly, lonely strangers within. I desperately want things to change between us. She used to think of Magic as her enemy, a force that separated us. Is it possible that she prefers it that way?

When Vic calls to see me three weeks after our futile meeting, I am surprised and unenthusiastic.

"Can I come over now?"

"You mean—"

"Yeah, right now."

Usually lookers set up an appointment weeks in advance. It's part of the ritual. For them, deal-talk is a momentous occasion. With Vic, you'd think he was calling to visit his barber.

"I don't have much time," I fib. "No more than fifteen minutes."

"That's more'n I need," he says.

Slouching as usual in the chair beside my desk, he hands me a sheet of paper on which he has crudely handwritten the salient figures of a new offer. From the first figure on he has me.

"You're in the ballpark," I say.

"Thought it would grab you," he responds.

The offer is still some distance from what I'm seeking, but it's unequivocally real.

"Your offer is certainly a basis for discussion," I say, priming myself to be flexible and open-minded. A hard-nosed attitude could well slam the door. I have no doubt I can get Vic to enhance the offer, which, after all, is only a feeler, a starting point.

"I'll leave it with you. Think it over. You and I have lots of time, eh?" he says. "Call me when you're ready to talk some more."

Our next meeting is at Vic's plant. Briefly Vic has me meet Gordon, the chairman of the board, in his luxurious lair and we exchange memories of the old days when I was his employee. Before dismissing us he says: "Good luck to you both. Be reasonable; make a deal."

"It's up to Vic," I say.

"It's up to Harry," Vic says and we all laugh as we depart Gordon's office.

Awaiting us in a plush conference room is Lionel, the man who would be Magicolor's president if we consummate a deal. As we talk I judge him to be a quiet, intense man in his mid-thirties, much less communicative than I, less inclined to reveal his thinking, and certainly less emotional and given to enthusiasm. He would take some getting used to, but I figure if he's fair and honest, if he has integrity, my people will easily adapt. I have long ago concluded that the substance of a man is more critical to the job of leadership than his style.

"How about your customer list?" Vic demands.

Reaching across the conference table, I hand him a folder of papers. The two men huddle for several minutes over the list.

"Very impressive," Lionel says, grinning.

"I had no idea you do business with so many big ones," says Vic.

"No wonder we couldn't ever crack them," Lionel says.

"You mean we've been locking horns?" I say.

"You needn't worry, Harry," Vic says. "Our technology is lousy in your product area."

"What really amazes me are your costs," Lionel says. "How do you get them so low? Look at that labor figure as a percent of sales, Vic. It's half ours."

"It's our culture," I say.

Puzzled, they look at each other.

"C'mon, Harry. What about your production methods, the equipment, overhead, and your material costs? Don't they figure in?" Lionel says defensively.

"Of course," I reply. "But you're asking the wrong question. Ask, why are those things cheaper? It's attitude, strictly attitude."

"Attitude?"

"That's right, Lionel. Everyone has an incentive, everyone is motivated, everyone participates in every decision that affects them. Take my advice, if we make a deal and you take over, don't change the culture. If you do, Magicolor will be just like any other company you can buy."

The two men glance at each other, eyebrows raised.

I remember Gordon was parental about his people and stuck his nose into every detail of their activities. You might say he was a benevolent dictator. Inevitably he'd remake Magic to conform to his style. Still, Gordon is decent and success oriented and his employees seem to stay with him. My people could do worse.

Lionel is mostly silent as Vic and I sculpt an agreement in less than a half hour. Taxes are one of my major considerations, since the original cost of Magic and the building is insignificant relative to the selling price. Consequently my taxable gain will be considerable. Indeed, that Vic is willing to structure the deal to my advantage taxwise is the main reason why I will accept less from him rather than try for more with another suitor.

Vic is willing to forego an asset purchase, with its adverse tax consequence to me, in favor of a stock purchase. Though it is early December, he is also willing to promptly consummate the deal before the first of the year. It is expected that the Congress will be considering a new tax bill early in 1985 that could, among other changes, eliminate the existing favorable capital gains rate. In other words, taxwise, this year is the best year to sell—a year of which less than a month remains because of the delay over Tim.

The deal is marvelously uncomplicated. To appreciate the spread between what I sought and what I got, here is a comparison of the deals with Tim (what I wanted) and Vic.

The Deal	Vic	Tim	Difference
Business	$1,600,000	$2,300,000	- 700,000
Building	1,000,000	725,000	225,000
Total	2,600,000	3,025,000	-425,000
Less Taxes	512,000	616,000	
Less Commissions	-----	60,000	
After Tax & Commissions	$2,088,000	2,349,000	-261,000

Vic and Lenny and I shake hands, agreeing that their attorneys will draw up the papers. I return to the office in a near manic state. The thing is done, done at last after two wearisome years of trying. I call my lawyer, Dan, to prepare him for the task ahead. Believing that I know my interests better than he does, I've excluded him from the negotiating, preferring to do without an attorney's complicating and adversarial presence, which seems peculiar to all such creatures. I've confined him instead to providing the agreements and contracts and ensuring that they are legally binding, that they comply with my intent and that they secure me. Then I meet with my key people to give them the news and answer any questions. They congratulate me coolly, warily, showing no enthusiasm for my accomplishment.

"Soon you'll meet Lenny, your president to be," I explain. "He's of a new generation, a man full of vigor.

He's bound to improve on my tired ways, bring a fresh approach to the business. And Gordon, the owner and chairman of the board, takes a very keen interest in the welfare of his employees. No one here will be just a number."

No one seems to share my sense of relief that an era of fear and struggle is over.

"Think of the hard times we've had," I remind them. "Our company has been like a small boat in a rough sea. Under the new owners it will be able to withstand the worst storms. Everyone will be secure."

"But we always felt secure, Harry," says Emma, as the others nod their heads. "We never doubted that you'd do what you set out to do." I am simply amazed.

The following memorandum appears in each pay envelope.

Dear Stockholder,

The proposed purchase of Magicolor stock last September by Mr. Van der Steele has not materialized due to his inability to raise sufficient funding.

Now a substantial corporation of excellent reputation, whose management philosophy is compatible with ours, has made a new offer, of which, in accordance with ESOP regulations, you are hereby notified. At $35.00 per share it is $10.00 higher than the price established in the most recent objective appraisal. I feel it is fair and equitable and its acceptance is in the best interest of Magicolor's stockholders and employees.

Sincerely,

Harry Simon,
President

DRIVEN

Everything is right and ready: the price, the deal, the attorneys, the employees, and me. Janet isn't ready; she has grown comfortable with the status quo. The business is no longer her competitor responsible for keeping us apart. After all, it has given her affluence and status. The fact that it separates us seems to suit her; the business is now her ally.

Cathy isn't ready. The business has always been her ally, driving me to her for comfort in times of stress. It has given her noncommittal love. She equates the sale of the business with losing me.

And Vic isn't ready either, which he calls to tell me after I arrived home on Friday night three days after we shook hands.

"Couple of small matters still have to be settled," he says.

"I thought all the t's were crossed at the last meeting," I say.

"About the in-ground fuel tank," he says.

"What about it?"

"The surveyor tells us part of it is over the line on the abutter's property."

"I mentioned that when I showed you the original plans of the building, Vic. You knew all about it."

"Uh-huh. Say, how about getting your neighbor to grant us an easement?"

Though I'm on the brink of becoming annoyed, I manage to remain cool—at least for now. "I approached him a few years ago. He had no objection to leaving the tank where it was, but he refused to make it legal. It could be a problem should he want to sell his parcel."

"Uh-huh. Let me put it this way: Half the tank is now legally his and it can't stay where it is. We think you should pay for moving it."

"I thought we had a deal, Vic."

"We do, Harry."

"You had all the facts at your disposal when we shook hands, including knowledge of the tank's location. I've held nothing back. Now you're asking me to give you more than we agreed to. No dice, Vic, no dice."

"Don't be unreasonable, Harry."

"I'm not being unreasonable. You are. I'm sticking by the deal. You're asking to change it."

"What are we talking about in dollars? Three, five, thousand? I think you're blowing this thing all out of—"

"That's right, it's small potatoes," I agree. "Gordon can afford it. You're the one who's being small."

"We're firm on this, Harry."

"So am I, Vic."

"You mean you'd drop the whole thing?"

"The whole damn thing. I'd rather not do business with a bunch of cheapies."

"If I hang up, it's over," Vic warns, his voice tremulous.

"Don't hang up. I'll hang up," I say and slam down the receiver.

My tendency to volcanic rage hasn't changed; hence big consequences come from such little things as wrongly placed fuel tanks. For a principle I'll let a deal go. After two years I've come to the end of my patience. Add a feather, the burden becomes too heavy.

I storm into the kitchen from my study. "It's over," I blurt to Janet. "The bastards called it off for a few thousand bucks."

"Can't you compromise?" she asks reasonably.

"What's to compromise? We had a deal. Either they live up to it, or they can shove it."

"I'm sure there'll be others coming along," she says sensibly.

"Not for a while, not for me. After this one I need to take a break."

My disappointment is deep and disturbing. I dare not show up at the office in my distraught condition. For the next five days I stay home, reading and watching TV and gathering in the lines of hope and trust and promise that I had extended. By Wednesday my spirit is substantially improved and I'm ready to return to work. Then Gordon, the chairman, calls.

"I understand we've had a misunderstanding, Harry," he says cheerily.

"That's one way to put it, I suppose," I reply just as cheerily.

"It's too bad, don't you think? Losing something we both want."

"Your people changed the deal after it was made, Gordon. I don't appreciate that."

"Neither do I. I'll bet if you and I sat down, just the two of us, we could settle the matter in two minutes."

Feeling joyous at his reaching out, at the suddenness of the reversal, at knowing that he wants the deal more than I, I reply, "I'll bet you're right."

"How about joining me for lunch?"

"Fine, when?"

"Noon, at the University Club."

"I'm two hours away. Make it twelve-thirty."

"You're the boss, Harry."

"Now that's a twist," I say and we both laugh.

Over wine and tuna sandwiches, lunch is an empathetic conversation about our businesses, of how well each of us has withstood the rigors of growing older, of raising our families, and of his sons having become major players in his management team. The matter of the underground fuel tank is simply dismissed as a non-item.

Gordon makes no demand except that I continue on the course Vic and I had originally agreed on. I insist on one new condition: that Gordon be there at the signing.

"If anything should come up that requires a decision, a change, I don't want to deal with Vic or any of your employees. I want to deal with you, one top dog to another."

"I'll be there, Harry."

And he is. We meet in his attorney's cavernous mahogany conference room in downtown Providence. Gordon's team consists of Vic, Gordon, his president, his company's in-house lawyer, his bank's vice-president and the bank's lawyer, and his law firm's lawyer with a striking female assistant, eight in all. My team consists of my lawyer, Dan, and me.

He and I, having reviewed the agreements in advance, have already decided how far we are willing to compromise on any item to which we take exception.

We begin by going over the thirty-six page stock purchase agreement, the first of four documents. Essentially it delineates the purchase price—the sum to be placed in escrow as security to indemnify the buyer against any misrepresentations I may have made. Included are statements confirming that I have truthfully revealed everything about Magicolor, its financial statements and so forth, and that all taxes have been paid, and scores of sundry items that cover every aspect of Magicolor's existence of concern to the buyer.

Paragraph by paragraph the lawyers either approve of or take exception to what is stipulated. If the latter, arguments often ensue, particularly with Gordon's youthful, hostile, overachieving, in-house lawyer.

The first difference arises when Dan objects to Gordon's requirement that I be held responsible for all receivables now on Magic's books — sums owed by customers — that would prove uncollectible.

"We won't budge on that," Gordon's in-house lawyer says.

Dan, a deceptively easygoing fellow, suddenly rears. "What you see is what you get. You're buying Magicolor's risks along with its secure assets. Your demand is unreasonable."

"Not from our point of view, sir. We're adamant," says Gordon's man.

"Let's avoid a deadlock. I'm sure there's a solution," says the law firm's lawyer, flashing a stern look at the in-house lawyer.

In a low voice, not to be overheard, I say near Dan's ear, "I'm not worried about the receivables, Dan. They're all good. I think we're arguing over nothing."

Dan concedes, and the in-house lawyer looks toward Gordon for recognition of his victory.

The next disagreement centers on the inclusion of Janet "to indemnify and to hold Magicolor and the Buyer harmless from and against any claim, expense, loss or liability arising from—"

"Out of the question," I say, jumping in before Dan can respond and staring down the pushy lawyer. "You can include me, but not her. Just because she owns a few shares, you can't do this. And I'm adamant."

After seeing Gordon nod, the lawyer gives in.

The third difference develops over the escrow. Gordon's team seeks to withhold $200,000 to be deposited in the bank for four years as the buyer's security against any claims that may arise from the past.

I balk, willing to set aside only $50,000. After some strenuous though polite bargaining, we compromise at a sum of $100,000 to be withheld for one year, precisely what Dan and I had decided on before the meeting.

Next develops an irreconcilable dispute regarding "Indemnification and Reimbursement." Dan refuses to agree that I indemnify the buyer, "at all times after the date of this agreement [against] any and all actions, suits, proceedings, claims, demands....incident to misrepresentation, non-collection of receivables and taxes (including without limitation accounting and legal fees)."

"This makes Harry vulnerable to unjustifiable and mistaken claims—especially from the IRS," Dan asserts. "We are warranting that all taxes are current and we have been audited by the IRS through last year. What more do you want?"

"I'm sorry. We can't give here, Dan," says the law firm's lawyer.

"Absolutely not," emphasizes the in-house lawyer. "Do you take us for fools?"

"Let's set a time limit—say a year," says Dan.

"No time limit," says the in-house lawyer.

Neither Gordon nor the law firm's lawyers speak up to break the impasse.

"Maybe we don't have a deal, after all, fella," Dan threatens the in-house lawyer icily, barely restraining his rising fury.

"Let's take a walk," I say to Dan, rising to leave the room.

When we are in a small hallway outside the door, Dan says, "That guy's a maniac. He's got to be stopped."

"I know, Dan. But please don't kill the deal."

"I'm doing what's in your best interest, Harry."

"Of course. I can see that. I'm not worried about the IRS or the possibility of any future claims. Magic is clean."

"You're taking a chance, Harry. Do you realize what you're saying?"

"I most certainly do. But it's okay. Let it go."

"Just so long as you understand."

"I don't think I'm taking too much of a chance."

Dan's stance is understandable. Not knowing how cleanly I conduct Magic's business, why should he not anticipate my vulnerability to all sorts of possible future claims? He is bound to doubt my claim of innocence, if for no reason other than my naivete. In matter of fact, how many businessmen can say they're immaculate? His assumption that most businesses have something to hide is generally correct. If Magic is an exception, the reason, obviously, is that I'm neurotic.

We return to the conference room and accept the provision as written. After Gordon's side grants, at my request, that it be three years rather than the five before I can enter into competition with Magic, the stock purchase agreement and escrow agreement are settled. Sending out for sandwiches and coffee, we work through lunch hour. A review of a fourth document, the real estate purchase and sale agreement, is uneventful, as is the fifth, the consulting agreement, which requires that I be available for consultation for a year at an annual salary of $50,000. The entire negotiation lasts five grueling hours.

To beat the new tax year, we all meet again in a week, at ten o'clock on the sunny wintry morning of December 28 in the same conference room. This time Janet and Emma are present because, being independent stockholders, (on my advice Emma picked up an option I had granted her years ago and Janet owns a few shares of stock as a gesture) their signatures are needed for the transfer of ownership.

All arguments and differences behind us, the atmosphere is relaxed and happy. Gordon and his entourage sit across the great mahogany table from Dan, Janet, Emma, and me. As the lawyers pass the seemingly endless stream of documents down the lines of pertinent parties, we crack witty exchanges and laugh easily.

Gordon, well into his seventies, is like a boy who has just received a new tricycle. I marvel at the vitality of his spirit.

"Do you think you'll ever retire, Gordon?" I ask.

"I am retired, Harry. I don't work anymore. I just have fun."

I can see he is somehow free, freer than I've ever been, and serene. On rare occasions I could say that work was fun, but most of the time it was serious.

"What are you going to do with your life, Harry?"

"Don't know yet, Gordon. I just sold most of it to you."

But I do know what I'll do: I'll bask in vast open time and write what I feel and read the books I've been meaning to since college and sail on the bay and build that neglected garden in our backyard at the Cape into the peaceful haven I imagined it could be and travel across the world, and I'll do it all in my own time on my own terms. Most of all, I plan to finally take time to share myself with Janet.

When the signing is completed, Gordon comes over to our side of the table and embraces Janet, then takes my hand and holds it.

"Have a happy, good life together," he says, as if Janet and I were just beginning. "Enjoy and good luck."

Except for my wedding day, this is the most momentous one of my life, more so than the day I joined Magic, more so than when I became an owner two years later. From this day on there is no obligation, no necessity, no responsibility, no goal to intervene between myself and myself. It's absolutely frightening.

The next day Gordon throws a party in Magicolor's lunchroom for all the employees. There's champagne and cold meats and beer and cake. I assure everyone that they are in good hands, that I will miss them all "at least for a week," and my eyes brim with tears. Gordon speaks of the fine job I've done, of his intention to do business in the same satisfying way, and of his plans to make Magicolor "the biggest color house in the industry."

After the speeches Gordon's team and I mingle with the employees.

"You've got it made, Mr. Simon," says Bud, a worker with five years to go before retirement. "Good luck, sir."

I shake my head. "Have it made? One thing I've learned, Bud, is never to believe that."

My God, how I want to, though.

EPILOGUE

1985

Being wealthy—having investments worth millions of dollars, which bring in hundreds of thousands of dollars of income each year without my having to lift a finger or fear that a competitor will threaten it or that the tribulations of the economy will seriously erode it or that I need suffer at all to earn it—being this well off gives me a feeling of freedom that I have never known before.

When Julie, now my personal accountant, asks me what I'm going to do with the money, he's not asking how I'm going to invest it, because he knows I'll be conservative and cautious, but rather how I'm going to live the rest of my life.

"Y'know, Harry," he says, "you're a survivor, but now that you don't have to fight to survive anymore, how are you going to survive?"

That's my wise and valued advisor for you. He knows just what to ask.

"No problem," I say. "I'll do all the things I've always wanted to do and never had time for."

"Harry," he says, "time isn't the fourth dimension you think it is, it's really a state of mind."

"How so?" I ask, intrigued and slightly uncomfortable.

"You've always run, not because time is actually short but because the clock inside you thinks it is. I don't believe you can be free until you're off the stopwatch."

I've stripped myself of all responsibilities, even the overseeing of my investments, which I've assigned to a professional advisor. Money and business are no longer a concern in my daily life. Instead I tend the garden and I sail and Janet and I travel. But I still rush around: to the post office, to the gate at the air terminal, to meet friends for an evening out.

Janet says that my rushing around is driving her crazy.

"You miss the business, the daily excitement and challenge and being a boss. You don't know what to do with yourself."

"Not at all," I say. "If Gordon called me today and said, 'Here, take Magic back for half what we paid you for it,' I'd tell him no dice."

"Then what's going on, Harry? For God's sake let up on yourself, let up on me. You run around like you're meeting a deadline every hour. I watch you mow the lawn, rushing back and forth, like you're mad at it. What's wrong?"

"Nothing's wrong. Absolutely nothing."

To find out what's wrong I follow the advice that I read someplace. I write down my thoughts in the form of an essay.

IS THERE LIFE AFTER RETIREMENT?

During the two years I tried to sell my company, I had time to prepare myself psychologically for life after work. When I decided to unload I had no intention of banking the fires of enthusiasm within myself. Rather I stopped asking, "What am I doing?" and began asking, "Why am I doing it?"

My job seemed to be done. True, I could have made my enterprise bigger. But the quantities of life—homes, cars, money, status—were sufficient; it was time to concentrate on the quality of life that I had sacrificed in the quantitative wars.

The question people ask now is what am I. When I apply for a credit card or a new bank account, I have trouble writing "retired" on the application form. When I meet new people, they usually ask what I did before. I find it hard to answer. What bothers me is that the world wants to know *what* I am rather than *who* I am.

Janet and I could become world travelers or live anyplace—London, Bora Bora, or right where we are. All our lives we've been tied down raising children and making a living. Janet is now ready to burst out and see what's out there. But I resist. During the traveling we've already done I can't wait to return home. Yet once I'm here, home isn't yet home; the roots haven't taken hold.

From my study window, between the tall hedges behind the house, I can glimpse tantalizing portions of the perennial garden I've been restoring after ten summers of neglect. I had vowed that one day when I left the rat race I'd make the garden beautiful again. One glass clear morning this spring, kneeling in the soil planting a bed of peonies, I became overwhelmed with sadness from the beauty and peace around me, and my eyes filled up with tears. What was this?

It happened again one brisk, shimmering June afternoon in my small catboat gliding across the bay on a broad reach. I was exhilarated with a sense of abandon, a feeling I used to dream about having and that I can now have practically at will. Yet after ten minutes I couldn't endure it any longer and felt suddenly afraid and empty. I've hardly sailed since.

For months I've had the same dream: I become lost, although not always in the same place. But the message is the same—I have no discipline. I need to show results—pure visible achievement—for my labor. I'm unaccustomed to my newfound freedom and security and ease. I can't make them my reality.

For years I handily survived deadly competition and the outrageous swings of the economy. I seemed to thrive on fear of failure. Was selling Magic my swan song? Has it left me only emptiness and trivia, nothing more?

I looked to my peers, once successful men like myself now retired, for the answer.

"How did you adjust to all the freedom, the glut of time?" I asked.

"I've never been busier," they answered. "In fact, I often wonder how I ever managed to find time to work before. You'll adjust soon enough, Harry."

But none of them said they were fulfilled by being busy.

One thing I've discovered: call it the law of compensating activity. With time cheaper and more available I find more things to do in which to use it up. Recently I stopped wearing my watch. The old day-to-day deadlines are gone. But I have more time to ponder that big deadline looming ahead in the misty future.

The other day the nursery delivered twenty-five boxwood shrubs for a border, part of my ten-year garden-improvement plan. Immediately I took the wheelbarrow and the spade and worked like a zealot planting the shrubs one after another.

"What are you trying to do?" Janet asked. "Complete the whole ten years in one?"

"Certainly not," I replied. "They're here to be planted, so I'm doing it."

Part way through the project, I removed my soggy hat and salt-streaked sunglasses and noticed a robin gingerly dipping its beak into the birdbath. A swath of brilliant Oriental poppies caught my eye. I watched the breeze billow across a hedge of tall ancient arbor vitae like a wave. I lay on the grass supported on an elbow, erasing time, doing nothing but enjoying the sweet ambience of time and place. In those moments I forgot, however briefly, what the culture and my upbringing had taught me, and what my internal drive had forbidden me ever to do. Is this what I had missed and needed all the years I had been in business?

APPENDIX A

Magicolor's Management Methods

Frequently I arrived at the plant to beat the shift change, to see off the third shift and greet the first coming in. Being there at the early hour brought me closer to the workers. Occasionally I appeared at the 11 P.M. shift change for the same reason. I would leave Cathy at a motel while I visited the plant and later return to her.

Having once worked the hateful second shift as a quality-control technician in a plastics factory, I knew the alienation that workers can feel from being ignored by management. Receiving no sign of recognition, not even that they exist, they can feel as if they're in exile. I attributed the high productivity of our third shift, traditionally the least productive one, partly to my visits. And our first shift may well have been discouraged from beating the norm by a surfeit of management recognition: They probably thought that the bosses were always breathing down their necks.

To Rob my visits were "a needless crock"; the high efficiency of the third shift was "only a fluke." In fact, Rob had never met anyone on that shift. To him it was a ghost shift. Yet it made a major contribution to our bottom line. The third shift reduced hourly overhead costs by virtue of its existence. It enabled us to run at a higher profit or to sell at a lower price. It made us more competitive and increased our sales. It forgave our mistakes, provides a margin for error.

After a recession set in a few years later, we had to shut down the third shift and lay off some of its best people. Profits plummeted, and the entire company grew dispirited. Only then did Rob appreciate their contribution.

Though starting time was normally 8:30 A.M., the two women who arrived at seven were taking advantage of Emma's policy that allowed the staff to regulate their hours to suit themselves, provided they worked forty hours a week and arranged for someone to perform their tasks in their absence. As a result, each office worker learned one or more jobs besides her own, a boon when someone became ill or her work load was temporarily excessive and she needed help. The two women quit work at 3:30 P.M. The freedom to schedule their own time was not only convenient—for example, giving mothers more time to be with their children—it also encouraged them to be more responsible. By having hours out of sync with the masses, they felt privileged. It enhanced their dignity.

The flexible work schedule benefited the company in small but important ways. By arriving early the office workers found they were more efficient without the distraction of phones, which began their assault at nine. They were also surprisingly generous with their time, actually working more hours rather than shaving a few minutes here and there—so typical under a traditional schedule. Furthermore everyone's attitude was always bright-spirited. They answered the phones with enthusiastic voices.

Encouraging creative solutions to our business problems, I made Magicolor an arena for constant

DRIVEN

experimentation. Emma's flexible time plan was one of scores of examples, a few of which will be described elsewhere. Although it bothered some who needed the security of the known, our daring prepared us for tackling the hard times that would lie ahead. Never satisfied with the status quo, I created a culture aimed at striving to improve. For no matter how well we performed when times were good, because that was easy, we could only be sure of our capability when the industry and our competitors were suffering.

APPENDIX B

More on Magicolor's Management Methods

Of the many factors contributing to Magicolor's success, perhaps the most important was our method of compensating salesmen, which consisted of a car, expenses, non-contributory liberal benefits, (such as medical and life insurance, retirement and profit-sharing plans, vacations up to four weeks), a salary sufficient to meet a family's basic needs, and a commission that increased as sales increased beginning with the first sales dollar.

Behind our novel commission schedule was the assumption that each incremental dollar of sales was harder to achieve; in other words, opportunity decreased as a market became increasingly saturated. Given a guaranteed fixed territory, a salesman was encouraged to cull from it whatever he could without any limit on his earnings. I told the salesmen that nothing would please me more than to have their income exceed mine or Rob's—not that Rob agreed.

Our sales compensation plan was a precise reversal of the typical plan extant in our country. Most American companies limit a salesman's income. In contrast, by imposing no cap on earnings combined with increasing reward as performance improved, we gave our salesmen the incentive to apply their entrepreneurial drive. The usual problem of declining income due to inflation was also solved: As the price of goods increased, so automatically did the salesman's commission. (In high inflation years, however, it was still necessary to adjust the base salary upward.)

The compensation plan was an important reason why Miller fought his dismissal and why Francis, burying his resentment against Rob, remained with Magicolor. Both men possessed strong egos, and an entrepreneurial spirit, and believed in themselves more than in others. Where else could such men find the earning potential that Magicolor offered, unless in their own businesses, of course.

Possibly the most important reason for Magicolor's success, was its commitment to excellence.

When I worked at MPI, I witnessed conditions that made disaster inevitable. If Cal was a prince of bosses, he was also an incompetent manager, failing to see that innocuous bad decisions gather and become enormously destructive. That Cal's incompetence was not discovered until too late reflects on his boss, MPI's president. When I fail to acknowledge the failing of one of my employees, it reflects on me.

Intuitively I knew that MPI had to go under sooner or later. The MPI experience taught me how NOT to run a business, which indeed may have been the best way to learn: The consequences of error in business are so stark and final. So at Magicolor I avoided doing what MPI did wrong. Whatever policy I pursued I did so with the compulsion and fanaticism of a revolutionary. I understood that the errors that led to MPI's demise — taking shortcuts, breaking rules, showing bias, procrastinating, seeing only the immediate, giving arbitrary rewards, ignoring details and minutia — were the result of poor discipline. I made sure at Magicolor that every activity was guided by reason and not convenience or human inclination.

This principle requires that every action taken must follow an established procedure, which can be changed only with the concurrence of all concerned. For example, no customer's order can be processed until the customer is approved for credit. As simple as this rule seems, were it not imposed, a company would soon find itself flooded with delinquent accounts.

Each person's function and authority were clearly defined and held sacred. No one dared encroach on another's domain. Protocol was adhered to. For instance, a salesman could discuss matters of mutual concern with our technical director, but he could not instruct him or ask for special attention. A salesman could not deal directly with the production manager, who was responsible for scheduling his customers' orders, but he could deal through the sales manager to ask for emergency treatment, in which case the schedule could be changed by agreement with the production manager. Turfs were protected, but not so rigidly that exceptions weren't made by mutual consent of the concerned parties.

Every accomplished task was subject to review, and errors were corrected without criticism unless repeated. For example, the lab oversaw production's quality and every customer invoice was checked before it was mailed by someone other than the preparer for extension errors and spelling.

All parties affected by a decision were involved in making the decision. The janitor decided which broom the company would buy, an office worker participated in the selection of the desktop computer, a truck driver chose which vehicle to lease. On matters affecting the entire company, all employees would meet and vote on them after lengthy discussion — for example, whether to work a four-day forty-hour week or to continue a five-day format.

Ten percent of pre-tax profits were distributed as a cash bonus every quarter to the workers and staff in proportion to their relative wages. (The salesmen, having their own incentive, were excluded.) Each month the department heads met to discuss item by item the prior month's profit and loss statement and to recommend remedial action if necessary.

After twenty consecutive months of profits and bonuses, however, we had our first loss and our first bonus-less month. Then a second and a third month of losses occurred — an entire quarter — due to a mini-recession in the industry. The workers grumbled, alleging that the company was hiding profits in order not to share them. I called a company-wide meeting.

"I don't expect to convince anyone that our figures are honest," I explained. "The issue here is not truth; the issue is trust. If anyone thinks I'm lying about our bottom line, I urge him to find another employer, someone he can believe in. He should not want to work here.

"But if you will accept the P and L's, the bad as well as the good, you will also understand what it is to be in business. It's just like your life and mine with its good and bad periods. In business, however, the way things are is summed up in one concise figure. So a business doesn't always win and often it suffers through hard times, never knowing how long they will last.

"All of you have shared in our profits without taking any risk. Would you also like to share in our losses? Of course not. You don't share in our losses for precisely the reason that you've taken no risk. But don't expect a bonus when there are losses. In such times we must conserve our financial strength.

"I'm afraid that our present system of reward doesn't work well. It breeds suspicion when times are bad. So from now on, there'll be no more profit sharing. Instead we will tie rewards directly to your own effort rather than the company's success. I'll tell you more about it at another meeting held just for that purpose."

Meetings were rare, but informal business discussion, even small talk, was constant. Except for instructions and formal written information fixed by procedure, there was minimal paperwork. The atmosphere was relaxed, a far cry from the pressure cooker I knew at MPI, simply because everyone knew the rules in a system that met all contingencies, including emergencies that often developed like dust devils on a clear day. In short, everyone felt secure.

All employees understood that quality was paramount, not to be sacrificed for quantity. In the manufacturing of color concentrates there were countless opportunities to screw up—from product contamination in the form of alien black specks, to a color match that under a particular light source does not match the customer's standard. Magicolor established quality checks at each step in the process. Thus our customers rarely encountered a defective product, whereas poor quality was rife among our competitors.

APPENDIX C

PROJECTED CASH FLOW
(Add 000)

	Year 1	Year 2	Year 3	Year 4	Year 5
INCOME:					
Sales	$3,850	$4,000	$4,400	$5,000	$5,500
EXPENSES:					
Operating	3,080	3,160	3,430	3,850	4,235
S,G & A*	655	640	682	750	825
ADD:					
Depreciation	68	68	70	70	73
Res. Bad Debts	10	11	12	13	15
NET PROFIT:					
Before Taxes	115	200	288	400	440
Taxes	52	100	155	212	233
After Taxes	63	100	133	188	207
NET CASH FLOW	141	179	215	271	295
ADD TO WORKING CAPITAL:**	98	119	125	148	232
Cash Generation	43	60	90	123	63

	Year 1	Year 2	Year 3	Year 4	Year 5
Equity:					
Added	220	30			
Withdrawn	-220	- 106	-106	-106	-106
Add'tl Bank					
Loans	25	30	100		
Cash Balance	43	52	35	83	140

*Selling, general and administrative.
**Machinery and equipment, inventory, accounts receivable, loan interest.

APPENDIX D

Buy/Sell Documents and the Purpose of Each

I BANK LOAN AGREEMENT and note between the corporation and the bank. A letter of credit guaranteeing the note to Rob.

II ESCROW AGREEMENT between Rob, me, the corporation and the bank, to place the necessary stock in the bank's possession.

III ASSIGNMENT of INSURANCE POLICIES to ESCROW AGENT, a life insurance policy on my life, assigned to the bank.

IV CORPORATION NOTES to MR. STARR are special clauses on interest, subordination to the corporation's secured notes, and the guaranty by me.

V ASSIGNMENT of INSURANCE POLICIES to STARR enables Rob to purchase from the corporation the life insurance policies on his life.

VI RELEASE of STARR removes Rob's name from the mortgage on the factory building.

VII REAL ESTATE involves preparing a new deed on the building, reassigning the lease to me by the corporation, and giving Rob a certified check for $25,000.

VIII RESIGNATIONS concerns Rob resigning as a corporate officer, director, and trustee of the company's benefit plans.

IX DISTRIBUTION from PROFIT SHARING TRUST in which the corporation pays Rob his vested interest in the Profit Sharing Plan as well as a bonus "in the gross amount of the unvested portion of Mr. Starr's interest in said Plan."

X SHARES of STOCK are brought by Rob and me to the closing, endorsed by each, and delivered to the bank.

XI CONSULTATION and NO COMPETITION AGREEMENT

XII CORPORATE VOTES by the board of directors ratifying the purchase agreement and authorizing the corporate actions.

Appendix E

Dear Mr. Van der Steele III:

Enclosed are Magicolor's sales figures by plant and month for the past eight and a half years and its financial figures for the last five years. Let me provide some historical background.

Eight years ago I consummated a deal to buy out a 50% shareholder (Rob Starr) on terms that consisted of a substantial consulting fee and payment of principal on an installment basis plus interest. Sales for the next three years improved steadily, profits were sufficient, but cash flow remained short because of the debt burden. Then in the third year our largest customer (Perfection Toys), making up 35% of our sales, withdrew to establish their own coloring facility—a rare event in our industry.

Clearly our third year was one of crisis. We struggled for the next two years to make up for the substantial loss of sales, with little success. As debt and ever increasing interest rates continued to erode cash flow, profits failed to improve. Contributing to this failure were also the increased costs of attempting to improve sales. But by the end of the third year we revised our strategy with dramatic results.

By restructuring our short-term into long-term debt, paying off the former shareholder, reducing our sales staff, streamlining all departments, and introducing an innovative incentive system throughout the company, we became lean and hungry. Within a year profits turned up, enabling us to chew away (as interest rates peaked at 21 1/2%) at our costly debt. The downward trend reversed; our momentum gathered such that even the weakening economy, despite stalling our growth, failed to derail our profitability.

For the recent five months sales have declined as our major accounts are experiencing serious production cutbacks, some as high as 60%. But we are confident that Magicolor is not suffering lost market share. Although the company's combined sales have dropped about 14%, past month's sales for the Chicago facility have increased 36% over last year. At the same time, in spite of overall reduced revenues, please note that profits are actually higher than a year ago. Our management strategy is working.

We agree with you and with the economic forecasters that a rebound is now in progress. Magicolor is presently financially strong, lean, productive, and turned on. With capacity in place, we are poised for doubling sales by expanding our sales effort geographically with plans to eventually establish satellite plants in Charlotte, North Carolina, and Cleveland, Ohio.

I hope, by giving you insight into the events and strategies behind the figures, you will interpret their significance with deeper appreciation. As you can see, Magicolor's present victory is no accident. It is the end result of seventeen years of trial and error. The wisdom gained from that experience constitutes the most valuable asset Magic has to offer.

Looking forward to your response, I remain,

Cordially yours,
Harry Simon